MAX WEBER

Class, Status and Power

MAX WEBER

Class, Status and Power

Amitabh Bhatt

CENTRUM PRESS
NEW DELHI-110002 (INDIA)

CENTRUM PRESS
H.O.: 4360/4, Ansari Road, Daryaganj,
New Delhi-110002 (India)
Tel: 23278000, 23261597, 23255577, 23286875
B.O.: No. 1015, Ist Main Road, BSK IIIrd Stage,
IIIrd Phase, IIIrd Block, Bengaluru-560085 (INDIA)
Tel: 080-41723429
Email: centrumpress@gmail.com
Visit us at: www.centrumpress.com

Max Weber: Class, Status and Power

First Edition, 2011

ISBN 978-93-81293-49-2

PRINTED IN INDIA

Printed at Suman Printers, Jagatpuri Extn., Delhi

Contents

Contents

Preface

Max Weber is undoubtedly one of the most outstanding social scientists of contemporary times. Weber developed a different approach to the study of social groups and classes than did Marx. For Marx, there were two primary groups in society and these were classes, the bourgeoisie and the proletariat, whose contradictory social relationship is the motive force for change in capitalism. Marx considers these classes to be defined and determined by whether they own the means of production or whether they do not own the means of production and must sell labour power to those who do. In contrast, for Weber, social groups and classes are in the sphere of power and are connected to the distribution of power. Given that there are various ways that power can be exercised, for Weber it is not possible to reduce the organization of all these groups to a single dimension or factor such as ownership or non-ownership of the means of production. Rather, for Weber there is a pluralism associated with class structure in that people attempt to achieve ends using various means – each of these may create a grouping such as a class, status group, or party. Social stratification has multiple and overlapping dimensions and groups that involve a complex set of social relationships.

For Weber, what we would call social stratification, social class, or social inequality is in the sphere of power, and can be analyzed by examining economic situation, status honour, or parties. In general, we understand by 'power' the chance of a man or of a number of men to realize their own will in a communal action even against the resistance of others who are participating in the same action. This is a very broad definition that could include political or economic power exercised at the level of community or society as a whole, or it could refer to smaller scale actions taken by groups in communities such as religious or peer groups, or even the exercise of power in institutions such as the family. The examples that Weber provides are usually quite specific though and he is concrete in his application of this definition. Weber did not ignore economic sources of power, and considered these to be among the more important sources, especially in capitalism. But he claimed that power emerged from other economic sources, ie. not just from class but status groups and parties.

In Weber's view every society is divided into groupings and strata with distinctive life-styles and views of the world, just as it is divided into distinctive classes. While at times status as well as class groupings may conflict, at others their members may accept fairly stable patterns of subordination and super ordination.

With this twofold classification of social stratification, Weber lays the groundwork for an understanding of pluralistic forms of social conflict in modern society and helps to explain why only in rare cases are such societies polarized into the opposing camps of the "haves" and the "have-nots." He has done much to explain why Marx's exclusively class-centred scheme failed to predict correctly the shape of things to come in modern pluralistic societies.

Weber's analysis of class is rooted in the economic sphere, in the domain of markets, and he does not consider classes to be groups or communities. Weber's approach is more diverse than that of Marx, in that Weber considers each of financiers, debtors, professional groups such as lawyers or doctors, landless, and workers to be classes. That is, for Weber there are many more possible classes than just capitalists and workers and he does not consider ownership or non-ownership of the means of production to be the major source of class formation in capitalism.

This book will interest all students, academics and scholars of sociological theory, Weberian sociology and research methodology.

—Editor

1

Introduction

Weber differed only marginally from Marx when he defined as a class a category of men who (1) "have in common a specific causal component of their life chances in so far as (2) this component is represented exclusively by economic interests in the possession of goods and opportunities for income, and (3) it is represented under the conditions of the commodity or labour market." He was even fairly close to Marx's view, though not necessarily to those of latterday Marxists, when he stated that class position does not necessarily lead to class-determined economic or political action. He argued that communal class action will emerge only if and when the "connections between the causes and the consequences of the 'class situation' " become *transparent*; Marx would have said when a class becomes conscious of its interests, that is, of its relation, as a class, to other classes. Yet Weber's theory of stratification differs from that of Marx in that he introduced an additional structural category, that of "status group."

Classification of men into such groups is based on their consumption patterns rather than on their place in the market or in the process of production. Weber thought Marx had overlooked the relevance of such categorization because of his exclusive attention to the productive sphere. In contrast to classes, which may or may not be communal groupings, status groups are normally communities, which are held together by notions of proper lifestyles and by the social esteem and honour accorded to them by others. Linked with this are expectations of restrictions on social intercourse with those not belonging to the circle and assumed social distance toward inferiors. In this typology we again find Weber's sociological notion of a social category as dependent on the definition that others give to social relationships. A status group can exist only to the extent that others accord its members prestige or degrading, which removes them from the rest of social actors and establishes the necessary social distance between "them" and "us."

Empirically there are fairly high correlations between standing in the class and in the status order. Especially i capitalist society, the economically ascendant class will, in the course of time, also acquire high status; yet in principle, propertied and propertyless people may belong to the same status group. At certain times, an economically weak element, such as the East Elbian Junkers, may exercise considerable influence and power because of its preeminent status. Generally, as much pos-Weberian analysis of American politics has shown, political behaviour may at times be influenced by men who are fearful of losing their status or who bridle at not having been accorded a status they think is their due; such influence may be as powerful as class-determined modes of political behaviour.

In Weber's view every society is divided into groupings and strata with distinctive life-styles and views of the world, just as it is divided into distinctive classes. While at times status as well as class groupings may conflict, at others their members may accept fairly stable patterns of subordination and super ordination.

With this twofold classification of social stratification, Weber lays the groundwork for an understanding of pluralistic forms of social conflict in modern society and helps to explain why only in rare cases are such societies polarized into the opposing camps of the "haves" and the "have-nots." He has done much to explain why Marx's exclusively class-centred scheme failed to predict correctly the shape of things to come in modern pluralistic societies.

In regard to the analysis of power in society, Weber again introduces a pluralistic notion. Although he agrees with Marx in crucial respects, he refines and extends Marx's analytical scheme. For Marx, power is always rooted, even in only in the "last analysis," in economic relations. Those who own the means of production exercise political power either directly or indirectly. Weber agreed that quite often, especially in the modern capitalist world, economic power is the predominant form. But he objects that "the emergence of economic power may be the consequence of power existing on other grounds." For example, men who are able to command large-scale bureaucratic organizations may wield a great deal of economic power even though they are only salaried employees.

Weber understands by power: the chance of a man, or a number of men "to realize their own will in communal action, even against the resistance of others." He shows that the basis from which such power can be exercised may vary considerably according to the social context, that is, historical and structural circumstance. Hence, where the source of power is located becomes for Weber an empirical question, one that cannot be answered by what he considers Marx's dogmatic emphasis on one specific source. Moreover, Weber argues, men do not only strive for power to enrich themselves. "Power, including economic power, may be valued 'for its own sake.' Very frequently the striving for power is also conditioned by the social 'honour' it entails."

INTRODUCTION TO MAX WEBER

Max Weber was born on April 21, 1864, in Erfurt, Thuringia (now East Germany), the eldest son of a well situated German family that valued education, culture and citizenship. Max was surrounded by good books from the day he was born and by the time he was fourteen could and did read Homer, Virgil, and Livy fluently in the original. By the time he finished the Gymnasium he had read his way through the forty-volume Weimar edition of Goethe's works, could quote Shakespeare in English and had exercised his critical faculties on the works of Spinoza, Schopenhauer and Kant. Weber began his serious studies at the University of Heidelberg on the faculty of law, but his interests carried over into the fields of economics and philosophy, in all of which he regularly attended lectures. Despite such a prodigious interest in learning, Weber's student days do not present a uniform picture of the budding bookworm. Max could not make up his mind whether to lead the life of the scholar or that of the gentleman. Probably in order to overcome his ascetic tendencies he joined one of the *Burschenschaften* (duelling fraternities) and quickly adopted their boisterous way of life and shallow nationalistic views. The picture of crude animal spirit that he presented on one of his visits home was enough to anger his mother into trying to slap some sense of decency back into him. The effect was lasting. This phase and the incident ate important because they signify Weber's continuous dilemma of having to choose between the life of scholarly isolation and that of personal involvement. Whenever he ventured too far afield from his chosen scholarly labours to become involved into political activities, a form of allegorical slap in the face always seemed to await him in the end!

In 1883, Weber began his year of voluntary military training that opened up reserve officer's status to university trained persons. Though he detested military service, he did not rebel—the part of him which enjoyed the fraternities acquiesced to the rigours and idiocies of military drill. When he finished his military training, he did not return to Heidelberg but matriculated at Berlin.

In Berlin he came under the influence of Gneist and Gierke, absorbing from the former a feeling for British parliamentary institutions and from the latter an understanding of German legal history and the role played in it by associations; but he also listened with mixed feelings to Treitschke's crude nationalism. After a brief stay at Goettingen, Weber returned to Berlin in 1866, where he took his examination in law and reluctantly accepted a position at a Berlin criminal court. Since the work bored him, he continued his studies with Professor Mommsen and eventually wrote his Ph.D. dissertation. This dissertation was entitled *A Contribution to the History of Medieval Business Organizations*, and it already showed his skilful handling of legal concepts, economic principles and historical documentation. At his oral examination Professor Mommsen paid him high compliments and foresaw a brilliant career as a scholar for Weber.

But Weber was still uncertain whether an academic career could command his full attention. J. P. Mayer, in his study *Max Weber and German Politics* (London, 1944), wrote in this respect: "The conflict whether he should turn to practical things or whether he should pursue the aim of achieving smoothing outstanding in the field of scholarship and academic teaching—and only an outstanding achievement would satisfy him—is profound. This conflict is, as it were, of constitutional significance for Max Weber's whole being." Weber was far from espousing a life of monastic asceticism; to him theoretical work acquired meaning only in the course of application and from this probably derived his later concern with scientific methodology rather than with metaphysical speculations. Still torn between his desires to become involved in more worldly affairs or to pursue a purely academic career, Weber prepared his habilitation study in order to qualify as an instructor in Law at the University of Berlin. This effort, constituting his second major work, took the form of a study of Roman agrarian history, but was really a penetrating analysis of the social, political and economic developments of Roman society. It was published in 1891.

While he was still working on the study and during his preparations for his tasks as instructor at the University of Berlin, Weber joined the Verein für Sozialpolitik. This association aimed at the improvement of labour's working conditions, regulation of banking and business practices and was generally prepared to grant the state greater latitude in its handling of social problems. The members of this association became known as *Katheder Sozialisten* (academic socialists), an early German version of the British Fabian society. In the Verein Weber found at least a limited outlet for his desire to combine theoretical investigations with practical applications and through these activities he became thoroughly conversant with the sociopolitical problems of his day.

In 1892, Weber married Marianne Schnitger and formally began his lectures at the University of Berlin. Two years later, Weber was offered and accepted a full professorship at the University of Freiburg. There he delivered his inaugural lecture in 1895 on *The National State and Germanic Policy*, which, in its essentials, forecast much of his later political thinking. His central point, as relevant then as it is now, was the question of whether the German bourgeoisie was politically mature enough to take on the political leadership of the nation. Though Weber answered it in the negative, he doubted that it was really too late to make good this lack of political education. But he admonished his listeners that the task was immense and that it must remain the serious duty of every German, "each in his narrow circle," to collaborate in the political education of his nation. Political education, he declared, must be the goal of political science.

Very soon afterwards Weber was appointed Professor of Economics at Heidelberg University, where he spent one of his intellectually most fruitful and enjoyable years. But within the year Weber suffered a nervous breakdown which resulted in the complete suspension of his work. For hours, his wife and biographer recalled later in her *Max Weber, Ein Lebensbild* (Tübingen, 1926), he would sit at the window and stare into space; his recovery took almost four years, during which time he never opened a book or wrote a line. Weber again returned to his scholarly labours in 1903, at which time he began a long series of studies to clarify the method of the social sciences. He was also appointed associate editor of the *Archiv für Sozial* wissenschaften, which flowered into Germany's foremost journal of the social sciences, a position which it held until the *advent of Hitler*.

In 1904, Weber made his first visit to the United States, to attend a scientific World Congress held in St. Louis. In the United States Weber thought he recognized the meaning of the Twentieth Century: the ascendency of the masses and the need of vast bureaucratic structures to govern them. The same year also saw the publication of his *The Protestant Ethic and the Spirit of Capitalism*. In this work Weber analyzed the beginnings of capitalism in order to gain a fuller appreciation of the significance and implications of capitalist economics in its contemporary phase. Weber foresaw the absence of any justification—religious or ethical—in the pursuit of wealth and feared its transformation in the United States into a mere sport, ending, possibly, in what he called "mechanized petrifaction."

Though the University of Heidelberg continued his appointment after his recovery, Weber was no longer able to lecture and in 1907, thanks to a substantial inheritance, he resigned and continued his work as a private scholar. The remaining years of his life were taken up with his studies of *Economics and Society*, in which he introduced the theme of the evolution of Western civilization in terms of its developing rationality and attempted to illuminate the emergence of industrial civilization, with emphasis on the characteristics that distinguish it from other, earlier forms of society. For the first time, according to Weber, the world witnessed the creation of a deliberately planned social order through the instrumentalities of capitalism in the economic sphere, the methods of science in the intellectual and the manipulation of bureaucracy in the political sphere.

Weber interrupted this work once during World War I, when he served in the administration of army hospitals, an experience which provided him with rich materials for the formulation of principles on bureaucratic systems, and again in 1918, when he accepted an appointment as consultant to the German Armistice Commission, and as expert advisor on the Confidential Committee for Constitutional Reform. The result of this latter experience, Weber's last brush with the world of politics, was the eventual introduction into the Weimar constitution of Article 41, which provided for the election of the President by popular vote. It represented the culmination of much of Weber's thinking on this subject; he regarded the position of President of the new Reich as the focal point for the development of charismatic leadership which, he felt, could emerge only if that office was open to election by all the people. A popular leader must be the center of any political system and not an institution whose authority was only delegated, i.e., a parliamentary assembly. As the ignominious use of Article 48 (emergency powers) by the popularly elected President later showed, Weber had completely and romantically misread the true meaning of "plebiscitarian democracy." Nevertheless his death in June, 1920, at the age of 56 came at a time when his involvement in the political education of his countrymen might have been of considerable benefit to them. More than any other figure later during the Weimar period, Weber had the intellectual stature and respect that might have commanded him a hearing when the first danger signs of catastrophe began to appear.

At his death Max Weber left behind him a number of incomplete studies, including his *Wirtschaft und Gesselschaft* (*Economics and Society*). Though most of these studies were farranging in scope and detailed in execution, there was among them one which represented, in effect, an effort by Weber to provide a set of definitions that would help to integrate his work and would also serve as a suitable introduction to it for the beginner. Since many of these definitions and principles were based on Weber's own empirical investigations, they had in fact been tested, and could be viewed as preliminary formulations for a general science of social behaviour. Such a formulation had been, for example, his statement on sociology which appeared in the journal *Logos*, Vol. IV (1913), and it is the reworked version of this article that makes up the following pages.

These methodological principles begin with Weber's definition of sociology as the science which aims at the interpretative understanding of social behaviour in order to gain an explanation of its causes, its course and its effects. The rest of the study is mainly concerned with the explanation of what is meant by such terms as social behaviour, understanding, causal explanation, and what typological means must be used for purposes of analysis. Here we can only briefly sketch the salient points of Weber's systematization. Readers who are interested in a fuller treatment are referred to the excellent studies by Theodore Able, *Systematic Sociology in Germany* (New York, 1929); Reinhard Bendix, *Max Weber, An Intellectual Portrait* (Garden City, 1960); H. Gerth and C. W. Mills, eds., *From Max Weber: Essays in Sociology* (New York, 1946); and A. M. Henderson and T. Parsons, eds., *Max Weber: The Theory of Social and Economic Organization* (Glencoe, 1947).

According to Weber, human conduct, in order to qualify as social behaviour must be clearly *intentional*, i.e., it must have meaning attached to it by the individuals engaged in it, who in turn orient themselves toward the similar behaviour of others. Merely introspective conduct such as meditation, or conduct that is oriented toward material objects of situations ranks only as nonsocial behaviour. In order to analyze social behaviour Weber proceeds to create certain typical ideal behaviour patterns for purposes of comparison with actual examples of behaviour that he had observed in his investigations.

We are thus introduced to Weber's term of the *ideal type*, by which he proposes that all conceptual formulations and definitions in sociology should be expressed. Such an ideal type is created by means of "a onesided emphasis and intensification of one of several aspects of a given event and represents a uniform mental structure" (Able). Weber is quite insistent on making clear that such an ideal type must be at least in the realm of probability and not merely possible; that is, there must be found somewhere at least a close empirical approximation. Thus, the construction of an ideal type can also be regarded as a working hypothesis, which, until its realistic worth has been proved by observation, may, like any other hypothesis, be of little analytical value. The ideal type, furthermore, is purely *descriptive* and should not be misused to explain the data it reveals; nor does it at any time indicate what action can or should be taken.

The ideal type is therefore primarily an instrument for classification, and as such useful for the systematic arrangement of several categories in each of which all observations—either quantitatively of qualitatively—that are covered by its descriptions may be grouped together. In this way it is possible, for example, to construct ideal types of bureaucracy, feudalism, parliamentary democracy of capitalism and then classify the observational data according to their greater proximity to one of these types rather than to others.

The most important form of social behaviour according to Weber is so-called reciprocal social behaviour, which terminologically becomes a *social relation* and whose study is considered by Weber to be the central theme of sociology. A social relation is present where individuals mutually base their behaviour on the expected behaviour of others. Some of the types of social relations that Weber singles out for explanation in the following pages are struggle, communalization, aggregation and corporate groups.

Struggle he defines as a form of social relation in which one individual behaves in such a way as to assert his will over and against the resistance of another individual. *Communalization* is a social relation based upon a subjective feeling, either emotional or traditional, of belonging together. *Aggregation* is a social relationship based upon a rationally motivated balance of a union of interests. A *corporate group*, in turn, constitutes a social relation in which authority is upheld by the activities of a leader and an administrative staff. The last three types of social relationships may be either *open* or *closed*, depending on whether participation in them is due to voluntary agreement or to authoritative imposition.

Undoubtedly one of the more complex terms in Weber's vocabulary of definitions is that of "understanding." It is difficult to render this term in English since here it is used in a much broader sense than the one which Weber reserves for it. According to Weber a course of behaviour may have an intended meaning, regardless of whether or not a person of persons involved in it "understands" the meaning of their behaviour. Neither does the observer of a course of behaviour always "understand" its meaning. The chief point of meaningful behaviour is simply that some "intention" is attached to it. Obviously certain actions are carried out with a more clearly defined purpose than others, and the means employed to achieve their goals are clearly discernible. Thus a reflex action is "meaningless" as the direction of that action may not be the one originally intended and the means to bring it about have not been selected with forethought. As usual Weber warns that there is no rigid separation between "meaningful" behaviour and behaviour that has no intent attached to it.

The importance of "understanding" lies for Weber in its strictly technical nature of providing a clue to the observation and theoretical interpretation of the subjective states of mind of individuals whose behaviour is being studied. In other words "understanding" becomes a tool of sociological research which aims at providing more insight than can be had, even by the most precise statistical proof, of the high correlation between a given situation and a corresponding course of behaviour. "Understanding" goes further by asking not only why an action has taken place but also why a certain "behaviour pattern" continues to be followed. In this way the search for motivation is introduced as basic to any kind of sociological interpretation. Merely functional understanding may suffice for the natural sciences, but not for the social sciences, which must probe the why and wherefore of any given course of social behaviour.

Thus, the discovery that a capacity for rational conduct is correlated with a specific cephalic index and that where such correlation exists there can be noted a greater desire for power and prestige is merely a *datum* of and not an *object* for sociological investigation. Sociological analysis begins only with the causal explanation of the *kind* of social behaviour that leads to the acquisition of power and prestige by showing such correlation, why or why not they succeeded in their undertaking, and what were the understandable consequences of their seeking of power under equally "meaningful" behaviour of other individuals. It is necessary therefore to gain knowledge of the whole social situation and not merely of isolated conditions of events, however uniform their appearance may be.

Weber insists that even though the process of "understanding" is essentially subjective, the individual engaging in it can do so with the necessary degree of objective detachment. Of course, because the individual can never detach himself completely from other individuals whose social behaviour he is interpreting, such interpretation will necessarily always be more fragmentary and hypothetical than a similar process of causal interpretation in the natural sciences. But in recognizing this difficulty, Weber also suggests means of overcoming it. He does this by distinguishing interpretation which is merely *adequate at the level of meaning* (i.e., it gives some single sufficient reason for a certain type of behaviour), from interpretation which is also *causally adequate.* A causally adequate interpretation is achieved when the probability of a recurrence of a phenomenon under the same circumstance is empirically determined. Thus, in order for sociology to achieve scientifically balanced explanation it must use both criteria of adequacy on the level of meaning and causal adequacy because "If no meaning attaches itself to such typical behaviour, then no matter how high the degree of uniformity or the statistical preciseness of probability, it still remains an incomprehensible statistical probability regardless of whether it deals with an overt or subjective process".

Weber suggests two *ways* by which "understanding" is obtained and two *kinds* of "understanding" that have to be taken into consideration. Thus we may understand the meaning of a given type of behaviour intellectually if the behaviour is rational. Such rationality depends on the behaviour pattern unfolding in a manner that to us appears to be logical, i.e., it conforms to a predictable sequence of behaviour. Again we may acquire "understanding" by empathy of a given type of behaviour if such behaviour appears to be irrational. Such empathy is achieved by projecting oneself into the irrational situation and experiencing its emotional impact. The more susceptible we are ourselves to a given type of irrationality, the more readily will such "understanding" occur.

By using either the intellectual or empathic approach we can achieve two *kinds* of "understanding." By mere observation of a familiar action we can obtain *actual understanding* (e.g., a person who reaches for the knob to shut a door). This is probably the most common form of understanding. Of we can try to discover the motives underlying the conduct just observed and in this way achieve what Weber calls *explanatory understanding*. In order to establish a meaningful connection between the performance of an act and its underlying motive, the observer must be able to project himself intellectually and emotionally into the same situation, with the knowledge that under similar conditions he would behave in the same way. To *actually understand* the meaning of a familiar form of conduct is merely an exercise in deduction. But to explain the motives behind it will always be a difficult fundamental question of methodology in the social sciences—difficult because any concern with motives must remain necessarily always incomplete, since even the individual engaging in a certain form of behaviour may not always be aware of his own motivation. Thus it would not be unusual for the same situation to be explainable in terms of two entirely different sets of motivation, each of which appears equally valid to the observer.

Weber's passion for scientific objectivity left him when he turned to a consideration of the state. Here his definition seems to echo the influence of Hegel, Treitschke and the highpitched nationalism of the Wilhelmine empire.

Already in his inaugural lecture at the University of Freiburg, Weber had declared that "the power and interests of the nation are the last and decisive interests which economic policy has to serve.... The national state is for us the secular power organization of the nation and in this national state the *raison d'etat* is for us the ultimate yardstick for economic considerations." Marianne Weber also informs us that "His passion for the national power state sprang clearly from an innate instinct which no reasoning could call into question. The powerful nation is the expanded body of a powerfully endowed man; its affirmation is his self-affirmation." The *Machtstaat* idea was, according to J. P. Mayer, central to Weber's admiration of Bismarck as the faithful and brilliant practitioner of Machiavellism. Hans Kohn, who in his *The Mind of Germany* (New York, 1960), subjects Weber's liberalism to searching criticism, noted that " Weber, like most German scholars, never understood the implications and limitations of Machiavellism. He was unable to see the moral element inherent in any political power."

Accordingly, Weber's definition of the state rests primarily on authority, bureaucracy, compulsory jurisdiction over a territory and monopolization of the legitimate use of force. He is careful to reject any definition of the modern state and its legal order that centers on either the purpose of the political community or some specific value judgments that inspire belief in its legitimacy. Instead he states that political communities have pursued all conceivable ends at one time or another without thereby losing the character of the modern state. All political formations are formations of violence to Weber, with the state singled out especially "as the last source of all legitimate violence."

"Power" Weber defines as the opportunity which permits one individual to impose his will on the behaviour of others even against their will. But he rejects his definition as being too elusive, in favor of the narrower concept of "domination," which is in effect political power. Domination is achieved by influencing others through the explicit articulation of what one wants them to do and having these "commands" obeyed implicity. However the two way relationship between ruler and ruled which this concept implies hinges on the belief by both sides in the legitimacy of the authority that exercises domination. Consequently, Weber considered it necessary to recognize three principles which permit this legitimate exercise of the power to issue commands.

MAX WEBER: LIFE AND CAREER

Karl Emil Maximilian Weber (1864–1920) was born in Erfurt, Thuringia to a family of notable heritage His father, Max Sr., came from a Westphalian family of merchants and industrialists in the textile business and went on to become a National Liberal parliamentarian of some recognizable influence in Wilhelmine politics. His mother, Helene, came from the Fallenstein and Souchay families, both of the long illustrious Huguenot line, which had for generations produced public servants and academicians. Evidently, Max Weber was brought up in a prosperous, cosmopolitan, and highly cultivated family milieu that was wellplugged into the political and social establishment of the German *Bürgertum*. Also, his parents represented two, often conflicting, poles of identity between which their eldest son would struggle throughout his life — worldly statesmanship and ascetic scholarship.

Educated mainly at the universities of Heidelberg and Berlin, Weber was trained in jurisprudence, eventually writing his *Habilitationsschrift* on Roman law and agrarian history. After some flirtation with legal practice and public service, he received an important research commission from the *Verein für Sozialpolitik* (the leading social science association under Gustav Schmoller's leadership) and produced the so-called East Elbian Report on the displacement of the German agrarian workers in East Prussia by Polish migrant labourers. Greeted upon publication with much praise and some political controversy, this early success led to his first university appointment at Freiburg to be followed shortly by a prestigious professorship in political economy at Heidelberg. Weber and his wife Marianne, an intellectual in her own right and early women's rights activist, soon found themselves at the center of the vibrant intellectual and cultural life of Heidelberg; the so-called "Weber Circle" attracted such intellectual luminaries as Georg Jellinek, Ernst Troeltsch, and Werner Sombart and later a number of younger scholars including Marc Bloch, Robert Michels, and György Lukács. Weber was also active in public life as he continued to play an important role as a Young Turk in the *Verein* and maintain a close association with the *Evangelischesoziale Kongress* (especially with the leader of its younger, liberal wing, Friedrich Naumann). It was during this time that he first established a solid reputation as a brilliant political economist and passionate public intellectual, albeit with a somewhat unpredictable and laconic temperament.

All these fruitful years came to an abrupt halt in 1896 when Weber collapsed with a nervousbreakdown shortly after his father's sudden death (precipitated by a heated confrontation with Weber). His routine as a teacher and scholar was interrupted so badly that he eventually withdrew from regular teaching duties in 1903, to which he would not return until 1919. Although severely compromised and unable to write as prolifically as before, he still managed to immerse himself in the study of various philosophical and religious topics, which resulted in a new direction in his scholarship as the publication of miscellaneous methodological essays, and especially that of *The Protestant Ethic and the Spirit of Capitalism,* testifies. After this stint essentially as a private scholar, he slowly resumed his participation in various academic and public activities. With Edgar Jaffe and Sombart, he took over editorial control of the *Archiv für Sozialwissenschaften u. Sozialpolitik*, turning it into the leading social science journal of the day as well as his new institutional platform. In 1909, he cofounded the *Deutsche Gesellschaft für Soziologie*, in part as a result of his growing unease with the *Verein*'s political orientation and lack of methodological discipline, becoming its first treasurer (he would resign from it in 1912, though). This period of his life, until interrupted by the outbreak of the First World War in 1914, brought the pinnacles of his achievements as he worked intensely in two areas: the comparative sociology of world religions and his contribution to the *Grundriss der Sozialökonomik*, in particular the sections on economic and legal sociology, which would be put together and published posthumously as *Economy and Society*. Along with the major methodological essays that he drafted during this time, these works would become mainly responsible for Weber's enduring reputation as one of the founding fathers of modern social science.

With the onset of the War, Weber's involvement in public life took an unexpected turn. At first a fervent nationalist supporter of the War, as virtually all German intellectuals of the time were, he grew disillusioned with the German war policies, eventually refashioning himself as one of the most vocal critics of the Kaiser government in a time of war. As a public intellectual, he issued private reports to government leaders and wrote journalistic pieces to warn against the Belgian annexation policy and the unlimited submarine warfare, which, as the War deepened, evolved into a call for overall democratization of the authoritarian state that was Wilhelmine Germany. By 1917, Weber was campaigning vigorously for a wholesale constitutional reform for postwar Germany, including the introduction of universal suffrage and the empowerment of parliament.

When defeat came in 1918, Germany found in Weber a public intellectual leader, even possibly a future statesman, with relatively solid liberal democratic credentials who was wellpositioned to influence the course of postwar reconstruction. He was invited to join the draft board of the Weimar Constitution as well as the German delegation to Versaille; albeit in vain, he even ran for a parliamentary seat on the liberal Democratic Party ticket. In those capacities, however, he opposed the German Revolution (all too sensibly) and the Versaille Treaty (all too quixotically) alike, putting himself in an honourable yet unsustainable position that defied the partisan alignments of the day. By all accounts, his political activities bore little fruit, except his advocacy for a robust plebiscitary presidency in the Weimar Constitution, and his political influence was marginal at best despite the widespread respect he commanded from the general public.

Frustrated with daytoday politics, he turned to his scholarly pursuits with renewed vigour. In 1919, he briefly taught in turn at the universities of Vienna (*General Economic History* was an outcome of this experience) and of Munich (where he gave the muchlauded lectures, *Science as a Vocation* and *Politics as a Vocation*), while compiling his scattered writings on religion in the form of massive three volume *Gesammelte Aufsätze zur Religionssoziologie* [*GARS* hereafter]. All these reinvigorated scholarly activities ended abruptly in 1920, however, when he suddenly died of pneumonia in Munich. Max Weber was fifty six years old.

Philosophical Influences

Putting Weber in the context of philosophical tradition proper is not an easy task. For all the astonishing variety of identities that can be ascribed to him as a scholar, he was certainly no philosopher at least in the narrow sense of the term. His reputation as a Solonic legislator of modern social science also tends to cloud our appreciation of the extent to which his ideas were embedded in the intellectual tradition of the time. Broadly speaking, Weber's philosophical worldview, if not coherent philosophy, was informed by the deep crisis of the Enlightenment project in findesiècle Europe, which was characterized by the intellectual revolt against positivist reason, a celebration of subjective will and intuition, and a neo-Romantic longing for spiritual wholesomeness. As such, the philosophical backdrop to his thoughts will be outlined here along two axes: epistemology and ethics.

Epistemology: Neo-Kantianism

Weber encountered the pan-European cultural crisis of his time mainly as filtered through the jargon of German Historicism. His early training in law had exposed him to the sharp divide between the reigning Labandian legal positivism and the historical jurisprudence championed by Otto von Gierke (one of his teachers at Berlin); in his later incarnation as a political economist, he was keenly interested in the heated "strife over methods" (*Methodenstreit*) between the positivist economic methodology of Carl Menger and the historical economics of Schmoller (his mentor during the early days). Arguably, however, it was not until Weber grew acquainted with the Baden or Southwestern School of NeoKantians, especially through Wilhelm Windelband, Emil Lask, and Heinrich Rickert (his onetime colleague at Freiburg), that he found a rich conceptual template suitable for the clearer elaboration of his own epistemological position.

In opposition to a Hegelian emanationist epistemology, briefly, Neo-Kantians shared the Kantian dichotomy between reality and concept. Not an emanent derivative of concepts as Hegel posited, reality is irrational and incomprehensible, and the concept only an abstract construction of our mind. Nor is the concept a matter of will, intuition, and subjective consciousness as Wilhelm Dilthey posited. According to Hermann Cohen, one of the early Neo-Kantians, concept construction is fundamentally a cognitive process, which cannot but be rational as Kant held. If our cognition is logical and all reality exists within cognition, then only a reality that we can comprehend in the form of knowledge is rational — metaphysics is thereby reduced to epistemology, and Being to logic. As such, the process of concept construction both in the natural (*Natur-*) and the cultural-historical sciences (*Geisteswissenshaften*) has to be universal as well as abstract, not different in kind but in their subject matters. The latter is only different in dealing with the question of values in addition to logical relationships.

For Windelband, however, the difference between the two kinds of knowledge has to do with its aim and method as well. Cultural-historical knowledge is not concerned with a phenomenon because of what it shares with other phenomena, but rather because of its own definitive qualities. For values, which form its proper subject, are radically subjective, concrete and individualistic. Unlike the "nomothetic" knowledge that natural science seeks, what matters in historical science is not a universal law-like causality, but an understanding of the particular way in which an individual ascribes values to certain events and institutions or takes a position towards the general cultural values of his/her time under a unique, never-to-be-repeated constellation of historical circumstances. Therefore, cultural-historical science seeks "ideographic" knowledge; it aims to understand the particular, concrete and irrational "historical individual" *with* inescapably universal, abstract, and rational concepts. Turning irrational reality into rational concept, it does not simply paint (*abbilden*) a picture of reality but transforms (*umbilden*) it. Occupying the gray area between irrational reality and rational concept, then, its question became twofold for the Neo-Kantians — one being in what way we can understand the irreducibly subjective values held by the historical actors in an objective fashion, and the other, by what criteria we can select a certain historical phenomenon as opposed to another as historically significant subject matter worthy of our attention. In short, the issue was not only the values to be comprehended by the seeker of historical knowledge, but also his/her own values, which are no less subjective. Valuation (*Werturteil*) as well as value (*Wert*) became a keen issue.

According to Rickert's definitive elaboration, valuation precedes values. On the one hand, he posits that the "in-dividual," as opposed to mere "individual," phenomenon can be isolated as a discrete subject of our historical inquiry when we ascribe certain subjective values to the singular coherence and indivisibility that are responsible for its uniqueness. In his theory of value-relation (*Wertbeziehung*), on the other, Rickert argues that relating historical objects to values can still retain objective validity when it is based on a series of explicitly formulated conceptual distinctions; that between the investigator's values and those of the historical actor under investigation, between personal or private values and general cultural values of the time, and between subjective value-judgment and objective value-relations.

In so positing, however, Rickert is making two highly questionable assumptions: one is that there are certain values in every culture that are universally accepted within that culture as valid, and the other that a historian free of bias must agree on what these values are. Just as natural science must assume "unconditionally and universally valid laws of nature," so, too, cultural-historical science must assume that there are "unconditionally and universally valid values." If so, an "individual" historical event has to be reduced to an "individual" manifestation of the objective process of history, a conclusion that essentially implies that Rickert returned to the German Idealist faith in the meaningfulness of history and the objective validity of the diverse values to be found in history. An empirical study in historical science, in the end, cannot do without a metaphysics of history. Bridging irrational reality and rational concept in historical science, or overcoming *hiatus irrationalis* (á la Lask) without recourse to a metaphysics of history still remained a problem as acutely as before. While accepting the broadly neo-Kantian conceptual template as Rickert elabourated it, Weber's methodological writings would turn mostly on this issue.

Ethics: Kant and Nietzsche

German Idealism seems to have exerted another enduring influence on Weber, discernible in his ethical worldview more than in his epistemological position. This was the strand of Idealist discourse in which a broadly Kantian ethic and its Nietzschean critique figure prominently.

The way in which Weber understood Kant seems to have been through the conceptual template set by moral psychology and philosophical anthropology. In conscious opposition to the utilitarian-naturalistic justification of modern individualism, Kant viewed moral action as simultaneously principled and self-disciplined *and* an expression of genuine freedom and autonomy. On this Kantian view, freedom and autonomy are to be found in the instrumental control of the self and the world (objectification) according to a law formulated solely from within (subjectification). Furthermore, such a paradoxical compound is made possible by an internalization or willful acceptance of a transcendental rational principle, which saves it from falling prey to the hedonistic justification of a subjectification that Kant found in Enlightenment naturalism and which he so detested. Kant in this regard follows Rousseau in condemning utilitarianism; instrumental-rational control of the world in the service of our desires and needs just degenerates into organized egoism. In order to prevent it, mere freedom of choice based on elective will (*Willkür*) has to be replaced by the exercise of purely rational will (*Wille*). Instrumental transformation of the self is thus the crucial benchmark of autonomous moral agency for Kant as well as for Locke, but its basis has been fundamentally altered in Kant; it should be done with the purpose of serving a higher end, that is, for Kant, the universal law of reason. A willful self-transformation is demanded now in the service of a higher law based on reason or, one might say, of an "ultimate value" in Weber's parlance.

Weber's understanding of this Kantian ethical template was strongly tinged by the Protestant theological debate taking place in the Germany of his time between (orthodox Lutheran) Albrecht Ritschl and Matthias Schneckenburger (of Calvinist persuasion), a context with which Weber became acquainted through his Heidelberg colleague, Troeltsch. Suffice it to note in this connection that Weber's sharp critique of Ritschl's Lutheran communitarianism seems reflective of his broadly Kantian preoccupation with radically subjective individualism and the methodical transformation of the self. All in all, one might say, as Ernest Gellner did, that: "the preoccupations of Kant and of Weber are really the same. One was a philosopher and the other a sociologist, but there ... the difference ends".

That which also ends, however, is Weber's subscription to a Kantian ethic of duty when it comes to the possibility of a universal law of reason. Weber was keenly aware of the fact that the Kantian linkage between growing self-consciousness, the possibility of a universal law, and principled and thus free action had been irrevocably severed. Kant managed to preserve the precarious duo of non-arbitrary action and subjective freedom by asserting such a linkage, which Weber believed to be antiquated in his allegedly Nietzschean age.

According to Nietzsche, "will to truth" cannot be content with the metaphysical construction of a grand metanarrative, whether it be monotheistic religion or modern science, and growing self-consciousness, or "intellectualization" à la Weber, can lead only to a radical skepticism, value relativism, or, even worse, nihilism. According to such a Historicist diagnosis of modernity that culminates in the "death of God," the alternative seems to be either a radical self-assertion and self-creation that runs the risk of being arbitrary (as in Nietzsche) or a complete desertion of the modern ideal of self-autonomous freedom (as in early Foucault). If the first approach leads to a radical divinization of humanity, one possible extension of modern humanism, the second leads inexorably to a "dedivinization" of humanity, a postmodern antihumanism.

Seen in this light, Weber's ethical sensibility is built on a firm rejection of a Nietzschean divination and Foucaultian resignation alike, both of which are radically at odds with a Kantian ethic of duty. In other words, Weber's ethical project can be described as a search for a non-arbitrary form of freedom (his Kantian side) in what he perceived as an increasingly post-metaphysical world (his Nietzschean side). According to Paul Honigsheim, his pupil and distant cousin, Weber's ethic is that of "tragedy" and "nevertheless." This deep tension between the Kantian moral imperatives and a Nietzschean diagnosis of the modern cultural world is apparently what gives such a darkly tragic and agnostic shade to Weber's ethical worldview.

Rationalization as a Thematic Unity

Weber's main contribution as such, nonetheless, lies neither in epistemology nor in ethics. Although they deeply informed his thoughts to an extent ruefully under-appreciated even today, his main preoccupation lay elsewhere. He was after all one of the founding fathers of modern social science. Beyond the recognition, however, that Weber is not simply a sociologist par excellence as Talcott Parsons's Durkheimian interpretation made him out to be, identifying an *idee maitresse* throughout his disparate oeuvre has been controversial ever since his own days and is still far from settled. *Economy and Society*, his alleged *magnum opus*, was a posthumous publication based upon his widow's editorship, the thematic architectonic of which is unlikely to be reconstructed beyond doubt even after its recent reissuing under the rubric of *Max Weber Gesamtausgabe*. *GARS* forms a more coherent whole since its editorial edifice was the work of Weber himself; and yet, its relationship to his other sociologies of, for instance, law, city, music, domination, and economy, remains controvertible. Accordingly, his overarching theme has also been variously surmised as a developmental history of Western rationalism (Wolfgang Schluchter), the universal history of rationalist culture (Friedrich Tenbruck), or simply the *Menschentum* as it emerges and degenerates in modern rational society (Wilhelm Hennis). The first depicts Weber as a comparative-historical sociologist; the second, a latter-day Idealist historian of culture reminiscent of Jacob Burckhardt; and the third, a political philosopher on a par with Machiavelli, Hobbes, and Rousseau. Important as they are for in-house Weber scholarship, these philological disputes need not hamper our attempt to grasp the gist of his ideas. Suffice it for us to recognize that, albeit with varying degrees of emphasis, these different interpretations all converge on the thematic centrality of rationality, rationalism, and rationalization in making sense of Weber.

At the outset, what immediately strikes a student of Weber's rationalization thesis is its seeming irreversibility and Eurocentrism. The apocalyptic imagery of the "iron cage" that haunts the concluding pages of the *Protestant Ethic* is commonly taken to reflect his dark fatalism about the inexorable unfolding of rationalization and its culmination in the complete loss of freedom and the evaporation of meaning in the modern world. The "Author's Introduction" (*Vorbemerkung* to *GARS*) also contains oft-quoted passages that allegedly disclose Weber's belief in the unique singularity of Western civilization's achievement in the direction of rationalization, or lack thereof in other parts of the world. For example:

> A product of modern European civilization, studying any problem of universal history, is bound to ask himself to what combination of circumstances the fact should be attributed that in Western civilization, and in Western civilization only, cultural phenomena have appeared which (as *we* like to think) lie in a line of development having *universal* significance and value.

Taken together, then, the rationalization process as Weber narrated it seems quite akin to a metahistorical teleology that irrevocably sets the West apart from and indeed above the East.

At the same time, nonetheless, Weber adamantly denied the possibility of a universal law of history in his methodological essays; even within the same pages of *Vorbemerkung,* he said, "rationalizations of the most varied character have existed in various departments of life and in all areas of culture". He also made clear that his study of various forms of world religions was to be taken for its heuristic value rather than as "complete analyses of cultures, however brief"; it was meant as a comparative-conceptual platform on which to erect the edifying features of rationalization in the West. If merely a heuristic device and not a universal law of progress, then, what is rationalization and whence comes his uncompromisingly dystopian vision?

Calculability, Predictability, and World-Mastery

Roughly put, taking place in all areas of human life from religion and law to music and architecture, rationalization means a historical drive towards a world in which "one can, in principle, master all things by calculation". For instance, modern capitalism is a rational mode of economic life because it depends on a calculable process of production. This search for exact calculability underpins such institutional innovations as monetary accounting (especially double-entry bookkeeping), centralization of production control, separation of workers from the means of production, supply of formally free labour, disciplined control on the factory floor, and other features that make modern capitalism *qualitatively* different from all other forms of economic life. The enhanced calculability of the production process is also buttressed by that in non-economic spheres such as law and administration. Legal formalism and bureaucratic management reinforce the elements of predictability in the sociopolitical environment that encumbers industrial capitalism by means of introducing formal equality of citizenship, a rule-bound legislation of legal norms, an autonomous judiciary, and a depoliticized professional bureaucracy. All this calculability and predictability in political, social, and economic spheres was not possible without changes of values in ethics, religion, psychology, and culture. Institutional rationalization was, in other words, predicated upon the rise of a peculiarly rational type of personality, or a "person of vocation" (*Berufsmensch*) as outlined in the *Protestant Ethic*. The outcome of this complex interplay of ideas and interests was modern rational Western civilization with its enormous material and cultural capacity for relentless world-mastery.

Knowledge, Impersonality, and Control

On a more analytical plateau, all these disparate processes of rationalization can be surmised as increasing knowledge, growing impersonality, and enhanced control. First, knowledge. Rational action in one very general sense presupposes knowledge. It requires some knowledge of the ideational and material circumstances in which our action is embedded, since to act rationally is to act on the basis of conscious reflection about the probable consequences of action. As such, the knowledge that underpins a rational action is of a causal nature conceived in terms of means-ends relationships and aspiring towards a systematic, logically interconnected whole. Modern scientific and technological knowledge is a culmination of this process that Weber called intellectualization, in the course of which, the germinating grounds of human knowledge in the past, such as religion, theology, and metaphysics, were slowly pushed back to the realm of the superstitious, mystical, or simply irrational. It is only in modern Western civilization, according to Weber, that this gradual process of disenchantment (*Entzauberung*) has reached its radical conclusion.

Second, impersonality. Rationalization, according to Weber, entails objectification (*Versachlichung*). Industrial capitalism, for one, reduces workers to sheer numbers in an accounting book, completely free from the fetters of tradition and non-economic considerations, as the market relationships do vis-à-vis buyers and sellers. For another, having abandoned the principle of Khadi justice (i.e., personalized *ad hoc* adjudication), modern law and administration also rule in strict accordance with the systematic formal codes and *sine irae et studio*, that is, "without regard to person." Again, Weber found the seed of objectification not in material interests alone, but in the Puritan vocational ethic (*Berufsethik*) and the life conduct that it inspired, which was predicated upon a disenchanted monotheistic theodicy that reduced humans to mere tools of

God's providence. Ironically, for Weber, modern inward subjectivity was born once we lost any inherent value *qua* humans and became thoroughly objectified vis-à-vis God in the course of the Reformation. Modern individuals are subjectified and objectified all at once.

Third, control. Pervasive in Weber's view of rationalization is the increasing control in social and material life. Scientific and technical rationalization has greatly improved both the human capacity for a mastery over nature and institutionalized discipline *via* bureaucratic administration, legal formalism, and industrial capitalism. The calculable, disciplined control over humans was, again, an unintended consequence of the Puritan ethic of rigorous self-discipline and self-control, or what Weber called "innerworldly asceticism (*innerweltliche Askese*)." Here again, Weber saw the irony that a modern individual citizen equipped with inviolable rights was born as a part of the rational, disciplinary ethos that increasingly penetrated into every aspect of social life.

MODERNITY: THE "IRON CAGE" AND VALUE-FRAGMENTATION

Thus seen, rationalization as Weber postulated it is anything but an unequivocal historical phenomenon. As already pointed out, first, Weber views it as a process taking place in disparate fields of human life with a logic of each field's own and varying directions; "each one of these fields may be rationalized in terms of very different ultimate values and ends, and what is rational from one point of view may well be irrational from another". Second, and more important, its ethical ramification for Weber is deeply ambivalent. To use his own dichotomy, the formal-procedural rationality (*Zweckrationalität*) to which Western rationalization tends does not necessarily go with a substantive-value rationality (*Wertrationalität*). On the one hand, exact calculability and predictability in the social environment that formal rationalization has brought about dramatically enhances individual freedom by helping individuals to understand and navigate through the complex web of institutions in order to realize the ends of their own choice. On the other hand, freedom and agency are seriously curtailed by the same force in history when individuals are reduced to a "cog in a machine," or trapped in an "iron cage" that formal rationalization has spawned with irresistible efficiency and at the expense of substantive rationality. Thus his famous lament in the *Protestant Ethic*:

> No one knows who will live in this cage (*Gehäuse*) in the future, or whether at the end of this tremendous development entirely new prophets will arise, or there will be a great rebirth of old ideas and ideals, or, if neither, mechanized petrification, embellished with a sort of convulsive self-importance. For the "last man" (*letzten Menschen*) of this cultural development, it might well be truly said: "Specialist without spirit, sensualists without heart; this nullity imagines that it has attained a level of humanity (*Menschentums*) never before achieved".

Third, Weber envisions the future of rationalization not only in terms of "mechanized petrification," but also of a chaotic, even atrophic, inundation of subjective values. In other words, the bureaucratic "iron cage" is only one side of the modernity that rationalization has brought about; the other is a "polytheism" of value-fragmentation. At the apex of rationalization, we moderns have suddenly found ourselves living "as did the ancients when their world was not yet disenchanted of its gods and demons". Modern Western society is, Weber seems to say, once again enchanted as a result of disenchantment. How did this happen and with what consequences?

Reenchantment *via* Disenchantment

In point of fact, Weber's rationalization thesis can be understood with richer nuance when we approach it as, for lack of better terms, a dialectics of disenchantment and reenchantment rather than as a one-sided, unilinear process. Disenchantment had ushered in monotheistic religions in the West; in practice, this means that *ad hoc* maxims for life-conduct had been gradually displaced by a unified total system of meaning and value, which historically culminated in the Puritan ethic of vocation. Here, the irony was that disenchantment was an ongoing process nonetheless. Disenchantment in its second phase pushed aside monotheistic religion as something irrational, thus delegitimating it as a unifying worldview in the modern secular world.

Modern science, which was singularly responsible for this late development, was initially welcomed as a surrogate system of orderly value-creation, as Weber found in the convictions of Bacon (science as "the road to *true* nature") and Descartes (as "the road to the *true* god"). For Weber, nevertheless, modern science is a deeply nihilistic enterprise in which any scientific achievement worthy of the name *must* "ask to be surpassed and made obsolete" in a process "that is in principle *ad infinitum*," at which point, "we come to the *problem of the meaning* of science." He went on to ask: "For it is simply not self-evident that something which is subject to such a law is in itself meaningful and rational. Why should one do something which in reality never comes to an end and never can?". In short, modern science has relentlessly deconstructed other value-creating activities, in the course of which its own meaning has also been demolished beyond repair. The result is the "*Götterdämmerung* of all evaluative perspectives" including its own.

Irretrievably gone as a result is a unifying worldview, be it religious or scientific, and what ensues is its fragmentation into incompatible value spheres. Weber, for instance, observed: "since Nietzsche, we realize that something can be beautiful, not only in spite of the aspect in which it is not good, but rather in that very aspect". That is to say, aesthetic values now stand in irreconcilable antagonism to religious values, transforming "value judgments (*Werturteile*) into judgments of taste (*Geschmacksurteile*) by which what is morally reprehensible becomes merely what is tasteless".

Weber is, then, *not* envisioning a peaceful dissolution of the grand metanarratives of monotheistic religion and universal science into a series of local narratives and the consequent modern pluralist culture in which different cultural practices follow their own immanent logic. His vision of polytheistic reenchantment is rather that of an incommensurable value-fragmentation into a plurality of alternative metanarratives, each of which claims to answer the same metaphysical questions that religion and (early modern) science strove to cope with in their own ways. The slow death of God has reached its apogee in the return of gods and demons who "strive to gain power over our lives and again ... resume their eternal struggle with one another".

Seen this way, Weber's rationalization thesis concludes with two strikingly dissimilar prophecies — one is the imminent iron cage of bureaucratic petrification and the other, the Hellenistic pluralism of warring deities. The modern world has come to be monotheistic and polytheistic all at once. What seems to underlie this seemingly self-contradictory imagery of modernity is the problem of modern humanity (*Menschentum*) and its loss of freedom and moral agency. Disenchantment has created a world with no objectively ascertainable ground for one's conviction. Under the circumstances, according to Weber, a modern individual tends to act only on one's own aesthetic impulse and express arbitrary convictions that cannot be communicated in the eventuality; the majority of those who cannot even act on their convictions, or the "last men who invented happiness" à la Nietzsche, lead the life of a "cog in a machine." Whether the problem of modernity is accounted for in terms of a permeation of objective, instrumental rationality or of a purposeless agitation of subjective values, Weber viewed these two images as constituting a single problem insofar as they contributed to the inertia of modern individuals who fail to take principled moral action. The "sensualists without heart" and "specialists without spirit" indeed formed two faces of the same coin that may be called the disempowerment of the modern self.

Modernity *contra* Modernization

Once things were different, Weber claimed. An unflinching sense of conviction that relied on nothing but one's innermost personality once issued in a highly methodical and disciplined conduct of everyday life — or, simply, life as a duty. Born amidst the turmoil of the Reformation, this archetypal modern self drew its strength solely from within in the sense that one's principle of action was determined by one's own psychological need to gain self-affirmation. Also, the way in which this deeply introspective subjectivity was practiced, that is, in self-mastery, entailed a highly rational and radically methodical attitude towards one's inner self and the outer, objective world. Transforming the self into an integrated personality and mastering the world with relentless energy, subjective value and objective rationality once formed "one unbroken whole". Weber calls the agent of this unity the "person of vocation" (*Berufsmensch*) in his religious writings, "personality" (*Persönlichkeit*) in the methodological essays, "genuine politician" (*Berufspolitiker*) in the political writings, and "charismatic individual" in *Economy and Society*. The much-celebrated Protestant Ethic thesis was indeed a genealogical account of this unique moral agency in modern times.

Once different, too, was the mode of society constituted by and in turn constitutive of this type of moral agency. Weber's social imagination revealed its keenest sense of irony when he traced the root of the cohesive integration, intense socialization, and severe communal discipline of the "sectlike society" (*Sektengesellschaft*) to the isolated and introspective subjectivity of the Puritan person of vocation. The irony was that the anxiety-ridden, egotistical, and even antisocial virtues of the person of vocation could be sustained only in the disciplinary environment of small-scale associational life. Membership in exclusive voluntary associational life is open, and it is such membership, or "achieved quality," that guarantees the ethical qualities of the individuals with whom one interacts. "The old 'sect spirit' holds sway with relentless effect in the intrinsic nature of such associations," Weber observed, for the sect was the first mass organization to combine individual agency and social discipline in such a systematic way. Weber thus claimed that "the ascetic conventicles and sects ... formed one of the most important foundations of modern individualism". It seems clear that what Weber was trying to outline here was an archetypical form of social organization that can empower individual moral agency by sustaining group disciplinary dynamism, a kind of pluralistically organized social life we would now call a "civil society".

To summarize, the irony with which Weber accounted for rationalization was driven by the deepening tension between modernity and modernization. Weber's problem with modernity originates from the fact that it required a historically unique constellation of cultural values and social institutions, and yet, modernization has effectively undermined the cultural basis for modern individualism and its germinating ground of disciplinary society, which together had given the original impetus to modernity. The modern project has fallen victim to its own success. Under the late modern circumstances characterized by the "iron cage" and "warring deities," then, Weber's question becomes: "How is it at all possible to salvage *any remnants* of 'individual' freedom of movement *in any sense* given this all-powerful trend" ?

Knowledge

Such an appreciation of Weber's main problematic, which culminates in the question of modern individual freedom, may help shed light on some of the controversial aspects of Weber's methodology. In accounting for his methodological claims, it needs to be borne in mind that Weber was not at all interested in writing a systematic epistemological treatise in order to put an end to the "strife over methods" (*Methodenstreit*) of his time. His ambition was much more modest and pragmatic. Just as "the person who attempted to walk by constantly applying anatomical knowledge would be in danger of stumbling"; translation altered], so can methodology be a kind of knowledge that may supply a rule of thumb, codified *a posteriori*, for what historians and social scientists do, but it could never substitute for the skills they use in their research practice. Instead, Weber's attempt to mediate historicism and positivism was meant to aid an actual researcher make a practical value-judgment (*Werturteil*) that is fair and acceptable in the face of the plethora of subjective values that one encounters when selecting and processing historical data. After all, the questions that drove his methodological reflections were what it means to practice science in the modern polytheistic world and how one can do science with a sense of vocation. In his own words, "the capacity to distinguish between empirical knowledge and value-judgments, and the fulfilment of the scientific duty to see the factual truth as well as the practical duty to stand up for our own ideals constitute the program to which we wish to adhere with ever increasing firmness". In short, Weber's methodology was as ethical as it was epistemological.

Understanding (*Verstehen*)

Building on the Neo-Kantian nominalism outlined above, thus, Weber's contribution to methodology turned mostly on the question of objectivity and the role of subjective values in historical and cultural concept formation. On the one hand, he followed Windelband in positing that historical and cultural knowledge is categorically distinct from natural scientific knowledge. Action that is the subject of any sociological inquiry is clearly different from mere behaviour. While behaviour can be accounted for without reference to inner motives and thus can be reduced to mere aggregate numbers, making it possible to establish positivistic regularities, and even laws, of collective behaviour, an action can only be interpreted because it is based on a radically subjective attribution of meaning and values to what one does. What a social scientist seeks to understand is this subjective dimension of human conduct as it relates to others. On the other hand, an understanding (*Verstehen*) in this subjective sense is not anchored in a non-cognitive empathy or intuitive appreciation that is arational by nature; it can gain objective validity when the meanings and values to be comprehended are explained causally, that is, as a means to an end. A teleological contextualization of an action in the means-end nexus is indeed the precondition for a causal explanation that can be objectively ascertained. So far, Weber is not essentially in disagreement with Rickert.

From Weber's perspective, however, the problem that Rickert's formulation raised was the objectivity of the end to which an action is held to be oriented. As pointed out, Rickert in the end had to rely on a certain transhistorical, transcultural criterion in order tc account for the purpose of an action, an assumption that cannot be warranted in Weber's view. To be consistent with the Neo-Kantian presuppositions, instead, the ends themselves have to be conceived of as no less subjective. Imputing an end to an action is of a fictional nature in the sense that it is not free from the subjective valuation that conditions the researcher's thematization of a certain subject matter out of "an infinite multiplicity of successively and coexistently emerging and disappearing events". Although a counterfactual analysis might aid in stabilizing the process of causal imputation, it cannot do away completely with the subjective nature of the researcher's perspective.

In the end, the kind of objective knowledge that historical and cultural sciences may achieve is precariously limited. An action can be interpreted with objective validity only at the level of means, not ends. An end, however, even a "self-evident" one, is irreducibly subjective, thus defying an objective understanding; it can only be reconstructed conceptually based on a researcher's no less subjective values. Objectivity in historical and social sciences is, then, not a goal that can be reached with the aid of a correct method, but an ideal that must be striven for without a promise of ultimate fulfilment. In this sense, one might say that the so-called "value-freedom" (*Wertfreiheit*) is less a methodological principle for Weber than an ethical virtue that a personality fit for modern science must possess.

Ideal Type

The methodology of "ideal type" (*Idealtypus*) is another testimony to such a broadly ethical intention of Weber. According to Weber's definition, "an ideal type is formed by the one-sided *accentuation* of one or more points of view" according to which "*concrete individual* phenomena ... are arranged into a unified analytical construct" (*Gedankenbild*); in its purely fictional nature, it is a methodological "utopia [that] cannot be found empirically anywhere in reality". Keenly aware of its fictional nature, the ideal type never seeks to claim its validity in terms of a reproduction of or a correspondence with social reality. Its validity can be ascertained only in terms of adequacy, which is too conveniently ignored by the proponents of positivism. This does not mean, however, that objectivity, limited as it is, can be gained by "weighing the various evaluations against one another and making a 'statesman-like' compromise among them", which is often proposed as a solution by those sharing Weber's kind of methodological perspectivism. Such a practice, which Weber calls "syncretism," is not only impossible but also unethical, for it avoids "the practical duty to stand up for our own ideals".

According to Weber, a clear value commitment, no matter how subjective, is both unavoidable *and* necessary. It is *unavoidable*, for otherwise no meaningful knowledge can be attained. Further, it is *necessary*, for otherwise the value position of a researcher would not be foregrounded clearly and admitted as such — not only to the readers of the research outcome but also to the very researcher him/herself. In other words, Weber's emphasis on "one-sidedness" (*Einseitigkeit*) not only affirms the subjective nature of scientific knowledge but also demands that the researcher be self-consciously subjective. The ideal type is devised for this purpose, for "only as an ideal type" can subjective value — "that unfortunate child of misery of our science" — "be given an unambiguous meaning". Along with value-freedom, then, what the ideal type methodology entails in ethical terms is, on the one hand, a daring confrontation with the tragically subjective foundation of our historical and social scientific knowledge and, on the other, a public promulgation of one's own subjective value. Weber's methodology in the end amounts to a call for the heroic character-virtue of clear-sightedness and intellectual integrity that together constitute a genuine person of science, or a scientist with a sense of vocation who has a passionate commitment to one's own specialized research, yet is utterly "free of illusions".

POLITICS AND ETHICS

Even more explicitly ethical than was his methodology, Weber's political project also discloses his entrenched preoccupation with the willful resuscitation of certain character traits in modern society. At the outset, it seems undeniable that Weber was a deeply liberal political thinker especially in a German context that is not well known for liberalism. This means that his ultimate value as a political thinker was locked on individual freedom, that "old, general type of human ideals". He was also a bourgeois liberal, and self-consciously so, in a time of great transformations that were undermining the social conditions necessary to support classical liberal values and bourgeois institutions, thereby challenging liberalism to attempt a radical self-redirection. To that extent, he belongs to that generation of liberal political thinkers in fin-de-siècle Europe who clearly perceived the general crisis of liberalism and sought to resolve it in their own liberal ways. Weber's own way was to address the problem of classical liberal characterology that was, in his view, being progressively undermined by the indiscriminate bureaucratization of modern society.

Charismatic Leadership Democracy

Such a concern with ethical character is clearly discernible in Weber's stark political realism. Utterly devoid of any normative qualities, for instance, the modern state is defined simply as "a human community that (successfully) claims the *monopoly of the legitimate use of physical force* within a given territory," whether that legitimacy derives from charisma, tradition, or law. Further, he held that, even in a democratic state, domination of the ruled by the ruler(s) is simply an unavoidable political fact. If the genuine self-rule of the people is impossible, the only choice is one between leaderless and leadership democracy (*Führerdemokratie*). When advocating a sweeping democratization of post-war Germany, thus, Weber envisioned democracy in Germany as a political marketplace in which strong charismatic leaders can be identified and elected by winning votes in a free competition, even struggle, among themselves. Preserving and enhancing this element of struggle in politics is important since it is only through a dynamic electoral process that national leaders strong enough to keep an otherwise omnipotent bureaucracy under control can be made. The primary concern for Weber in devising democratic institutions has, in other words, less to do with the values and institutions that can realise the ideals of democracy as such than with the breeding of a certain character fit for national leadership. So far, Weber's theory of democracy seems to contain certain authoritarian elements that can support Jürgen Habermas's famous critique that Carl Schmitt, "the *Kronjurist* of the Third Reich," was "a legitimate pupil of Weber's".

Leadership democracy is, however, not solely reliant upon the quality of its leaders, let alone that of a caesaristic dictator.

In addition to electoral competition, Weber saw localized, yet public associational life as a breeding ground for the formation of charismatic leaders. When leaders are identified and trained at the level of, say neighborhood choral societies and bowling clubs, the alleged authoritarian elitism of leadership democracy comes across as more pluralistic in its conceptualization, far from its usual identification with demagogic dictatorship and unthinking mass following. Insofar as a civil society, or "sectlike society" in his own parlance, functions as an effective medium for the horizontal diffusion of charismatic qualities among lay people, his notion of charisma can retain a strongly democratic tone to the extent that he also suggested social pluralism as a sociocultural ground for the political education of the lay citizenry from which genuine leaders would hail. In short, the charismatic leadership ideal in Weber's political project also requires a heterogeneous and pluralistically organized civil society as its corollary. Together, Weber expected, strong national leadership and a robust civil society would form a bulwark of political dynamism in times of bureaucratic petrification.

Nationalism and Power-Politics

Weber's preoccupation with civic education runs like a thread through his nationalism as well. There can be no denying that Weber was an ardent nationalist. And yet, his nationalism was unambiguously free from the obsession with primordial ethnicity and race that was prevalent in Wilhelmine Germany. Even in the Freiburg Address of 1895, which unleashed his nationalist sentiments with an uninhibited and youthful rhetorical force, he makes it clear that the ultimate rationale for the nationalist value-commitment that should guide all political judgments, even political and economic sciences as well, has less to do with the promotion of the German national interests per se than with a civic education of the citizenry in general and political maturity of the bourgeois class in particular. At a time when "the ultimate, most sublime values have retreated from the public sphere", Weber found an instrumental value in nationalism insofar as it can imbue patriotic feelings among the citizenry and thereby increase their participation in public affairs.

Crucial to this civic educational project was, according to Weber, exposing citizens to the harsh reality of "eternal struggle," or power-politics (*Machtpolitik*) among the nation-states with which Germany had to engage actively. Weber observed with more than a hint of envy, for example, that it was "the reverberation of a position of world power" that exposed the English citizens "to 'chronic' political schooling," and it was this political education that made possible both the empire-building *and* liberal democracy. In this sense, Weber's nationalism can be surmised as a variant of liberal imperialism, or social imperialism (*Sozialimperialismus*) as it was called in Germany; to that extent, one might say that his political thinking is not free from the problems of liberalism in turn-of-the-century Europe. Such a diatribe notwithstanding, what is of more significance in our context is Weber's obsession with a liberal characterology and civic education. The next question that Weber's ethico-political project raises is, then, what kind of character virtues are necessary for the kind of leadership and citizenship that can together make a great nation, while holding inevitable bureaucratization in check.

The Ethics of Conviction and Responsibility

Weber suggested two sets of ethical virtues that a proper political education should teach — the ethic of conviction (*Gesinnungsethik*) and the ethic of responsibility (*Verantwortungsethik*). According to the ethic of responsibility, on the one hand, an action is given meaning only as a cause of an effect, that is, only in terms of its causal relationship to the empirical world. The virtue lies in an objective understanding of the possible causal effect of an action and the calculated reorientation of the elements of an action in such a way as to achieve a desired consequence. An ethical question is thereby reduced to a question of technically correct procedure, and free action consists of choosing the correct means. By emphasizing the causality to which a free agent subscribes, in short, Weber prescribes an ethical integrity between action and consequences, instead of a Kantian emphasis on that between action and intention. According to the ethic of conviction, on the other hand, a free agent should be able to choose autonomously not only the means, but also the end; "this concept of personality finds its 'essence' in the constancy of its inner relation to certain ultimate 'values' and 'meanings' of life". In this respect, Weber's problem arises from the recognition that the kind of rationality applied in choosing a means cannot be used in choosing an end. These two kinds of reasoning represent categorically distinct modes of rationality, a boundary further reinforced by modern value fragmentation. With no objectively ascertainable ground of choice provided, then, a free agent has to create a purpose *ex nihilo*: "ultimately life as a whole, if it is not to be permitted to run on as an event in nature but is instead to be consciously guided, is a series of ultimate decisions through which the soul — as in Plato — chooses its own fate" [Weber 1917/1949, 18]. This ultimate decision and the Kantian integrity between intention and action constitute the essence of what Weber calls an ethic of conviction.

It is often held that the gulf between these two types of ethic is unbridgeable for Weber. Demanding an unmitigated integrity between one's ultimate value and political action, that is to say, the *deontological* ethic of conviction cannot be reconciled with that of responsibility which is *consequentialist* in essence. In fact, Weber himself admitted the "abysmal contrast" that separates the two. This frank admission, nevertheless, cannot be taken to mean that he privileged the latter over the former as far as political education is concerned.

Weber clearly understood the deep tension between consequentialism and deontology, but he still insisted that they should be forcefully brought together. The former recognition only lends urgency to the latter agenda. Resolving this analytical inconsistency in terms of certain "ethical decrees" did not interest Weber at all. Instead, he sought for a moral character that can produce this "combination" with a sheer force of will. He called such a character a "politician with a sense of vocation" (*Berufspolitiker*) who combines a passionate conviction in supra-mundane ideals that politics has to serve and a sober rational calculation of its realizability in this mundane world. Weber thus concluded: "the ethic of conviction and the ethic of responsibility are not absolute opposites. They are complementary to one another, and only in combination do they produce the true human being who is *capable* of having a 'vocation for politics'".

In the end, Weber's ethical project is not about formal analysis of moral maxims, nor is it about substantive virtues that reflect some kind of ontic telos. It is too formal to be an Aristotelean virtue ethics, and it is too concerned with moral character to be a Kantian deontology narrowly understood. The goal of Weber's ethical project, rather, aims at cultivating a character who can wilfully bring together these conflicting formal virtues to create what he calls "total personality" (*Gesamtpersönlichkeit*). It culminates in an ethical characterology or philosophical anthropology in which passion and reason are properly ordered by sheer force of individual volition. In this light, Weber's political virtue resides not simply in a subjective intensity of value commitment nor in a detached intellectual integrity, but in their willful combination in a unified soul.

Concluding Remarks

Seen this way, we find a remarkable consistency in Weber's thought. Weber's main problematic turned on the question of individual autonomy and freedom in an increasingly rationalized society. His dystopian and pessimistic assessment of rationalization drove him to search for solutions through politics and science, which broadly converge on a certain *practice of the self*. What he called the "person of vocation," first outlined famously in *The Protestant Ethic*, provided a bedrock for his various efforts to resuscitate a character who can wilfully combine unflinching conviction and methodical rationality even in a society besieged by bureaucratic petrification and value fragmentation. It is also in this entrenched preoccupation with an ethical characterology under modern circumstances that we find the source of his enduring influences on twentieth-century political and social thought.

On the left, Weber's articulation of the tension between modernity and modernization found resounding echoes in the "Dialectics of Enlightenment" thesis by Theodor Adorno and Max Horkheimer; György Lukács's own critique of the perversion of capitalist reason owes no less to Weber's problematization of instrumental rationality on which is also built Jürgen Habermas's elaboration of communicative rationality as an alternative. Different elements in Weber's political thought, e.g., intense political struggle as an antidote to modern bureaucratic petrification, leadership democracy and plebiscitary presidency, uncompromising realism in international politics, and value-freedom and value-relativism in political ethics, were selected and critically appropriated by such diverse thinkers on the right as Carl Schmitt, Joseph Schumpeter, Leo Strauss, Hans Morgenthau, and Raymond Aron. Even the postmodernist project of deconstructing Enlightenment selfhood finds, as Michel Foucault does, a precursor in Weber. All in all, across the vastly different ideological and methodological spectrum, Max Weber's thought will continue to be a deep reservoir of fresh inspiration as long as an individual's fate under (post)modern circumstances does not lose its privileged place in the political, social, cultural, and philosophical self-reflections of our time.

2

Multiple Sources of Power, Class, Status and Party

Weber developed a different approach to the study of social groups and classes than did Marx. For Marx, there were two primary groups in society and these were classes, the bourgeoisie and the proletariat, whose contradictory social relationship is the motive force for change in capitalism. Marx considers these classes to be defined and determined by whether they own the means of production (bourgeoisie) or whether they do not own the means of production and must sell labour power to those who do (proletariat).

In contrast, for Weber, social groups and classes are in the sphere of power and are connected to the distribution of power. Given that there are various ways that power can be exercised, for Weber it is not possible to reduce the organization of all these groups to a single dimension or factor such as ownership or non-ownership of the means of production. Rather, for Weber there is a pluralism associated with class structure in that people attempt to achieve ends using various means – each of these may create a grouping such as a class, status group, or party. Social stratification has multiple and overlapping dimensions and groups that involve a complex set of social relationships.

Power

For Weber, what we would call social stratification, social class, or social inequality is in the sphere of power, and can be analyzed by examining economic situation, status honour, or parties (organizations formed by people to achieve certain ends). In a section of *Economy and Society* concerned with the distribution of power, Weber begins his analysis of class status and party. Weber's definition of power is as follows (quote 14)

In general, we understand by 'power' the chance of a man or of a number of men to realize their own will in a communal action even against the resistance of others who are participating in the same action.

This is a very broad definition that could include political or economic power exercised at the level of community or society as a whole, or it could refer to smaller scale actions taken by groups in communities such as religious or peer groups, or even the exercise of power in institutions such as the family. The examples that Weber provides are usually quite specific though and he is concrete in his application of this definition. Weber did not ignore economic sources of power, and considered these to be among the more important sources, especially in capitalism. But he claimed that power emerged from other economic sources, ie. not just from class but status groups and parties.

CLASSES

Weber's analysis of class is rooted in the economic sphere, in the domain of markets, and he does not consider classes to be groups or communities. Weber's approach is more diverse than that of Marx, in that Weber considers each of financiers, debtors, professional groups such as lawyers or doctors, landless, and workers to be classes. That is, for Weber there are many more possible classes than just capitalists and workers and he does not consider ownership or non-ownership of the means of production to be the major source of class formation in capitalism.

Class Situation

Weber begins his analysis by defining class situation as the relationship of a person or number of people to a particular market that has an important effect on the lives of these people. Weber notes (quote 15)

The typical chance for a supply of goods, external living conditions, and personal life experiences, in so far as this chance is determined by the amount and kind of power, or lack of such, to dispose of goods or skills for the sake of income in a given economic order. .

From this approach, Weber argues that there are three features of class. These are as follows:

Life Chances. "A number of people have in common a specific causal component of their life chances". That is, a group of people in a similar situation so that they have their life chances determined more or less in common, by some factor that strongly affects this. The ownership or non-ownership of property is one factor that affects life chances. For example, the wealth, income and property of two people may be similar, and this tends to imply a similar outcome to their actions. To each of the sets of causes is attached a probability of a set of possible outcomes, so that people with the same life chances may end up in different positions. The meaning each person attaches to these, and the manner these are used, may differ quite considerably. Weber notes how the power of those with property, compared to those without property, gives the former great advantages over the latter. But Weber does not restrict the definition to property in the means of production though, and notes that it could emerge in the area of distribution, for example in sales, where owners of different types of sales operations could form different classes – wholesale, retail, mining, forestry, etc.

Economic Interest. "This component is represented exclusively by economic interests in the possession of goods and opportunities for income".

Markets. This component "is represented under conditions of the commodity or labour markets".

Together, items ii. And iii. mean that class situation refers to a similar position with respect to the ownership of property or goods, or having (or lacking) opportunities to obtain specific types of income on the market (e.g. lawyers, entertainers). That is, those having similar economic interests with respect to particular markets are in a similar position. And note that these need not just be markets in labour or means of production, but could be an interest in any form of market, where that market has a strong effect on life chances. Examples of non-Marxian forms of class situations might be professionals (lawyers, doctors, accountants), technicians with different specialties (carpenters, computer programmers), entertainers, or professionals in sports. While individuals in each of these may have different backgrounds, in conducting their profession and selling their expertise, each has a common relationship to a market.

Class

"The term 'class' refers to any group of people that is found in the same class situation". Together these three aspects define the class situation, and those with a common class situation form a class. For example, the working class is a social class for Weber, since this is a grouping of people who each have the same relationship to labour markets, and their connection to this market determines their life chances. The petty bourgeoisie is another class, since its members have in common the characteristic that they have ownership of means of production, but in such limited manner, that they must also use their own labour as well.

While Weber considers classes to be important, especially for life chances, he does not think that the common class situation will necessarily form the basis for social action. He notes "In our terminology, 'classes' are not communities; they merely represent possible, and frequent, bases for communal action". With respect to the working class, Weber notes (quote 17), the direction in which the invididividual worker, for instance, is likely to pursue his interests may vary widely, according to whether he is constitutionally qualified for the task at hand to a high, to an average, or to a low degree. ... The rise of societal or even of communal action from a common class situation is by no means a universal phenomenon.

Types of Classes

Classes may be distinguished in several ways and since there are many markets, interests, and class situations, there are potentially a multiplicity of classes in any society. Weber develops the following classification for different possible types of classes.

Ownership Classes. These are the positively privileged who own mines, cattle, slaves, capital goods, stocks, money, land and real estate, buildings, and in today's world new forms of property such as forests, water, technology (patents), communications (media sells audiences), franchises, and intellectual property. Capital becomes highly differentiated depending on how it is used in the market, and how the owner of capital employs it. One can lend money and merely collect interest or a return on this money (rentier), or the owner of capital can become actively involved as an entrepreneur. Weber does not consider capital as merely a technical aspect of production, but examines the meanings which the owners of this capital attach to its use. The consequences of each different type of use of capital can be quite different, in terms of societal effects.

Commercial Classes. Among the possible forms taken by the commerical class are merchants, bankers and financiers, professionals, and industrial and agricultural entrepreneurs. Where there were different classes of this sort, there could be struggles if there was some difference in economic interests, e.g. between debtors and creditors.

The positively privileged portions of this class have great wealth. At the opposite end of the spectrum are those who are negatively privileged – those without property. These are not necessarily an undifferentiated group. Just as there are several types of property ownership, there are also many ways in which individuals or groups may lack property. Debtors represent a class situation where net assets may be positive, but where the benefit of the asset is taken by others (farmers and small businesses). This is different than those with no property at all. Some of those without any property may be slaves (unfree), the poor, paupers, or homeless. These latter groups differ from proletarians, in that they have reached a condition where they are unable to sell even their labour power. Further, some with no property, may have something else which can improve their market situation, the acquisition classes. Even the proletarians of Marx must have something to sell – their labour power or their ability to work. The lumpenproletariat may lack even this.

Acquisition Classes. These are individuals who have no (or very little) tangible, marketable property but have certain skills or abilities which can be offered on the market, and which are likely to receive a return over and above that received by those who have only labour power to offer on the market. There are many different types of marketable skills, both in terms of specific type, and the value of this type. Specialists, or those with unusual or rare talents, such as entertainers or sports professionals, may be able to be well situated with respect to some market. Those who are able to exercise a monopoly over their skills by keeping others from acquiring these skills (monopoly or some closure to the group) are able to be well situated. Those who have higher levels of education, qualifications and credentials may be similarly well situated.

Major Classes. While there could be such a pluralism of classes that it would be difficult to analyze class structure, Weber also argued that at a particular time and place there were a number of major classes that are most important. In "Status Groups and Classes", Weber identifies the major social classes as

- the working class as a whole, the more so the more automated the work process becomes
- the petty bourgeoisie
- the propertyless intelligentsia and specialists (technicians, various kinds of white-collar employees, civil servants – possible with considerable social differences depending on the cost of their training)
- the classes privileged through property and education.

For the latter two groups, Weber notes that members of the propertyless intelligentsia may have a chance to move become members of the classes privileged through property or eduction, and Weber notes that "money increasingly buys *everything*."

Weber's methodology could be applied to Saskatchewan or Canada today and, with some additions and modifications, the major classes might be farmers, petty bourgeoisie, lower level white collar (clerical and sales), industrial working class and trades, upper level white collar and professional, and propertied. The latter differs in this province from that of large centres with very wealthy capitalists having greater amounts of control over capital and the economy. There are also different sections of the propertied – real estate, industrial, financial, oil, or mining.

Sociologists since Weber have distinguished groups from aggregates, sets, or collections of individuals who may have a common situation. An aggregate of individuals may have a common class situation, they may be considered a class, but this class may not be a group. This collectivion of people may have a common set of values, ideas and norms, but do not interact in a sustained or patterned fashion.

A group carries with it the notion of interaction among group members. Two examples of sociological definitions of groups are as follows. Quote 18: "Social groups are collectivities of individuals who interact and form social relationships.... They have their own norms of conduct and are solidaristic. Within this category may be included the family, groups of friends and many work groups.". Groups could be considered (a) to have an ongoing and independent reality, with individuals coming and going but the group remaining active, (b) to have an effect on the attitude of members, and vice versa, socializing new members, and (c) there will be some difference of opinion among group members. The group may be a community, and it may cut across class lines, or at least across class situations.

Weber notes the possibility that classes may form groups, but considers this to be unlikely. The common class situation does not usually lead to social action on the basis of the common class situation. In order for such social action to take place, there have to be proper cultural and intellectual conditions, and the nature of the contradictory market situation would have to be relatively transparent to all. These struggles are likely to be most clearly expressed when other aspects, such as status differences, are removed. Weber notes that there is class conscious organization where (a) there are no groups between the real adversaries, (b) large numbers of persons are in the same class situation, (c) it is technically easy to organize those in the common class situation, and (d) where the goals of the class are well understood, and this understanding is led by those outside the class (intelligentsia).

Note how different this is from Marx's view of class. For Marx, class involved not only a common market situation or position (and one restricted primarily to the capital-labour relation), but also the recognition of this common position by members of the class, the ability to act as a class, and the opposition of the class to the interests of another class. Marx's expectation was that this class consciousness would develop. Weber is much more skeptical of consciousness developing on the basis of class and argues that there are many different bases for common class situation.

Status and Status Groups

Definition. Weber argues that groups are more likely to be formed on the basis of status or status honour. He notes in quote 19:

> In contrast to classes, *status groups* are normally communities. They are, however, often of an amorphous kind. In contrast to the purely economically determined 'class situation' we wish to designate as 'status situation' every typical component of the life fate of men ... is determined by a specific, positive or negative, social estimation of *honour*. this honour may be connected with any quality shared by a plurality, and, of course, it can be knit to a class situation: class distinctions are linked in the most varied ways with status distinctions.

Honour refers to any distinction, respect, or esteem that is accorded to an individual by others. Such social recognition may be a formal process (titles, awards) or it may be in ordinary forms of social interaction whereby we respect or disrespect others (forms of greeting, inclusion or exclusion in a formal or informal group, nature of friendships). Social honour is expressed in social relationships, in how we interact with each other. Social esteem may be either positive or negative, so that an individual may be given a high level of social esteem or honour, or at the other ending, a low level of such esteem.

For Weber, social honour is social in nature, in that it does not automatically result from some market or property relationship in the economic sphere, but is an expression of social relationships. It can be associated with any quality that is socially valued (positive) or is not desirable (negative).

Status honour is linked to social evaluations, whereas class is related to the economic or market situation. Weber considers status honour to be a more important basis for people forming themselves into groups or communities. Or communities may be formed, and this community and its mode of behaviour and norms become the basis for status honour in this community. This may be more subjective (social esteem) than objective (common market situation). It can also be considered to be a difference between consumption (standards and levels of living associated with particular status) as opposed to production (position within this is the basis for class).

Forms of Status Groups. A status group could be formed on the basis of any characteristic that is socially recognized by others, and which becomes the object of social honour. For example, social honour could recognize ethnic or religious characteristics, male-female characteristics, or lifestyle characteristics such as bikers, musical tastes, sports, etc. There is a multiplicity of status groups, but in terms of the major types of social honour that can form the basis for power, affecting the life chances of individuals and groups, Weber identifies three. Note that the status situations and groups that interest Weber are those in the sphere of power, where life chances are related to the status groups. Thus peer groups or groups based on musical tastes or some lifestyles factors may be important in terms of status honour, but are not really status groups in the Weberian sense.

Property is an important basis for a status group, especially where markets prevail. Those with considerable property or wealth have the means to develop a certain style of life, and those without property are not able to exercise this style. Because of this, or on the basis of property alone, social honour may also be accorded these same people. Hadden notes that status "may get in the way of communal action on a class basis". Markets concern gains and losses through exchange and do not have honour associated with them. If markets were allowed to operate fully, this would destroy status differences and only market considerations would influence life chances. While property can form an important basis for status, property alone is not the key to status, and status "normally stands in sharp opposition to the pretensions of sheer property". Those who acquire property may not be accorded the same status privileges are those who originally held property. One example of this is the distinction between established society and the nouveau riche. Status groups may thus attempt to hinder some market activities, or may give market privileges only to those with the proper status levels (old boys network).

Note how this might be developed into a model of gender stratification, with male status denied to females. Male status privileges may extend across property or income lines, denying women the same levels of status. The factors associated with male status may even be denied to those women who have property or have acquired a prominent or high income position. While Weber develops this approach for ethnic groups, an analysis of sex or gender stratification comes from recent feminist writers.

Styles of life based on consumption differences commonly form status groups in the Weberian sense. Property and income are the source of funds required for consumption. It not so much the source of the income that forms the status group as the set of objects and services consumed which leads to the social honour associated with group interaction. Groups may form around residential neighbourhoods, professions, and educational levels (community associations, professional associations, restrictions based on educational qualifications).

Groups unrelated to property could also be formed. These could be ethnic groups, religious groups, groups around sexual orientation, and the various urban communities and groups which form around common sets of interests. In each, there is likely to be some social honour accorded members, there is likely to be some closure of the group, and membership may carry with it certain duties and privileges. Some of these groups may have effect on life chances, especially where religion or ethnicity is an important feature of social organization.

Features of Status Groups. Status groups may cut across property and class lines. This is especially the case with ethnic groups, where social honour is accorded those with the same ancestry, and disrespect or dishonour may be associated with those who do not have this ancestry. This honour or dishonour can form the basis for awarding jobs, opportunities for promotion, and privileges in the political sphere. Characteristics of this type that affect life chances may be more meaningful to people than is relationship to markets (class situation), so that social status is the basis on which groups are formed. Another example is where groupings of men create "old boy networks" which control hiring, promotion, and rewards within institutions. When these men act together as a group, they exercise control over life chances to almost the same degree, or even more so, than do labour markets.

Since honour and dishonour are socially formed, those who are members of a status group associate meaning with the characteristics honoured. While this may be income and a particular style of life, it is not so much the relationship of the individual to the means of production as the meaning associated with the income and style of life. In this sense, relationship to the market and class situation may be an underlying factor, but it is the status honour or dishonour associated with lifestyle which Weber regards as more crucial to group formation.

Status groups are usually associated with some restrictions on social intercourse or interaction. That is, there is some degree of closure to outsiders, and the status group exercises some degree of management of relationships of those within the group. In ethnic or religious groups, marriage may be endogamous within the group. Those who are members are likely to belong to a circle or community. Various religious groups may operate in this manner, with fairly close guidelines concerning who one can associate with, and with whom marriage is to be arranged.

In contemporary society, with great geographic and social mobility, it may be difficult to maintain this closed nature. In contrast, where there is little social or geographic mobility, Weber notes that social status groups may solidify into castes.

Parties

Parties are organizations, rather than communities or groups, and they involve striving for a goal in a planned manner. They are associations of people that attempt to influence social action. Since they are concerned with achieving some goal, they are in the sphere of power in that. In Weber's words,

Whereas the genuine place of 'classes' is within the economic order, the place of 'status groups' is within the social order, that is, within the sphere of the distribution of 'honour.' From within these spheres, classes and status groups influence one another and they influence the legal order and are in turn influenced by it. But 'parties' live in a hose of 'power.' Their action is oriented toward the acquisition of social 'power,' that is to say, toward influencing a communal action no matter what its content may be.

That is, classes are in the economic order, status groups in the social order, and parties in the sphere of power. In some senses, power is not a separate order, in that classes and status groups are concerned with power. The difference between parties on the one hand, and status groups and class on the other, is in the level of analysis. Parties are organizations, whereas classes and status groups are groupings of people. If status groups or classes become well organized, they may form parties, or their parties may become the organizational wing of the class or status group. Trade unions, professional associations, ethnic organizations, and religious institutions are examples.

Parties also differ from classes or status groups in that they attempt to achieve goals in a planned manner, and thus are rational. There are various aims, goals, or purposes that the party attempts to achieve. It considers various possible ways of achieving these, and selects a course of action that it considers the most likely to achieve that goal. The structure of the party is also rational in that these actions are not a byproduct of social interaction, but are carefully considered and selected. The party is likely to have a constitution, a set of officers, and means of filling these positions with people most suited for them.

Parties may be political parties, or they may be other organizations aimed at achieving other goals. As such, they can cut across both status and class lines, expressing interests that may be common to those from many different sectors of society. Examples could be groups organized around helping to solve the problems of specific diseases (Cancer Society, Arthritis Society), groups such as the Wildlife society, or even sporting and recreation organizations. Some may have political ends, others may merely attempt to pursue a particular aim of those in the organization. Adams and Sydie note that parties are likely to be mixes of class or status group interests, "they are more likely to be mixed types".

For political parties to gain political power, they must attempt to represent a fairly broad range of interests. Putting together a political program involves identifying issues which are key, and other issues which will pull in various groups. Some parties, such as the British Labour Party, may primarily represent a specific class. Other parties, such as the Canadian Liberal Party or the Saskatchewan NDP attempt to put together programs which appeal to a wide variety of interests.

It might also be noted that these parties may acquire a life of their own and pursue ends that are not part of their original purposes. Weber noted how social actions can have unintended consequences which may be no part of the original intentions of the class, status group, or party. The most famous example is the Protestant ethic, which was established for purely religious or spiritual reasons. Weber argued that the establishment and power of this ethic had the unintended consequences of assisting the development of capitalism. Particular political parties are established with certain ends in mind, but as organizations, especially ones with some power, become subject to a variety of social influences which may change their purposes. Some long-time NDP supporters claim that the NDP has become more interested in maintaining power than in pursuing principles of social democracy. Parties tend to be a feature of modern societies, where power is exercised in a more formal, rational, and planned manner than in traditional societies. They do not operate in traditional societies, where personal relations or patronage may dominate. Parties are means of organization to achieve specific ends in modern society and, once organizations are developed as parties, they become more rational, that is systematic and permanent.

Weber's discussion of class, status and party give an idea of how markets affect people, and how people form themselves into groups, partly as a result of markets and partly on the basis of other factors that are socially important. To some extent, Weber's status groups would appear to be ways in which people in capitalism protect themselves from the effects of markets, but at the same time using the market as they can, and using the means of power they have at their disposal.

In spite of the myriad factors that must be taken into consideration when looking at these social structures and institutions, Weber concludes that there are relatively few dominant features of social structure. In terms of classes, the major classes are the working class, the capitalist class, and the middle professional group. For Weber there are also a number of major status groups and parties, not necessarily identical to or determined by the same factors as are classes. That is, one may consider some of the major styles of life as those of upper class, middle class, and lower class. Within this system of stratification, the working class does not fit, although the working class has been and continues to be an important social class in capitalism. Finally, people in societies create some major parties, political parties and other organizations, each aiming to achieve some end. Again, it is likely that only a few of these organizations will acquire major importance for people at any one time.

Weber's writings can thus be used as a guide, but one should not get lost in the mass of details to be considered. Rather, one must attempt to reconstruct the major groups and classes in society, determine how people related to these, and how these interact.

STATUS GROUP

The German sociologist Max Weber formulated a three-component theory of stratification in which he defines status group (also known as status class or status estate) as a group of people (part of a society) that can be differentiated on the basis of non-economical qualities like honour, prestige and religion. Since Max Weber, the issue of status inconsistency has been the object of many studies, particularly in the post-industrial societies and also because of an intervening factor: religion, particularly in emerging nations.

Weber writes that status groups emerge out of "the house of honour."

Such status honour is contrasted with:

- social class, based on economically determined relationship in the house of the marketplace.
- party, based on affiliations in the political domain, or the house of power.

Weber's discussion of the relationships between status groups, social class, and political parties is found in his essay "Class, Status, Party" which was written in German before World War I. The first English translation was done by Hans Gerth and C. Wright Mills and published in the 1940s. This version has been republished many times since. A new English translation called "The distribution of power within the community: Classes, Stände, Parties" and translated by Dagmar Waters and her colleagues was recently published in the Journal of Classical Sociology (2010).

INTERPRETATIONS OF WEBER'S LIBERALISM

There are varying interpretations of Max Weber's liberalism due to his well known sociological achievements. Max Weber is considered an eminent founder of modern social sciences, rivaled by the figures of Emile Durkheim and Karl Marx. Some students of Weberian thought have paid less attention to Weber's extensive and often passionate engagement with the politics of his day, particularly in the United States. However, European intellectuals have given more attention to his political thought. Most of Weber's political writings have not been published in translation, or have been translated only recently in a piecemeal form.

Weber's political ideas have inspired disagreement in Germany for decades. His conception of democracy has been the subject of particularly heated debate. Weber rejected the Wilhelmine regime's authoritarian political structure. He advocated parliamentary and democratic reform. Weber championed the freedoms of what he called the "age of the Rights of Man". Some find the liberalism of Weber as problematic.

Raymond Aron has noted that Weber was not a "liberal in the American sense," and not, "strictly speaking, a democrat in the sense that the French, the English, or the Americans gave the term." Aron saw Weber to have looked to place the "glory of the nation and the power of the state" above all other things.

Stephen P. Turner and Regis A. Factor have concluded that Weber rejected the philosophical basis for most Western formulations of Enlightenment liberalism. Weber conceived "parliamentarization" primarily for selecting leaders. Weber was strongly technocratic.

Political Views

Jacob Peter Mayer wrote a 1944 critique of Max Weber, entitled *Max Weber and German Politics: a study in political sociology*. Published in England during the war, this work never appeared in German translation. Mayer had been an archivist for the Social Democratic Party (SPD) and the primary book reviewer for the *Vorwärts*, the SPD party paper. He was a target of Nazi persecution, from which he escaped to England. There he became involved with the Labour Party and was a member of the faculty at the London School of Economics during the last part of the Second World War.

Mayer labelled Weber's philosophy as the "new Machiavellianism of the steel age." The conception of the state that Weber supported was viewed as a middle phase in a destructive tradition of German realpolitik-a tradition that Mayer saw to extend from Bismarck to Hitler. Mayer interpreted a "tragic" satisfaction with which Weber was seen to embrace "the empty character" of Heinrich Rickert's neo-Kantian philosophy of value. Mayer viewed Weber's value theory as a nihilistic contribution to the rise of National Socialism.

Wolfgang J. Mommsen initiated debate by arguing this in the 1959 German publication of *Max Weber and German Politics 1890-1920*. Mommsen questioned the sociologist's liberal reputation. According to Mommsen, Weber's sociological idea of charismatic authority was evident in his political views, and was "close to fascist notions of plebiscitary leadership." Mommsen wrote that Weber's theory of democracy "lent itself all too readily to an authoritarian reinterpretation" Mommsen also associated Weber with the rise of Hitler: "Weber's teachings concerning charismatic leadership coupled with the radical formulation of the meaning of democratic institutions, contributed to making the German people inwardly ready to acclaim the leadership position of Adolf Hitler."

Max Weber's call for the democratic reform of the Wilhelmine state, and his involvement in the drafting of the Weimar Constitution, had led German intellectuals in the 1950s to consider him as an authority who could justify the democratic character of the new Federal Republic of Germany. Mommsen's thesis, that Max Weber supported parliamentary democracy as a means to serve the power interests of the German nation-state, met a sharp response, because, in Raymond Aron's words, this removed "the new German democracy of a 'founding father,' a glorious ancestor, and a spokesman of genius."

Politics and Sociology

Weber's political views have been considered to threaten the reputation of his sociology. Günther Roth, Reinhard Bendix, and Karl Loewenstein have defended Weberian sociology by arguing that it stands separate from his political convictions. They consider Weber's distinction between scientific value-neutrality and evaluative politics to support this claim. In their view, Weber's politics should be interpreted as separate from the interpretation of his sociology. This idea was rejected by Mommsen. Mommsen wrote of continuities between Weber's "value-neutral" sociology and his "evaluative" politics. The second edition of *Max Weber and German Politics 1890-1920* argued that "values and science, in Weber's thought, were interdependent." Critics were dismissed as attempting "to shield Max Weber's sociological works against any possible criticism based on political aspects." Günther Roth responded in a 1965 American sociological journal, stating that Weber was a major target for a series of critiques aimed at political sociology in general, if not at most of social science. Roth also stated that Mommsen was removed from the interest of American sociologists in Weber, and his treatment becomes questionable when he interprets Weber's sociological analysis as political ideology. Roth stated that his "major intent" was "not to provide an historical defense of Weber but a review of critiques as they seem to bear on the raison d'etre of political sociology." He claimed that Weber "must appear relativist and Machiavellian to all those who, for ideological reasons, cannot recognize any dividing line between political sociology and political ideology. Weber emphatically insisted on such a distinction, while his critics refuse to distinguish between his scholarship and his politics." Raymond Aron did not consider Weber's sociology to stand above politics. He viewed Weber, in both politics and sociology, to be a typical "power-politician." Aron wrote in 1971 that Weber "belongs to the posterity of Machiavelli as much as to the contemporaries of Nietzsche," and that "the struggle for power between classes and individuals" seemed to Weber as the "essence" of politics.

MAX WEBER, DISENCHANTMENT AND CRITICAL THEORY

Weber's major works in economic sociology and the sociology of religion dealt with the rationalization, secularisation, and so called "disenchantment" which he associated with the rise of capitalism and modernity. In sociology, rationalization is the process whereby an increasing number of social actions become based on considerations of teleological efficiency or calculation rather than on motivations derived from morality, emotion, custom, or tradition. Rather than referring to what is genuinely "rational" or "logical", rationalization refers to a relentless quest for goals that might actually function to the *detriment* of a society. Rationalization is an ambivalent aspect of modernity, manifested especially in Western society; as a behaviour of the capitalist market; of rational administration in the state and bureaucracy; of the extension of modern science; and of the expansion of modern technology.

Weber's thought regarding the rationalizing and secularizing tendencies of modern Western society (sometimes described as the "Weber Thesis") would blend with Marxism to facilitate critical theory, particularly in the work of thinkers such as Jürgen Habermas. Critical theorists, as antipositivists, are critical of the idea of a hierarchy of sciences or societies, particularly with respect to the sociological positivism originally set forth by Comte. Jürgen Habermas has critiqued the concept of pure instrumental rationality as meaning that scientific-thinking becomes something akin to ideology itself. For theorists such as Zygmunt Bauman, rationalization as a manifestation of modernity may be most closely and regrettably associated with the events of the Holocaust.

MODERN THEORIES

When the critique of classical social evolutionism becamc widely accepted, modern anthropological and sociological approaches changed respectively. Modern theories are careful to avoid unsourced, ethnocentric speculation, comparisons, or value judgements; more or less regarding individual societies as existing within their own historical contexts. These conditions provided the context for new theories such as cultural relativism and multilineal evolution.

In the 1920s and 30s, Gordon Childe revolutionized the study of cultural evolutionism. He conducted a comprehensive pre-history account that provided scholars with evidence for African and Asian cultural transmission into Europe. He combated scientific racism by finding the tools and artifacts of the indigenous people from Africa and Asia and showed how they influenced the technology of European culture. Evidence from his excavations countered the idea of Aryan supremacy and superiority. Childe explained cultural evolution by his theory of divergence with modifications of convergence. He postulated that different cultures form separate methods that meet different needs, but when two cultures were in contact they developed similar adaptations, solving similar problems. Rejecting Spencer's theory of parallel cultural evolution, Childe found that interactions between cultures contributed to the convergence of similar aspects most often attributed to one culture. Childe placed emphasis on human culture as a social construct rather than products of environmental or technological contexts. Childe coined the terms "Neolithic Revolution", and "Urban Revolution" which are still used today in the branch of pre-historic anthropology. In 1941 anthropologist Robert Redfield wrote about a shift from 'folk society' to 'urban society'. By the 1940s cultural anthropologists such as Leslie White and Julian Steward sought to revive an evolutionary model on a more scientific basis, and succeeded in establishing an approach known as neoevolutionism. White rejected the opposition between "primitive" and "modern" societies but did argue that societies could be distinguished based on the amount of energy they harnessed, and that increased energy allowed for greater social differentiation (White's law). Steward on the other hand rejected the 19th-century notion of progress, and instead called attention to the Darwinian notion of "adaptation", arguing that all societies had to adapt to their environment in some way.

The anthropologists Marshall Sahlins and Elman Service prepared an edited volume, *Evolution and Culture*, in which they attempted to synthesise White's and Steward's approaches. Other anthropologists, building on or responding to work by White and Steward, developed theories of cultural ecology and ecological anthropology. The most prominent examples are Peter Vayda and Roy Rappaport. By the late 1950s, students of Steward such as Eric Wolf and Sidney Mintz turned away from cultural ecology to Marxism, World Systems Theory, Dependency theory and Marvin Harris's Cultural materialism.

Today most anthropologists reject 19th-century notions of progress and the three assumptions of unilineal evolution. Following Steward, they take seriously the relationship between a culture and its environment to explain different aspects of a culture. But most modern cultural anthropologists have adopted a general systems approach, examining cultures as emergent systems and argue that one must consider the whole social environment, which includes political and economic relations among cultures. There are still others who continue to reject the entirety of the evolutionary thinking and look instead at historical contingencies, contacts with other cultures, and the operation of cultural symbol systems. As a result, the simplistic notion of "cultural evolution" has grown less useful and given way to an entire series of more nuanced approaches to the relationship of culture and environment. In the area of development studies, authors such as Amartya Sen have developed an understanding of "development" and 'human flourishing' that also question more simplistic notions of progress, while retaining much of their original inspiration.

Neoevolutionism

Neoevolutionism was the first in a series of modern multilineal evolution theories. It emerged in the 1930s and extensively developed in the period following the Second World War and was incorporated into both anthropology and sociology in the 1960s. It bases its theories on empirical evidence from areas of archaeology, palaeontology and historiography and tries to eliminate any references to systems of values, be it moral or cultural, instead trying to remain objective and simply descriptive.

While 19th-century evolutionism explained how culture develops by giving general principles of its evolutionary process, it was dismissed by the Historical Particularists as unscientific in the early 20th century. It was the neoevolutionary thinkers who brought back evolutionary thought and developed it to be acceptable to contemporary anthropology.

Neoevolutionism discards many ideas of classical social evolutionism, namely that of social progress, so dominant in previous sociology evolution-related theories. Then neoevolutionism discards the determinism argument and introduces probability, arguing that accidents and free will greatly affect the process of social evolution. It also supports counterfactual history—asking "what if" and considering different possible paths that social evolution may take or might have taken, and thus allows for the fact that various cultures may develop in different ways, some skipping entire stages others have passed through. Neoevolutionism stresses the importance of empirical evidence. While 19th-century evolutionism used value judgments and assumptions for interpreting data, neoevolutionism relied on measurable information for analysing the process of sociocultural evolution.

Leslie White, author of *The Evolution of Culture: The Development of Civilization to the Fall of Rome* (1959), attempted to create a theory explaining the entire history of humanity. The most important factor in his theory is technology. *Social systems are determined by technological systems*, wrote White in his book, echoing the earlier theory of Lewis Henry Morgan. He proposes a society's energy consumption as a measure of its advancement. He differentiates between five stages of human development. In the first, people use the energy of their own muscles. In the second, they use the energy of domesticated animals. In the third, they use the energy of plants (so White refers to agricultural revolution here). In the fourth, they learn to use the energy of natural resources: coal, oil, gas. In the fifth, they harness nuclear energy. White introduced a formula, P=E*T, where E is a measure of energy consumed, and T is the measure of efficiency of technical factors utilising the energy. This theory is similar to Russian astronomer Nikolai Kardashev's later theory of the Kardashev scale.

Julian Steward, author of *Theory of Culture Change: The Methodology of Multilinear Evolution* (1955, reprinted 1979), created the theory of "multilinear" evolution which examined the way in which societies adapted to their environment. This approach was more nuanced than White's theory of "unilinear evolution." Steward rejected the 19th-century notion of progress, and instead called attention to the Darwinian notion of "adaptation", arguing that all societies had to adapt to their environment in some way.

He argued that different adaptations could be studied through the examination of the specific resources a society exploited, the technology the society relied on to exploit these resources, and the organization of human labour. He further argued that different environments and technologies would require different kinds of adaptations, and that as the resource base or technology changed, so too would a culture. In other words, cultures do not change according to some inner logic, but rather in terms of a changing relationship with a changing environment. Cultures therefore would not pass through the same stages in the same order as they changed—rather, they would change in varying ways and directions. He called his theory "multilineal evolution".

He questioned the possibility of creating a social theory encompassing the entire evolution of humanity; however, he argued that anthropologists are not limited to describing specific existing cultures. He believed that it is possible to create theories analysing typical common culture, representative of specific eras or regions. As the decisive factors determining the development of given culture he pointed to technology and economics, but noted that there are secondary factors, like political system, ideologies and religion. All those factors push the evolution of a given society in several directions at the same time; hence the application of the term "multilinear" to his theory of evolution.

Marshall Sahlins, co editor with Elman Service of *Evolution and Culture* (1960), divided the evolution of societies into 'general' and 'specific'. General evolution is the tendency of cultural and social systems to increase in complexity, organization and adaptiveness to environment. However, as the various cultures are not isolated, there is interaction and a diffusion of their qualities (like technological inventions). This leads cultures to develop in different ways (specific evolution), as various elements are introduced to them in different combinations and at different stages of evolution.

In his *Power and Prestige* (1966) and *Human Societies: An Introduction to Macrosociology* (1974), Gerhard Lenski expands on the works of Leslie White and Lewis Henry Morgan. He views technological progress as the most basic factor in the evolution of societies and cultures. Unlike White, who defined technology as the ability to create and utilise energy, Lenski focuses on information—its amount and uses. The more information and knowledge (especially allowing the shaping of natural environment) a given society has, the more advanced it is. He distinguishes four stages of human development, based on advances in the history of communication. In the first stage, information is passed by genes. In the second, when humans gain sentience, they can learn and pass information through by experience. In the third, humans start using signs and develop logic. In the fourth, they can create symbols and develop language and writing. Advancements in the technology of communication translate into advancements in the economic system and political system, distribution of goods, social inequality and other spheres of social life. He also differentiates societies based on their level of technology, communication and economy: (1) hunters and gatherers, (2) agricultural, (3) industrial, and (4) special (like fishing societies).

Talcott Parsons, author of *Societies: Evolutionary and Comparative Perspectives* (1966) and *The System of Modern Societies* (1971) divided evolution into four subprocesses: (1) division, which creates functional subsystems from the main system; (2) adaptation, where those systems evolve into more efficient versions; (3) inclusion of elements previously excluded from the given systems; and (4) generalization of values, increasing the legitimization of the ever more complex system. He shows those processes on 4 stages of evolution: (I) primitive or foraging, (II) archaic agricultural, (III) classical or "historic" in his terminology, using formalized and universalizing theories about reality and (IV) modern empirical cultures. However, these divisions in Parsons theory is the more formal ways in which the evolutionary process is conceptualized and should not be mistaken for with Parsons' actual theory. Parsons develops a theory, where he tries to reveal the complexity of the processes which take form between two points of necessity, the first is the cultural "necessity," which is given through the values-system of each evolving community; the other is the environmental necessities, which most directly is reflected in the material realities of the basic production system and reflected in the relative capacity of each industrial-economical level at each window of time. Generally, Parsons highlights that the dynamics and directions of these process is shaped by the cultural imperative embodied in the cultural heritage and more secondary an outcome of sheer "economic" conditions.

3

Max Weber: The Rationalization of Society

METHODOLOGICAL APPROACH

Weber stressed the need for social theory to break through materialist and idealist models of explanation to indicate the "elective affinity" of different social conditions. However, his interests were not revolutionary oriented to praxis (Marx), nor scientifically directed at the establishment of a science of society (Durkheim), rather, his sociology is inspired by the concrete political concerns of Weber as a citizen of Germany: his attention goes out to the ways in which German political life should be ordered with the advent of bureaucracy and industrial capitalism and the decline of traditional world-views.

Objectivity and Value-Freedom

An Objective Sociology of Subjectivity : The differentiation of subject and object (and the corresponding distinctions between social and natural sciences) does not mean that the social sciences, which necessarily deal with ideal phenomena, cannot be objective. Social sciences cannot scientifically establish the ideals or normative principles which define what ought to be. But one can distinguish means and ends of action, and science can determine what the best means are, given that end. Sociology can, then, also say that some ends are useless since there are, and can be, no means to achieve those goals. Or sociology can also determine and explicitly state the axioms on which certain attitudes and statements rest.

There is therefore no universal ethics. No single set of ideals can be shown scientifically to be right or wrong. This is why there is religion, it is directed towards ultimate ends (*Gesinnungsethik*). On the other hand, sociology can assist in an ethics of responsibility (*Verantwortungsethik*), which seeks to find the rational calculus by which means are employed to ends, and the consequences they actually have, regardless of (despite of) the intentions.

Causality and Ideal-Types : Science seeks causes, but it also rests on ideals which it cannot justify scientifically, mainly the selection of relevant facts out of reality. So we must know the values that guide knowledge. This cannot lay in the formulation of laws; the uniqueness of historical events has to be explained (e.g. why is there capitalism only in the West?). Note that the natural sciences also seek to unravel the uniqueness of things.

The identification of causes of effects necessarily rests on certain assumptions, as a minimum this involves the selection of events, and the identification of the one factor or set of factors, in a broader frame of factors (which is basically a stream of events), without which a certain effect would not have been brought about. This identification is selective, and in this sense, subjective, but any such identification, then, must be verifiable by others (a sort of consensus theory of truth).

Ideal-types are specifically constructed with the purpose of interpreting and explaining a historical event. It is constructed by abstracting and combining a limited number of elements which are seldom found, in purity, in reality. However, the ideal-type is not an ideal, it is, rather, an idealization with a purpose: the ideal-type is not description nor hypothesis, but it is a metrological device that aids in describing and explaining, it makes reality describable and explainable at all.

Value-Freedom : Scientists should be value-free (in the meaning indicated above), but this does not mean, according to Weber, that scientists cannot have and propagate values. The scientist as educator must seek to specialize in knowledge and education, but the scientist can, not as scientist but as 'political animal', outside the university, express political and moral judgments. The sphere of science and politics, then, must and can be kept separate.

UNDERSTANDING AND EXPLANATION

Interpretative Sociology : Weber was interested in the formulation of general principles of social action, but these cannot be conceived as laws: sociology must seek to understand human action inasmuch as it is (non-)meaningful. Human action is subjective: it is guided by the motivations and intentions of the actors involved. Sociology seeks to understand those motives and meanings from an emphatic attitude (*Sinverstehen*). This does not exclude explanation: sociology understands human action, with reference to an ideal-type or with regard to a specific meaning of action, and thereby explains its course and consequences. Also, sociology can identify both the meaningful and non-meaningful elements of action. The techniques to grasp meaning must be replicable, and verifiable on the basis of the established standards of methodology. These techniques include a) direct observation of emotive action (e.g. anger), and b) explanatory understanding by identifying an intervening motivational link between meaning and action (e.g. chop wood). The latter implies the identification of a particular motive which is always linked to a broader frame of 'normativity'. This does not mean psychological reductionism (cf. there are explainable structures within which meaning is given).

Social Relationships : A social relationship is defined as a reciprocal interaction between two or more individuals, which does not necessarily mean that the meanings of all actors are identical, but that there must be meaning involved in any case on the part of the inter-actors (an orientation to).

Weber distinguishes four ideal-typical types of orientation in social relationships: 1) Purposive rational action is directed by the successful calculation of means towards a give end; 2) Value rational action is directed towards an ideal and is carried out for its own sake; 3) Affective action is also carried out for its own sake, yet it lacks a clear ideal, and rests on an emotive state; and 4) Traditional action is carried out under the influence of a custom or habit.

THE PROTESTANT ETHIC AND THE SPIRIT OF CAPITALISM

The Problem : There is the statistical fact that in modern capitalist societies, the high-skilled workers and the entrepreneurs are overwhelmingly Protestant. The connection between economic rationality in capitalism and Protestantism Weber will trace in the character of Protestant beliefs. This connection in itself is nothing special (Marx saw Protestantism as the ideological reflection of capitalism), but Weber suggest an alternative explanation. He will focus on cultural elements which, he will show, have are a peculiar independent factor in the formation of Western capitalism, defined as, an this is crucial, the rational capitalistic organization of free labour.

The Spirit of Capitalism : The methodical conduct of life under capitalism is not just a practice, it is also an ethic, a conviction which emphasizes the duty of the individual to increase capital, the making of money as a goal in and by itself. This conduct is specific to Western capitalism (other forms of capitalism may lack it). This capitalist spirit goes beyond the traditionalistic conception of the manipulation of nature to sustain one's livelihood.

Note from the start that what Weber is talking about is a very precise conception of capitalism (it is not what Marx meant by it): "capitalism is identical with the pursuit of profit, and forever renewed profit, by means of continuous, rational, capitalistic enterprise". Capitalist rational action Weber describes as "one which rests on the expectation of profit by the utilization of opportunities for exchange, that is on (formally) peaceful chances of profit... The important fact is always that a calculation of capital in terms of money is made". Capitalism for Weber, then, is first and foremost the desire to use the most rational, i.e. most efficient, means to accumulate wealth, a desire which serves no other end than itself. For the acquisition of more and more money, and at the same time the avoidance of pleasure, there is employed a very rational procedure. The method is rational (in terms of efficiency), and the goal is irrational, namely the acquisition of money for an end (to have it) which defies the main characteristic of money (namely a means of exchange, i.e. to be used). Note that this method of conduct, as inspired by the Protestant ethos of Calvinism, applies only to a limited number of people for a short period of time, and only in the West. It is then, by all standards, not true that Weber suggests that Protestantism led to capitalism, let alone caused it.

Luther's Concept of the Calling : The concept of the calling is a product of the Reformation. It refers to the joining of the mundane affairs of life with an over-arching religious influence (away from the ideal of Catholic monastic isolation to the inner-worldly worship of the outer-worldly god). One had to perform one's duties in the world to serve god. But Luther's concept of the calling was still traditionalistic since it implied an absolute acceptance of the way things are. Later Protestant sects changed this. Then four (ideal-typical) kinds of ascetic Protestantism emerged: Calvinism, Methodism, Pietism, and Baptism.

Calvinism : Calvinism has the following idea(l)s: the universe exists for god, the motives of god are humanly incomprehensible, and, most importantly, only a small number of people are chosen to receive grace, i.e. the notion of predestination. The consequences of these beliefs for the believer were an unprecedented feeling of inner loneliness: one could not know whether one was chosen, this is decisive, the crucial break from Catholicism (for the thesis Weber seeks to defend). Therefore, one had the duty to convince oneself that one was chosen, self-confidence would be a sign of weakened faith, and this self-confidence can best be secured by an intensely inner-worldly activity. For this reason, labour in the material world became the highest positive ethical attitude: the instrumental spirit of capitalism is an unintended offshoot of Calvinism.

Asceticism and the Spirit of Capitalism : The spirit of ascetic Protestantism gave birth to capitalist economic rationalism because of its emphasis on the ascetic rational motives with a denouncement of pleasure. Puritanism restricted pleasure, and at the same time broke with traditionalism, to see the acquisition of wealth as directly willed by god. Then, once capitalism is established, this religious core does not have to be there anymore. The economic rational conduct of life becomes a power independent of religion. The idea of the calling is a support for capitalism that, in the end, it no longer needs. Then, the cloak of the care for external goods has become an "iron cage."

So Weber concludes that the rationality of capitalism is connected with the irrationality of a value commitment (against a naive historical materialism), but Weber does not present a unified alternative theory. Weber states that there is an elective affinity between certain sorts of Calvinism and the ethics of capitalism. He adds that it is necessary "to investigate how Protestant Asceticism was in turn influenced by its character by the totality of social conditions, especially economic". A one-sided approach, materialist or idealist, is in any case useless. Also Weber did not maintain "such a foolish and doctrinaire thesis as that the spirit of capitalism... could only have arisen as the result of certain effects of the reformation, or even that capitalism as an economic system is the creation of the Reformation". Instead Weber argues that the Protestant ethic which holds that the acquisition of material goods is good in itself, even willed by god, has shaped the particular course capitalism has taken in the West, and that the ethic of Protestantism is co-responsible for the qualitative formation and quantitative expansion of the capitalist culture.

Addendum: The Protestant Sects and the Spirit of Capitalism : In this paper, Weber tries to account for the fact that, while (in the USA) state and church are separated and the state authorities accordingly never ask for a person's denomination, the question of religious affiliation was always posed in social and business life. Admission to a religious congregation was seen as a certificate of business morals, an absolute guarantee of the moral qualities of a gentleman, especially of the qualities required in business. This is because a sect, unlike a church, is a voluntary association of those who are religiously and morally qualified to become one of its members. Today the particular kind of denomination is rather irrelevant, but it is decisive that one is admitted to membership by ballot, after an examination of moral worth and an ethical probation in the sense of virtues which will guarantee inner-worldly asceticism and credit worthiness in business life. The methodical way of life in the sects nowadays appears in a complex of voluntary associations: one must belong to a club of whatever kind. These clubs, which are a secularized version of their predecessors (sects), share the formal qualities of being voluntary, exclusive and based upon an examination of worthiness. Not only the ethic of Protestantism, but also the social premiums, means of discipline, and, in general, the whole organization of Protestantism still find their derivatives today.

In history, three principles of protestant organization are revealed. 1) Voluntarism: Only qualified persons are admitted to the Lord's Supper. The voluntaristic nature of this admission is demonstrated by the fact that baptism is reserved for adults. This poses the problem of who is to decide who will and has to, and who cannot be admitted. 2) Sovereignty: Only the local sacral community can judge whether a member is qualified. The community stands jointly before god. Only charisma, not training or office (of professional theologians or spiritual authority) is recognized. 3) Moral discipline: Externally, expelled persons are boycotted, while, internally in the sects, brotherliness and mutual aid secure the cohesiveness of the group.

The modern functions of sect-like organizations in the USA follow the same pattern. The discipline of the sects was vested in the hands of laymen, it worked through the necessity to hold one's own, and it bred and selected qualities. This last element is most important: one has to have certain qualities and constantly has to prove this. Therefore, this inner-worldly asceticism is a methodical, rational way of conduct. It is the foundation of modern individualism since it legitimates the economic individualism of modern capitalism.

THE ECONOMIC ETHICS OF THE WORLD RELIGIONS

Weber's sociology of law is opposed to the organicist model of society, there is more than a one-to-one relationship, much more interdependence between different parts. Also, he is opposed to evolutionary theories that readily assume inevitable historical patterns. Weber is interested in finding the economic ethic of the religions of the world, i.e. the practical impulses for action found in the pragmatic contexts of religion. The economic ethic of a religion does not enjoy a one-to-one status with economic organization, but it is important to note that the economic ethic is not just a function of economic organization (contrary to Marx), nor of religion. Note for instance how religious ethics has evaluated suffering. Suffering can be seen as a reflection of possession by a demon. Therefore, the advantaged feel blessed, they are 'the chosen ones' that deserve grace (as a legitimation of inequality). The disadvantaged, on the other hand, must be purified, e.g. by magicians. Thus sacred values always include worldly matters (health, wealth, etc.). And, irrational values have led to very rational ways of life, and how this differently affects different social strata.

Religions of the World and Capitalism

The distinct characteristic of religion is the worship of divine entities, with priests, a cult, and a system of beliefs (magical forces, on the other hand, are subordinated to human needs by the use of formulae, with magicians, cults, and a low degree of systematic beliefs). The prophet of religion is an individual bearer of charisma who proclaims a religious doctrine, and is instrumental for change; prophets can (not necessarily) de-mystify the world or remove magic (cf. disenchantment). The doctrine of the prophet may be inconsistent, but, more importantly, his practical orientation to the world give unity. It is important to note that Weber did not simply conduct ex-post-facto experiments: there exist in history different combinations of material and ideal factors which are decisive for the (non-)formation of capitalism.

Religious Rejections of the World and Their Directions

Asceticism moves in two directions: it negates the world, and simultaneously wants to master it through the powers of abnegation, in different spheres of action:

1) The traditional community: the religiosity of the congregation no longer appeals to the community of villagers, members of the sib, guilds and so on, but, as religion of brotherliness, to the relations among the believers. This leads to tensions between the order and

universalist ethic demands of the brethren of the faith and the orders and values of this world.

2) The economic sphere: the religions of salvation warn against the impersonal mechanisms of the money-market. Therefore, asceticism routinized work in the world into serving god's will, and mysticism resorts to an objectless devotion for anybody, not for the person's sake, but for devotion.

3) The political sphere: to the powers of the state, claiming the monopoly of the legitimate use of force, puritanism reacts by acting against the world with the means of that world (violence). Mysticism, on the other hand, takes on a radical anti-political attitude: it completely withdraws from the pragma of violence. Tensions with the political world are unavoidable, but compromises are always made. The rationalization of politics and economy, leading action to be more and more considered in terms of means-ends relations (purposive rationality), increase these tensions. In the end, the religion of brotherliness could entirely reject purposive rational action.

4) The esthetic sphere: just like economy and politics, the esthetic sphere is rationalized into a separate social domain, claiming independence with regard to beauty and form. In the religions of brotherliness art is supposed to have a meaning (in relation to god) and not be just a thing of form. Again, this leads to tensions, but alliances or compromises are made.

5) The erotic sphere: eroticism has been raised into the sphere of conscious enjoyment, acquiring a sensational character as a salvation from rationalization, an escape from means-ends directed relations. Of course, a principled ethic of religious brotherhood is sharply opposed to this "brutality" an denial of bondage to god.

6) The intellectual sphere: the tension between religion and scientific knowledge is the greatest. Science has disenchanted the world into a causal mechanism (loss of freedom) and pushed religion away into the irrational

realm. Every religion, on the other hand, in the end asks for a sacrifice of the intellect; in religion the world is understood by virtue of a charisma of illumination, not by intellect. The scientification of the world has also led to a loss of meaning (senselessness), and religion, in turn, has become ever more other-worldly, more alienated from all structured forms of life, confining itself to the specific religious essence.

STATE, BUREAUCRACY, AND LAW IN THE AGE OF MODERNITY

One of Weber's most famous contributions to sociology is his approach to politics, bureaucracy and the state. First, note that political societies exercise their might over a territory by the threat or use of force, and by reference to some kind of legitimacy. Political legitimacy can be of three kinds: 1) Traditional authority is based on the belief in the age-old sanctity of power; 2) Legal domination is typical for the bureaucracy of the state; and 3) charismatic domination is based on the belief in the extraordinary qualities of a person.

When a political society uses force in such a way that it results in a successful monopoly over force, there is a state. Weber defines the state as "a compulsory association which organizes domination. It has been successful in seeking to monopolize the legitimate use of physical force as a means of domination within a territory. The domination of the state implies that its subordinates belief in the legitimacy of their subordination.To secure its legitimate monopoly over force, the state has combined the material means of organization in the hands of its leaders, and it has "expropriated all autonomous functionaries of estates who formerly controlled these means in their own rights. The state has taken their positions and now stands in top place". The crucial elements in Weber's definition of the state, then, refer to 1) the legitimate use of force, 2) the territorial boundaries which delineate the state's domination, and 3) the appropriation of the means of control.

The Legitimacy of the State

First, Weber contends that the modern state cannot be defined in terms of its ends, but only in terms of its means:

the state has acquired a monopoly over the use of force. Unlike the commonly held view at Weber's time of viewing the state as one of the noblest of man's creations, the means of the state should in Weber's view be conceived in terms of violence and coercion. The threat or use of physical force is not the only means of the state but it is specific to the state. The appropriation of the means of violence is necessary for the formation of the state, but it is not sufficient for its further development. States also fulfil the following functions: the enactment of law (legislation), the protection of personal safety and public order (police), the protection of vested rights (administration of justice), the cultivation of cultural interests (in the administration), and the organized armed protection against outside attack (the military).

The Territory of the State

Second, Weber holds the view that the state has a monopoly of force within a given territory. The authority of the state is binding within a particular territorial area only. After having given his definition, Weber stresses: "Note that 'territory' is one of the characteristics of the state (as it is of any political formation). Any kind of political association is therefore defined, next to legitimate force, as having a territorial basis: "Whenever corporate groups which make use of force are also characterized by a claim to territorial jurisdiction..., they must be regarded by definition to that extent as political groups". This does not mean, according to Weber, that every form of organization with territorial claims is a state; the monopoly of force and its legitimacy through legality are just as necessary conditions for there to be a state. He draws a comparison with churches: "The prevailing hierocratic territorial and parochial organization is in accordance with the normal striving of a church after complete domination;... But unlike the political corporate group, the church historically has not felt nearly as much the need for exclusive territorial domination and this is especially true today.

The Bureaucracy of the State

As a third element in Weber's definition of the state, he contends that the right to use force is given to other institutions only to the extent to which the state permits it. These institutions are the bureaucracies in the sphere of public government ("bureaucratic authority") and in the market-economy ("bureaucratic management"). Bureaucratic authority is bound by obedience to the power-holder: the means of power are separated from the formally autonomous power-holders to the bureaucratic apparatus of the state.

Bureaucracies are for Weber one of the most important characteristics of modern, rationalized societies. they indicate the extent to which the world has become 'calculable' in terms of efficiency, the extent to which the previous mysteries of the world, as embodied in traditionalistic ethical life, have become disenchanted (demystified).

Legal legitimacy rests on the validity of impersonal norms which have been consciously established in the context of purposive or value rationality. This accounts for the following characteristics of bureaucracies: 1) they are subject to the principle of fixed jurisdictional areas; 2) because of their hierarchy they are firmly ordered; 3) the modern office is based upon written documents (files); 4) the public equipment of the official are divorced from his private property, and the executive office is separated from the household; 5) specialized training is required; 6) official activity is a full-time job; 7) the management of offices is guided by general rules which can be learnt. Only within modern capitalist societies, do bureaucracies take on this form, directly affected by the division of labour: bureaucracies are specialization and therefore efficient.

Bureaucracies perform administrative tasks (management) to secure an efficient functioning of state and market-economy. Like capitalist enterprises, bureaucracies also concentrate the material means of management. In the military, for instance, war has become war of machines, and in the field of science, the bureaucratization of institutes and universities involves an increasing demand for material means of research and education. Bureaucracies are also based on a leveling of social differences: they create mass democracies which level the governed in opposition to the ruling. The bureaucratic apparatus is stable, permanent, indispensable, and the machine is "easily made to work for anybody who knows how to gain control over it". The administrative functions of bureaucracies are specialized and based on calculable rules: bureaucracy is dehumanized, and objective experts take control. The political master may find himself in the role of dilettante who stand opposite the expert.

Characteristic for modern bureaucracies is the discipline with which they operate. The discipline in the army and in monasteries is, according to Weber, a central force in the process of bureaucratization. Indeed, discipline emerged out of the techniques of the organization of warfare (not just the technological means), and it was military discipline that affected social and economic life. Under these conditions, mainly to satisfy the needs of professional soldiery, charismatic political power structures become routinized and rational, transforming into legal-rational power under bureaucratic control. Note, however, that as a formal means of organization, discipline can accompany any political power structure, whether traditional, charismatic or legal-rational.

The notion of discipline refers to, first, an institutional form of organization, which gradually extends throughout society. It refers to the "consistently rationalized, methodically trained and exact execution of the received order, in which all personal criticism is unconditionally suspended". Discipline reduces the significance of individual action, it is a matter purely of formal routine and efficiency. The official's position in a bureaucracy is therefore characterized by a) the social esteem he enjoys from the governed, b) the fact that he is appointed (not elected), c) that it is a life-long appointment, d) that he reserves regular salaries, and e) that he can have a career with fixed conditions for advancement. Second, the spread of discipline throughout society also transforms the individual psychology: people have developed a passion for bureaucratization. At the same time, Weber sees it important to "oppose this machinery in order to preserve a vestige of humanity from this fragmentation of the soul". The idea of democracy is inherently ambivalent towards bureaucracies since it opposes the status of bureaucratic specialist and seeks to replace them by the (just as arbitrary) influence of the governed and their representatives in political parties.

CLASS, STATUS, AND PARTY

Discipline is also an important mechanism in the power potentials of classes, status groups and parties. A class in Weber terminology's are determined by economic interest in the possession of goods (property) and opportunities for income (sale of labour service), a definition for which Weber is largely indebted to Marx. However, Weber contends that class interests are not uni-directly determined by ownership: class struggles do not necessarily have to result from the inequalities in ownership. Class consciousness must be mobilized under certain circumstances, which can be non-economic, such as the visibility of the class enemy, the menas of communication to organize a group, and so on. The relevance of classes as classes, however, is by definition solely restricted to market conditions.

Status

Status groups are determined by a social estimation of honour and prestige: unlike classes, status groups do not necessarily consist of economically privileged people, but of symbolic qualities and a particular life-style, and, unlike classes, they are mostly conscious of their common position (example: professional organizations). The potential of status groups for political and communal action is clear from their characteristic of social closure: groups tend to improve their lot by restricting access to rewards and privileges to a small circle of chosen ones. Certain social or physical attributes are selected and function as criteria of eligibility. It does not matter what these criteria are as long as they lead to distinguish insiders from outsiders. Exclusionary social closure thus enables status groups to secure advantages and resources for itself.

Party

Parties, finally, are exclusively related to power and domination. Parties strive to realize planned change in communal action (sometimes based on class, on status, on both, or neither). Parties can reach "beyond the frontiers of politics... But their aim is not necessarily the establishment of new international political, i.e. territorial, dominion". While discipline, class, status and party are related to aspects of power, it is noteworthy that Weber does not discuss them in relation to state and bureaucracy. Classes, status groups and parties can strive for power and mobilize political action, but they nevertheless operate in the realm of civil society or the nation. The nation refers to a group held together by sentiments of solidarity in the face of other groups. It is not identical with the people of a state but may cross through different states, or any one state can harbour different nations. A nation does not necessarily share the same language, religion, race or common descent but each of these or any other cultural values may be focused on to define the nation. Nations do tend to produce their own state, but are nevertheless in the first instance cultural entities.

THE RATIONAL STATE OF LAW

Weber's sociology of law is intimately related to his notion of state and bureaucracy (note: Giddens says that legitimacy is not necessarily related to the state or to state-law; but legal-rational legitimacy is, as Parsons rightly claims). The state not only has a monopoly of force, it is also a political community that successfully claims a legitimate monopoly of force. State domination is legitimated by legality, the belief in the rational validity of legal rules.

This rational-legal legitimation derives from the systemic rationalization of law and constitutionalism, from bureaucracies and from doctrines of sovereignty. Weber is clearly directed against materialist and idealist interpretations of law. He defines law in the following way: "An order will be called law if it is externally guaranteed by the probability that coercion (physical or psychological), to bring about conformity or avenge violation, will be applied by a staff of people holding themselves specially ready for that purpose". The element of staff, the organized coercive apparatus including "judges, prosecutors, policemen, or sheriffs" is decisive (not coercion itself). This does not mean that legal legitimacy is always tied up to the state, and it does not always imply adherence to law. The criminal, for instance, also recognizes the legitimacy of law, namely because he has to carefully plan the execution of a crime, he is aware that it is a violation of law. The coercive apparatus does not have to be a political agency; there must simply be a body that applies sanctions, whether bound to the state or not.

The Rationality of Modern Law

In spite of the attention Weber pays to the legitimacy of law, which resides in the legal subjects, he interprets the law positivistically as a set of reliable techniques for producing legally consistent answers. Rationalized law is formal, abstract, exemplifying the disenchanted modernized world. A sense of justice may play a role in the development of law, but such an emotional factor "cannot be expressed except in a few very general and purely formal maxims". Legal formalism can be challenged by social law, based on emotionally coloured ethical postulates like justice or human dignity, but this value-irrationalism has equally been opposed by attempts to re-establish objective standards of value and law as a technical tool. The legal-rational authority of the state's bureaucracies is governed by procedures, by a system of laws, not of men, which formally regulates social affairs.

THE RATIONALITY OF THE CAPITALIST ECONOMY

Weber considered the Western type of capitalist organization as "the most fateful force in our modern life". Indeed, throughout his writings, Weber discusses the influences of the capitalist economy on nearly every other sphere of modern society. The rise of bureaucracies, for instance, Weber explains partly by economic conditions. The money market is necessary to provide the income to maintain bureaucracies (based on a system of taxation) since bureaucracies cannot be derived from private profits. Other conditions of the expansion of bureaucracies are political. Bureaucratic structures grow larger and change qualitatively with the expansion of the state: "The increasing demand of a society, accustomed to absolute pacification, for order and protection ('police'), in all fields exerts an especially persevering influence in the direction of bureaucratization. A steady road leads from modifications of the blood feud, sacerdotally, or by means of arbitration, to the present position of the policeman as 'the representative of God on earth.'". Weber also mentions several technical developments that favor the rise of bureaucracies. The characteristically modern means of communication enter the picture as pacemakers of bureaucratization; public roads, telegraph and so on must be publicly administered. These technical developments are crucial for the possibilities of bureaucracies: "The modern Occidental state can be administered the way it actually is only because the state controls the telegraph network and has the mails and railroads at its disposal". Technological developments in the modern means of communication do not completely determine the operation of bureaucracies, they also respond to the demand of the capitalist market economy. Unambiguity, knowledge of the files, continuity and unity are all raised to the optimum point: "the extraordinary increase in the speed by which public announcements, as well as economic and political facts are transmitted, exerts a steady and sharp pressure in the direction of speeding up the tempo of administrative reaction towards various situations".

Note that Weber does not conceive the interplay of numerous, political, economic and cultural factors as an inevitable evolutionary trend. The extension of market capitalism he very likely sees as dominant. Also note that the antinomy between formal rationality (conduct organized according to calculable principles) and substantive rationality (calculable conduct applied to the furtherance of certain goals or value) cannot be resolved in modern capitalism.

The rise of modern rationalized law Weber also attributes to economic and political factors. Rational law is guided by general rules to create stable, predictable and patterned regularities in social actions and social institutions. Rationalized law is executed in the bureaucratic apparatus of the state, but it also serves the free-market economy. Specifically, law prevents a war of all against all on the economic battlefield. A rational free-market economy is not possible without the legal order of the state, but contractual freedom leads to the free use of resources without legal restraints: "The market is a relationship which transcends the boundaries of neighborhood, kinship group, or tribe". Laws leaving everything free to the market imply "a relative reduction of that kind of coercion which results from the threat of mandatory and prohibitory norms".

4

Max Weber: Concepts of Sociology

DEFINITIONS OF SOCIOLOGY AND SOCIAL ACTION

Sociology is a science which attempts the interpretive understanding of social action to arrive at a casual explanation of its course and effects. Sociology seeks to formulate type concepts and generalized uniformities of empirical processes. (History, on the other hand, is interested in the causal analysis of particular events, actions or personalities.)

Action is human behaviour to which the acting individual attaches subjective meaning. It can be overt or inward and subjective. Action is social when, by virtue of the subjective meaning attached to it by the acting individual(s), it takes account of the behaviour of others and is thereby guided. Social action may be oriented to past, present, or predicted future behaviour of others. Others may be concrete people or indefinite pluralities.

Not all action is social: if it ain't oriented to the behaviour of others, it ain't social. Also, it is not merely action participated in by a bunch of people (crowd action) or action influenced by or imitative of others. Action can be causally determined by the behaviour of others, while still not necessarily being meaningfully determined by the action of others. If I do what you do because it's fashionable, or traditional, or leads to social distinction, its meaningful. Obviously the lines are blurred (pp 113-114), but it's important to make a conceptional distinction.

Modes of Orientation of Social Action

Uniformity of social action = action which is wide-spread, frequently repeated by the same individual or simultaneously performed by many individuals and which corresponds to a subjective meaning attributable to the same actors.

Usage: probability of a uniformity in the orientation of social action, when the probability is determined by its actual practice ('it is done to conform with the pattern).

Custom: usage when the actual performance of the action rests on long familiarity. Non-conformance is sanctioned externally.

Action can also be uniform if the actor acts in his self-interests. The uniformity rests insofar as behaviour is determined by purely rational actions of actors to similar ulterior expectations.

Types of Social Action, identified by mode of orientation:

1) rational orientation to a system of discrete individual ends. individuals can choose and adjudicate between both means and ends, though these considerations may be with reference to other absolute values.
2) rational orientation to an absolute value, involving conscious belief in the absolute value entirely for its own sake and independent of prospects for external success. Can choose b/t means, but only with relation to absolute, fixed end. Absolute values are always irrational.
3) affectional orientation. If this is uncontrolled reaction to some exceptional stimulus, it is not meaningful — grey areas.
4) traditional orientation. If this is strict imitation, it is not meaningful — grey areas.

METHODOLOGICAL FOUNDATIONS OF SOCIOLOGY

There are 2 kinds of meaning: 1) actually existing meaning in a given concrete case of a particular actor, or average or approximate meaning attributed to a given number of actors; and 2) theoretically conceived pure types of subjective meaning attributed to hypothetical actor(s) in a given type of action (like an ideal type).

The line between meaningful action and reactive behaviour w/o subjective meaning is blurry. The basis for understanding meaning may be either rational (logical or mathematical — clear intellectual grasp of things) or emotionally empathetic or artistically appreciative (though sympathetic participation we grasp the emotional context in which the action took place).

For purposes of ideal type analysis, it's convenient to treat irrational (from the point of view of rational pursuit of a given end) action as deviation from a conceptually pure type of rational action. We compare this analytically clear type to empirical reality, and that increases our understanding of how actually action is influences by irrational factors. The more sharp and precise the ideal type (and thus the more abstract and unrealistic) the more useful it is in clarifying terminology and formulating classifications and hypotheses.

Some phenomena are devoid of subjective meaning. What is intelligible about an object is its relation to human action in its role either of means or of end, a relation which actors can be said to be aware of and to which their action has been oriented. If you can't make this relation (for example a hindering or favourable circumstance) it's not meaningful in the sense we care about.

There are 2 kinds of understanding: 1) direct observational understanding of subjective mean of a given act (eg, if i start to shout at you, you could directly observe my irrational emotional reaction by virtue of my shouting). 2) explanatory understanding: we understand motive, or, what makes an individual do a particular thing in a particular circumstance. Since we are interested in the subjective meaning of action, we must place an action in the complex of meaning in which it took place. A motive is a complex of subjective meaning which seems to the actor and/OR the observer an adequate ground for the conduct in question.

In most cases, actual action goes on in a state of inarticulate half-consciousness or actually unconsciousness of its subjective meaning. The ideal type case of meaning is where meaning is fully conscious and explicit: this rarely happens in reality. Adequacy on the level of meaning: a subjective interpretation of a coherent course of conduct when its component parts in their mutual relation are recognized as a 'typical' complex of meaning. Eg, according to our current norms of calculation and thinking, the correct solution to an arithmatical problem. Casual adequacy: there's a probability it will always actually occur in the same way. Eg, statistical probability, according to verified generalization from experience, that there would be a correct or incorrect solution to the arithmatical problem.

Subjectively understandable action exists ONLY as the behaviour of one or more individual human beings. States, for instance, are results of particular acts of individual persons. There is no such things as a collective personality that acts. These concepts of collective entities DO HAVE meanings in the minds of individual persons, and so actors orient their actions to them as if they existed or should exist.

Functional analysis is a good starting point for sociology. We need to know what kinds of action is functionally necessary for survival, and also for the maintenance of a cultural type and the corresponding modes of social action. We are interested, though, in the subjective meaning of actions to component individuals. The interesting question, then, is what motives determine and lead the individual members and participants in this situation to behave in such a way that the situation came into being in the first place.

THE CONCEPT OF SOCIAL RELATIONSHIP

Social relationship: the behaviour of actors in so far as, in its meaningful content, the action of each takes account of the others and is oriented to the behaviour of others. Mere group membership is not sufficient. The relation of the actors may be solidary, or the opposite. Eg, a 'state' ceases to exist when there is no longer a probability that certain kinds of meaningfully oriented social action will take place.

The subjective meaning need not be the same for all parties to the relationship. The relationship may be temporary or long term. Its subjective meaning may change over time.

The Concept of Legitimate Order

The validity of an order is the probability that people will orient their action to it.

Types of Legitimate Order

Legitimacy of an order can be upheld in 2 ways:

1) purely disinterested motives a) purely affectual, b) rational belief in absolute validity of an order as an expression of ultimate values, c) religious attitudes, through belief in need to follow order for salvation
2) entirely through self-interest based on ulterior motives

Convention: system of order where infraction meets with sanctions of disapproval and orders are considered binding.

Law: system of order where the above is enforced by a functionally specialized agency (e.g., the police).

A system of order with external sanctions may also be guaranteed by disinterested subjective attitudes. Eg, it can be both morally wrong and illegal to murder.

Bases of Legitimacy

Legitimacy may be ascribed to an order by those subject to it in the following ways:

1) tradition, belief in legitimacy of what has always existed.
2) affectual attitudes, legitimizing the validity of what is newly revealed or is a model to imitate
3) rational belief in its absolute value
4) legality. Readiness to conform with rules which are formally correct and have been imposed by accepted procedure.

Submission to an order is almost always determined by a variety of motives.

MAX WEBER'S CLASS, STATUS, PARTY

All communities are arranged in a manner that goods, tangible and intangible, symbolic and material are distributed. Such a distribution is always unequal and necessarily involves power. "Classes, status groups and parties are phenomena of the distribution of power within a community". Status groups makes up the social order, classes the economic order, and parties the legal/political order. Each order affects and is affected by the other.

Power

Power is the "chance of a man or a number of men to realize their own will in a social action even against the resistance of others who are participating in the action".

Power may rest of a variety of bases, and can be of differing types. "Economically conditioned power is not identical with power... The emergence of economic power may be the consequence of power existing on other grounds. Man does not strive for power only to enrich himself economically. Power, including economic power, may be valued for its own sake. Very frequently the striving for power is conditioned by the social honour it entails. Not all power entails honour." Power is not the only basis of social honour, and social honour, or prestige, may be the basis of economic power.

"Power, as well as honour, may be guaranteed by the legal order, but... [the legal order] is not their primary source. The legal order is rather an additional factor that enhances the chance to hold power or honour; but it cannot always secure them".

Class

Class is defined in terms of market situation. A class exists when a number of people have in common a specific casual component of their life chances in the following sense: this component is represented exclusively by economic interests in the possession of goods and opportunities for income under conditions of the commodity or labour markets.

When market conditions prevail (eg, capitalism), property and lack of property are the basic categories of all class situations. However, the concept of class-interest is ambiguous. Collective action based on class situations is determined by the transparency of the connections between the causes and the consequences of the class situation. If the contrast between the life chances of different class situations is merely seen as an acceptable absolute fact, no action will be taken to change the class situation.

A class in and of itself does not constitute a group (Gemeinschaft). "The degree in which social action and possibly associations emerge from the mass behaviour of the members of a class is linked to general cultural conditions, especially those of an intellectual sort". "If classes as such are not groups, class situations emerge only on the basis of social action."

Status Groups and Honour

Unlike classes, status groups do have a quality of groups. They are determined by the distribution of social honour. A specific style of life is shared by a status group, and the group itself is defined by those with whom one has social intercourse. Economic elements can be a sort of honour; however, similar class position does not necessitate similar status groups. People from different economic classes may be members of the same status group, if they share the same specific style of life.

The way in which social honour is distributed in the community is called the status order. Criteria for entry into a status group may take forms such as the sharing of kinship groups or certain levels of education. The most extreme of a status system with a high level of closure (that is, strong restriction of mobility between statuses) is a caste system. There, status distinctions are guaranteed no only by law and convention, but also by religious sanctions.

Relationships between Class and Status group; between Class situation, Status Situation, and Stratification.

Status groups can sometimes be equal to class, sometimes be broader, sometimes more restrictive, and sometimes bear no relation to class (duh). In most cases, status situation is the apparent dimension of stratification: "stratification by status goes hand in hand with a monopolization of ideal and material goods or opportunities". Class situation can take precedence over status situation, however. "When the bases of the acquisition and distribution of goods are relatively stable, stratification by status is favoured". Technological and economic changes threaten stratification by status, and "push class situation to the foreground.... Every slowing down of the change in economic stratification leads, in due course, to the growth or status structures and makes for a resuscitation of the important role of social honour".

Parties

"Parties reside in the sphere of power". "Parties are... only possible within groups that have an asssociational character, that is, some rational order and a staff of persons". Parties aim for social power, the ability to influence the actions of others, and thus may exist in a social club, the state, or a cohort of graduate students at the University of Chicago.

Parties may represent class or status interests, or neither. They usually represent a mix.

"The structure of parties differs in a basic way according to the kind of social action which they struggle to influence.... [T]hey differ according to whether or not the community is stratified by class or status. Above all else, they vary according to the structure of domination".

MAX WEBER: THE PROTESTANT ETHIC AND THE SPIRIT OF CAPITALISM

Though knowledge and observation of great refinement have existed elsewhere, only in the West has rationalization in science, law and culture developed to such a great degree. The modern West absolutely and completely depends for its whole existence, for the political technical, and economic conditions of its life, on a specially trained organization of individuals, so that the most important functions of everyday life have come to be in the hands of technically, commercially and above all legally trained government officials. Nowhere else does this exist to such a degree as it does in the West.

The most fateful force in modern life is capitalism. The impulse to acquisition has existed always and everywhere and has in itself nothing to do with capitalism. Capitalism is the pursuit of profit, and forever renewed profit, by means of continuous, rational, capitalistic enterprise. This enterprise must be continuous, because in a capitalistic society, anyone who did not take advantage of opportunities for profit-making would be doomed to extinction.

A capitalistic economic action rests on the expectation of profit by the utilization of opportunities for exchange, on (formally) peaceful chances for profit. Where this is rationally pursued, calculations in terms of money are made, whether by modern bookkeeping or more primitive means. Everything is done in terms of balances of money income and money expenses. Whether the calculations are accurate, or whether the calculation method is traditional or by guess-work affects only the degree of the rationality of capitalistic acquisition.

Characteristics of modern Western capitalism: rational industrial organization (that is, attuned to a regular profit and not to political nor irrational speculative opportunities for profit); separation of business from the household; rational bookkeeping. Capitalistic adventurers (in search of booty, whether by war or exploitation) have existed everywhere, but only in the modern West has developed... the rational capitalistic organization of (formally) free labour.

The rationality of MWC is dependent on the calculation of technical factors, and so is dependent on the development in science of the exact and rational experiment. C'ism did not cause this development: but, the continuing development of this type science is supported by capitalistic interests in practical economic applications.

The peculiar rationalism of Western culture extends to many fields — science, mystical contemplation, military training, law and administration. Each of theses fields may be rationalized in terms of very different ultimate values and ends, and what is rational from one point of view may well be irrational from another. The development of economic rationalism is partly dependent on rational technique and law, but it also requires people to have a favourable disposition toward adopting certain types of practical rational conduct.

In this book, we will treat ONLY ONE SIDE OF THE CAUSAL CHAIN, the connection of the spirit of modern economic life with the rational ethics of ascetic Protestantism.

Religious Affiliation and Social Stratification

Catholics show a stronger propensity to remain in their crafts, and become master craftsmen, while Protestants are attracted to a larger extent to the upper ranks of skilled labour and administrative positions in factories. Protestants own a disproportionate share of capital. All other things equal, Protestants have been more likely to develop economic rationalism than Catholics. Weber seeks the explanation in 'the permanent intrinsic character of their religion,' and not only in their temporary external historico-political situations.

The Reformation meant not the elimination of the church's control over everyday life, but a substitution of a new form of control for the previous one. While the Catholic church was fairly lax, Calvinism 'would be for us the most absolutely unbearable form of ecclesiastical control of the individual which could possibly exist.'

Protestantism must not be understood as joy of living or in any other sense connected with the Enlightenment. Early Protestantism (e.g., Luther, Calvin) had nothing to do with progress in an Enlightenment sense. Not all Protestant denominations had an equally strong influence on the development of members' business acumen and spirit of hard work.

The Spirit of Capitalism

The spirit of capitalism is "an historical individual: a complex of elements associated in historical reality which we united into a conceptual whole from the standpoint of their cultural significance".

Ben Franklin is an example of someone who espouses a philosophy of avarice which is: the ideal of an honest man of recognized credit. It includes a duty on the part of an individual toward the increase of his capital, which is assumed as an end in itself. It is not mere business astuteness, it is an ethos; infraction of its rules is not foolishness or bad business, but forgetfulness of duty.

In this ethic, economic acquisition is no longer considered a means of subsistence: it is the ultimate purpose of a man's life. This is combined with the strict avoidance of all spontaneous enjoyment of life..

People now are born into a capitalistic economy which presents itself to them as the unalterable order of things in which they must live. In so far as a person born now is involved in the system of market relationships, he must conform to capitalistic rules of action. Today's capitalism selects the subjects it needs through economic survival of the fittest. The interesting question, according to Max, is WHERE DID THIS SITUATION COME FROM?

It did NOT arise as the superstructure or reflection of economic situations. For example, the spirit of capitalism such as espoused by our buddy Ben Franklin was present before capitalistic order.

In order to arise, the spirit of capitalism had to struggle with its 'most important opponent,' traditionalism. For instance, workers will respond to an increase in piece rates by doing less work, collecting the usual amount of money, and going home early. Men do not "by nature" wish to earn more and more money, they simply wish to live as they are accustomed to and to earn as much as is necessary for that purpose.

Another way of attempting to increase productivity is to lower wages or piece rates, so that workers must work harder and longer to earn the same amount as before. This method has its limits. It (and capitalism) requires a surplus population which can be hired cheaply in the market. Also, too large a surplus population can encourage the development of labour intensive methods, rather than more efficient methods: low wages do not equal cheap labour. And, if you pay people too little, their efficiency and attentiveness decreases.

Thus, it would be better if labour were performed as if it were an absolute end in itself. This can only be the process of a long and arduous education (for example, being raised Pietist). Capitalism "now in the saddle" can fairly easily recruit the required workers, but this was not always the case.

Capitalism can exist with a traditionalistic character. The animating spirit of the entrepreneur may be the traditional rate of profit, the traditional amount of work, the traditional manner of labour-management relations, and the essentially traditional circle of customers and manner of attracting new ones. Take the example of the putting out system.

In such a system, this leisureliness can be destroyed, without any essential change in the form of work organization (such as vertically integrated factories). The spirit of capitalism is the cause of this change. Where the spirit of capitalism appears and is able to work itself out, it produces its own capital and monetary supplies as the means to its ends, but the reverse is not true.

Protestantism was not merely a stage prior to the development of a purely rationalistic philosophy, however. Rationalism shows a development which by no means follows parallel lines in the various departments of life. Since life may be rationalized from fundamentally different basic points of view and in very different directions, we must ask the origin of the irrational element which lies at the basis of this particular concrete form of rational thought: the conception of a calling.

Luther's Conception of The Calling

The idea of a calling — a life-task, a definite field in which to work — is peculiar to Protestants. Protestantism had a further new development, which was the valuation of the fulfilment of duty in worldly affairs as the highest form which the moral activity of an individual could assume. The only way of living acceptably to God was solely through the fulfilment of the obligations imposed upon the individual by his position in the world (his calling), NOT by trying to surpass worldly morality by monastic asceticism. Remember important part of Reformation: By faith, not works, shall ye be saved. You are justified by faith, etc. So all those indulgences earned by crawling on your knees up stairways, etc. don't get you anything.

For the time being (before Calvin et al. got hold of it), the idea of the calling remained traditionalistic and its only ethical result negative: worldly duties were no longer subordinated to ascetic ones; obedience to authority and acceptance of things as they were, were preached.

The Religious Foundations of Worldly Asceticism

However, this idea of the calling was not sufficient for the development of the spirit of capitalism. We needed the effects of forms of ascetic Protestantism: Calvinism, Pietism, Methodism and the Baptist sects.

An important thing to keep in mind is that these folks were not motivated by acquisitive lusts, but rather by salvation of the soul.

Calvinists believed in predestination. God designated before the creation of the world who would be saved and who would get to rot in hell. All creation exists for the sake of God, and has meaning only as means to the glory and majesty of God. Human merit or guilt plays no part in the possession of grace, since that would make God's decrees subject to human influence. This doctrine 'must above all have one consequence... a feeling of unprecedented inner loneliness of the single individual'. The individual was forced to follow the path of his own destiny decreed for him from eternity without help from others or from the Church — complete elimination of salvation through the Church and the sacraments (which Lutheranism retained). This meant the elimination of magic from the world. [It also meant the doing away with a periodical discharge of the emotional sense of sin (confession).]

Now, the elected Christian should glorify God in life by fulfilling God's commandments to the best of his ability. This requires social achievements of the Christian because God decrees that social life shall be organized according to his commandments.

Fear and lack of knowledge of whether or not one is going to rot in hell led to a need for ordinary men to find certitudo salutis (certainty of salvation). Pastoral advice to these poor, tortured dudes contained two themes: 1) an absolute duty to consider oneself chosen and to combat all doubts as temptations of the devil, since lack of self-confidence is the result of insufficient faith, hence of imperfect grace. 2) Intense worldly activity as the most suitable means to attain that self-confidence [thus we eliminate the free rider problem]. The Calvinist sought to identify true faith by its fruits: a type of Christian conduct which served to increase the glory of God. Good works do not affect salvation, but they are indispensable as a sign of election. In practice, this means God helps those who help themselves. The Calvinist creates a conviction of his own salvation. For Catholics, good works were not a part of a rationalized system of life — they could be performed sporadically, to atone — whereas for Calvinists they are. The God of Calvinism demanded not single good works, but a life of good works combined into a unified system. The moral conduct of the average man was subjected to a consistent method for conduct as a whole. The end of this asceticism was to be able to lead an alert, intelligent life: the most urgent task the destruction of spontaneous, impulsive enjoyment. The most important means was to bring order into the conduct of its adherents. Hence we have methodically rationalized ethical conduct. The Calvinistic doctrine of predestination was only one of several possible motives which could have supported the methodical rationalization of life. However, it had not only a unique consistency (by virtue of being based on logical deduction, rather than religious experience) and was psychologically extraordinarily powerful.

Pietism

This sect sought to make the invisible Church of the elect visible on this earth. By means of intensified asceticism these folks hoped to enjoy the blissfulness of community with God in this life. Sometimes this latter tendency led to displays of emotion, which were antithetical to Calvinist restraint. Other than that, however, the practical effect of Pietistic principles was an even stricter ascetic control of conduct in the calling:

1) Methodical development of one's own state of grace to a higher and higher degree of certainty and perfection in terms of the law was a sign of grace.
2) A belief that God's Providence works through those in such a state of perfection.

Since some of these folks believed grace subject to repentance, by the creation of methods to induce repentance even the attainment of divine grace became in effect an object of rational human activity.

Methodism

Though rebirth, an emotional certainty of salvation as the immediate result of faith was an important factor, the emotional act of conversion was methodically induced. Emotion, once awakened, was directed into a rational struggle for perfection. This provided a religious basis for ascetic conduct after the doctrine of predestination had been given up by these folks.

Nothing new was added to the idea of the calling.

The Baptist Sects

The church was viewed as a community of personal believers of the reborn. Salvation was achieved by personal, individual revelation; it was offered to everyone, though not everyone took it. The injunction was to be in the world but not of it, so worldly enjoyments and unnecessary social intercourse with non-reborn folks was avoided. The Holy Spirit worked in daily life, and spoke directly to any individual who was willing to hear. This leads to an eventual elimination of all that remained of the doctrine of salvation through the Church and sacraments. This accomplished the religious rationalization of the world in its most extreme form.

Conscience is the revelation of God to the individual.

The rationalization of conduct within the world, but for the sake of the world beyond, was the consequence of the concept of calling of ascetic Protestantism.

Asceticism and The Spirit of Capitalism

In Puritan thinking, the real moral objection to possession of wealth is to relaxation in the security of possession, the enjoyment of wealth with the consequence of idleness and the temptations of the flesh, above all distraction from the pursuit of a righteous life. It is only because possession involves this danger that it is suspect at all. Not leisure and enjoyment, but only activity serves to increase the glory of God. Waste of time is thus the first and in principle the deadliest of sins. Thus, inactive contemplation at the expense of work is right out.

Labour is an approved ascetic technique, but is also considered in itself an end of life as ordained by God.

Unwillingness to work is symptomatic of the lack of grace. Wealth does not exempt anyone from this.

The division of labour, which has a providential purpose in the thought of the Puritans, leads to qualitative and quantitative improvements in production, and thus serves the common good. But, in addition, specialization is encouraged by the calling, to which it provides an ethical justification; for, "outside of a calling the accomplishments of a man are only casual and irregular and he spends more time in idleness than in work." If God presents to His elect a change for profit, he must pursue it: the Christian must follow the call by taking advantage of the opportunity. The acquisition of wealth in the performance of a calling is morally permissible and enjoined.

— Asceticism turned against the spontaneous enjoyment of life. So, sport, for instance, is acceptable only if it serves a rational purpose, say, increasing physical efficiency.

— The powerful tendency toward uniformity of life, which today so immensely aids the capitalistic interest in the standardization of production, had its ideal foundation in the repudiation of all idolatry of the flesh (eg, non-ascetic, flashy or attractive clothing).

The Puritan outlook on life 'stood at the cradle of modern economic man'. This religious epoch bequeathed to its utilitarian successors "an amazingly good... conscience in the acquisition of money, so long as it took place legally". In addition, the power of religious asceticism provided owners with sober, conscientious and industrious workmen. And, it provided comforting assurance that the unequal distribution of goods in the world was ordained by God.

The religious basis had died away by Ben Franklin's time. Limitation to specialized work is now a condition of any valuable work in the modern world. "The Puritan wanted to work in a calling; we are forced to do so. For when asceticism was carried out of monastic cells into everyday life, and began to dominate worldly morality, did its part in building the tremendous cosmos of the modern economic order This order is now bound to the technical and economic conditions of machine production and today determine the lives of all the individuals who are born into this mechanism, not only those directly concerned with economic acquisition, with irresistible force."

The Religious Rejections of the World and Their Directions

Motives for the Rejections of the World: The Meaning of Their Rational Construction.

Individual spheres of value presented here as ideal types have a rational consistency rarely found in reality. This essay proceeds from the most rational forms reality can assume; it attempts to find out how far certain rational conclusions, which can be established theoretically, have been drawn in reality. Perhaps, also, we can find out why those rational conclusions have not been drawn.

Typology of Asceticism and Mysticism

Two contrasting abnegations of the world:

1) active asceticism that is a God-willed ACTION of the devout who are God's tools. Rationally active asceticism, in mastering the world, seeks to tame what is creatural and wicked through work in a worldly vocation (inner-worldly asceticism);

2) contemplative POSSESSION of the holy as found in mysticism. The individual is not a tool, but a vessel of the divine. Desired: other-worldly religious state; contemplative flight from the world.

Active asceticism may confine itself to controlling wickedness in the actor's own nature; in this case, it avoids any action in the orders of the world (asceticist flight from the world). In external bearing, it thereby comes close to contemplative flight. Conversely, the mystic may determine s/he need not flee from the world, and so be an inner-worldly mysticist, remaining in the orders of the world.

Directions of the Abnegation of the World

Formulated abstractly, the rational aim of redemption religion has been to secure for the saved a holy state, and thereby a habitude that assures salvation. This takes the place of an acute and extraordinary, and thus a holy state which is transitorily achieved by means of orgies, asceticism, or contemplation. Most prophetic and redemptory religions have lived not only in an acute, but a permanent state of tension in relation to the world and its orders. The more the religions have been true religions of salvation, the greater has this tension been. The tension has been greater the more religion has been sublimated from ritualism and towards 'religious absolutism.' Indeed, the further the rationalization and sublimation of external and internal possession of — in the widest sense — things worldly has progressed, the stronger has the tension on the part of religion become. For the rationalization and conscious sublimation of man's relations to the various spheres of values, internal and external, as well as religious and secular, have then pressed towards making conscious the internal and lawful autonomy of the individual spheres; thereby letting them drift into those tensions which remain hidden to the original naive relation with the external world. The more comprehensive and the more inward the aim of salvation has been, the more it has been taken for granted that the faithful should ultimately stand closer to the savior, the prophet, the priest, the brother in the faith than to natural relations and to the matrimonial community. Prophecy has created a new social community; thereby the relationships of the sib and of matrimony have been devalued.

Communities of villages, members of the sib, the guild or of partners in seafaring, hunting and warring expeditions have known two elemental principles: first, the dualism or in-group and out-group morality. For in-group morality the principled obligation to give brotherly support in distress has existed. All this followed the principle of "your want of today, may be my want of tomorrow" (this principle was not rationally weighed, but it played its part in sentiment). Accordingly, haggling in exchange and loan situations, as well as permanent debt-enslavement and similar kinds of enslavement, were confined to outgroup morality and applied only to outsiders.

The religiosity of the congregation transferred the ancient economic ethic of neighborliness (I'll help you out today, since

I may need you to help me out tomorrow) to the relations among brothers of the faith. What had previously been the obligations of the noble and the wealthy became the fundamental imperatives of all ethically rationalized religion (to care for orphans and widows, to give alms). The principle that constituted the communal relations among the salvation prophesies was the suffering common to all believers (whether or not the suffering actually existed or was a constant threat, whether it was internal or external). The more imperatives that issued from the ethic of reciprocity among neighbors were raised, the more rational the conception of salvation became, and the more it was sublimated into an ethic of absolute ends.

The Economic Sphere

The tension between brotherly religion and the world has been most obvious in the economic sphere. All the primeval magical or mystagogic ways of influencing spirits and deities have pursued special interests. The sublimated religions of salvation, however, had been increasingly tense in their relationships with rationalized economies.

A rational economy is a functional organization oriented to money-prices which originate in the interest-struggles of men in the market. Calculation is not possible without estimation in money prices and hence without market struggles. Money is the most abstract and impersonal element that exists in human life. The more the world of the capitalist economy follows its own immanent laws, the less accessible it is to any imaginable relationship with a religious ethic of brotherliness. Ultimately no genuine religion of salvation has overcome the tension between their religiosity and a rational economy.

The paradox of all rational asceticism is that rational asceticism has created the very wealth it rejected.

There have only been two consistent avenues for escaping the tension between religion and in the economic world in a principled and inward manner:

1) the Puritan ethic of the vocation. Puritanism, as a religion of virtuosos, renounced the universalism of love and rationally routinized all work in this world into

serving God's will and testing ones state of grace. Puritanism accepted the routinization of the economic cosmos, which, along with the whole world, it devalued as creatural and depraved. It involved a renunciation of salvation in favor of the groundless and always only particularized grace. Actually, this standpoint of unbrotherliness was no longer a genuine religion of salvation. A genuine religion of salvation can exaggerate brotherliness to the height of the mystic's acosmism of love.

2) Mysticism. The mystic's benevolence does not inquire into the man to whom and for whom it sacrifices. Mysticism is not interested in his person. Mysticism is a unique escape form this world in the form of an objectless devotion to anybody, not for man's sake, but purely for devotion's sake.

The Political Sphere

The consistent brotherly ethic of salvation religions has come into an equally sharp tension with the political orders of the world. Local (community, tribe, household, etc.) gods and magic were not a problem The problem arose when these barriers of locality, tribe and polity were shattered by universalistic religions. And the problem arose in full strength only when this god was a god of 'love.' The problem of tension with the political order emerged for redemption religions out of the basic demand for brotherliness. In politics as in economics, the more rational the political order became, the sharper the problems of these tensions became.

The brotherliness of a group of men bound together in war appears valueless in brotherly religions; it is seen as a mere reflection of the technically sophisticated brutality of the struggle. It's consecration appears as the glorification of fratricide.

The only two consistent solutions (first three guesses don't count...): puritanism and mysticism. Puritanism believes God's commands should be imposed on the world by the means of the world — violence, so "just war" is not a problem for Puritanism

(God is on their side). The mystics take a "radical political attitude" of "turning the other cheek" which makes them appear "necessarily vulgar and lacking in dignity in the eyes of every self-assured worldly ethic of heroism."

Organic social ethics (where religiously substructured) stands on the soil of brotherliness, but, in contrast to mystic and acosmic love, is dominated by a cosmic, rational demand for brotherliness. It point of departure is the experience of the inequality of religious charisma. The fact that the holy should be accessible to some and not all is unbearable to organic social ethics. It therefore attempts to synthesize this inequality of charismatic qualifications with secular stratification by status, into a cosmos of God-ordained services which are specialized in function. Certain tasks are given to every individual and every group according to their social and economic position as determined by fate. Without something like the Indian doctrine of Karma (which says there's a reason why you're bottom dog), every organic social ethic unavoidably represents an accommodation to the interests of the privileged strata of the world.

From the standpoint of inner-worldly asceticism, the organic ethic lacks the drive for an ethical and thorough rationalization of individual life. In such matters, it has no premium for the rational and methodical patterning of personal life in the interest of the individual's own salvation. The organic pragmatism of salvation must consider the redemptory aristocracy of inner-worldly asceticism, with its rational depersonalization of life orders, as the hardest form of lovelessness and lack of brotherliness. It must also consider the redemptory pragmatism of mysticism as a sublimated and unbrotherly indulgence of the mystic' s own charisma. Both inner-worldly asceticism and mysticism ultimately condemn the social world to absolute meaninglessness (or, at least they hold that God's aims concerning the world are utterly incomprehensible).

The rationalism of religious and organic doctrines of society cannot stand up under this idea; for it seeks to comprehend the world as an at least relatively rational cosmos in spite of all its wickedness: the world must hear at least traces of the divine plan of salvation. The organic ethic of society is an eminently conservative power hostile to revolution. Virtuoso religion is a potentially revolutionary force. Its revolutionary turn may assume two forms:

1) (from inner-worldly asceticism, with an absolute divine law) it becomes a religious duty to realize this divine natural law. This corresponds to an obligation to crusade.
2) (from mysticism) The commands of the world do not hold for the man who is assured in his obsession with god.

The Aesthetic Sphere

The development of intellectualism and the rationalism of life make art become a cosmos of more and more consciously grasped independent values which exist in their own right. Art comes to provide a salvation from the routines of everyday life, and begins to compete directly with salvation religion. [The refusal of modern man to assume responsibility for moral judgements tends to transform judgements of moral intent into judgements of taste.]

The Erotic Sphere

The brotherly ethic of salvation religion is in profound tension with the greatest irrational force of life: sexual love. The more sublimated sexuality is, and the more principled and relentlessly consistent the salvation ethic of brotherhood is, the sharper is the tension between sex and religion. A principled ethic of religious brotherhood perceives that inner, earthly salvation by mature love competes in the sharpest possible way with devotion to a supra-mundane God. Inner-worldly and rational asceticism (vocational asceticism) can accept only the rationally regulated marriage.

The Intellectual Sphere

The tension between religion and intellectual knowledge comes to the fore wherever rational, empirical knowledge has consistently worked through to the disenchantment of the world. Every increase of rationalism in empirical science increasing pushes religion from the rational into the irrational realm; but only today does religion become the irrational or anti-rational supra-human power.

The less magic or merely contemplative mysticism and the more pure doctrine a religion contains, the greater is its need of rational apologetics. The more religion became book-religion and doctrine, the more literary it became and the more efficacious it became in provoking rational lay-thinking, freed of priestly control. However, there is no "unbroken" religion working as a vital force which is not compelled at some point to demand the credo non quod, sed quia absurdum (some saint said this, but i can't remember which one, it means "i believe it because it is absurd". i think it was said in reference to the trinity), the sacrifice of the intellect.

Redemptory religion defends itself against the attack of the self-sufficient intellect, by raising the claim that religious knowledge moves in a different sphere.

The need for salvation, consciously cultivated as the substance of religiosity, has resulted from the endeavour of a systematic and practical rationalization of life's realities. All religions have demanded as a specific presupposition that the course of the world be somehow meaningful, at least in so far as it touches upon the interests of men (this claim arises first as the problem of unjust suffering and just compensation for the unequal distribution of individual happiness in the world). From here, the claim has tended to progress toward an ever increasing devaluation of the world. For, the more intensely rational thought has seized upon the problem of a just and retributive compensation, the less an entirely inner-worldly solution could seem possible, and the less an other-worldly solution could appear probable or even meaningful.

The intellect, like all culture values, has created an aristocracy based on the possession of rational culture and independent of all personal ethical qualities of man. The aristocracy of intellect is hence an unbrotherly aristocracy. Worldly man has regarded the possession of culture as the highest good. In addition to the burden of ethical guilt, however, something has adhered to this cultural value which was bound to depreciate it with still greater finality, namely, senselessness (if the cultural value is to be judged in terms of its own standards).

The pure inner-worldly perfection of self by a man of "culture", the ultimate value to which "culture" has seemed to be reducible is meaningless for religious thought. This meaninglessness follows for religious thought from the obvious meaninglessness of death when viewed from the inner-worldly standpoint. The cultivated man can die weary of life, but never satiated with it; for, the perfectibility of the man of culture, in principle, progresses indefinitely, as do the cultural values.

Culture appears as man's emancipation from the organically prescribed cycle of natural life. For this reason, culture's every step forward seems condemned to lead to an every more devastating senselessness. The advancement of cultural values seems to become a senseless hustle in the service of worthless, moreover self-contradictory, and mutually antagonistic ends. The advancement of cultural values appears the more meaningless the more it is made a holy task, a "calling."

The need for salvation responds to this devaluation by becoming more other-worldly, more alienated from all structured forms of life, and by confining itself to the strict religious essence. The reaction is the stronger the more systematic the thinking about the "meaning" of the universe becomes, the more the external organization of the world is rationalized, the more the conscious experience of the world's irrational content is sublimated.

These specific intellectual and mystical attempts at salvation in the face of these tensions succumb in the end to the world dominion of unbrotherliness. One the one hand, their charisma is not accessible to everyone. Hence, in intent, mystical salvation means aristocracy; it is an aristocratic religiosity of redemption. And, in the midst of a culture that is rationally organized for a vocational workaday life, there is hardly any room for the cultivation of acosmic brotherliness, unless it is among the strata of the economically carefree. Under the technical and social conditions of rational culture, an imitation of the life of Buddha, Jesus or Francis seems condemned to failure for purely external reasons.

MAX WEBER: GENERAL ECONOMIC HISTORY

The industrial provision for the needs of a human group is carried out by the method of enterprise. A rational capitalistic enterprise is one with capital accounting, according to the methods of modern bookkeeping and the striking of a balance. In a given economy, parts may be capitalistically organized, and other parts not so. An epoch is capitalistic if the provision of its wants is organized capitalistically to such a degree that the whole economic system would collapse if we take away the capitalistic form of organization.

General presuppositions for the existence of modern day capitalism (thinking along the ideal type line):

1) Rational capital accounting. This involves the appropriation of all physical means of production as the property of autonomous private enterprises.
2) Freedom of the market, in the sense of the absence of irrational limits on trading in the market.
3) Rational technology, to permit the required calculability. This implies mechanization.
4) Calculable law, the dependability of calculable adjudication and administration.
5) Free (not slave or serf) labour, people legally in the position to, and economically compelled to, sell their labour on the market without restriction.
6) Commercialization of economic life: general use of commercial instruments to represent share rights in enterprise and also in property ownership.

The Development of Industrial Technique

Real distinguishing characteristic of the modern factory: the concentration of ownership of workplace, means of work, source of power and raw material in the hands of the entrepreneur.

Key: Shift from nature's power (water) to more manageable, reliable, calculable forces (like steam). This, along with mechanization, permits rationalization of work.

Development of use of coal, and subsequent production of iron had 3 important consequences:

1) released technology and productive capabilities from the limits inherent in the qualities of organic industry (eg, horses get tired, the wind doesn't always blow, etc.)
2) mechanization of the production process thorough the steam engine liberated production from the organic limitations of human labour (it ain't just horses that get tired; and people can't lift as much, work as fast, as reliably, etc.)
3) through union with science, the production of goods was emancipated from the bonds of tradition and came under the dominance of freely roving intelligence.

Recruitment of the labour force for this new form of production was carried by means of indirect compulsion. The enclosure movement and changes in agricultural production left a bunch of people wandering around without jobs, who were forced into jobs by being threatened with the "workhouse" if they didn't take jobs in the new factories. From the beginning of the 18th c., there began to be laws to regulate employers conduct toward their employees, to ensure labourers were paid in money and not in kind.

War needs and luxury consumption fed capitalism's growth. However, all those silly folks who've argued that war was the driving force are wrong. While the desire of nobility and the upperclasses for luxury goods was important, the increasing production of tapestries and carpets was a key marker of the democratization of luxury, which is the crucial direction of capitalistic production. The decisive impetus for c'ism could only come from mass market demand.

Citizenship

Outside the occident there have not been cities in the sense of a unitary community. Occidental cities originally arose through the establishment of a fraternity; it was in its beginnings first above all a defense group, an organization of those economically competent to bear arms, to equip and train themselves. These folks owned their own arms: this is key.

In places like Egypt, Asia, India and China, irrigation was a big issue, and so kings' bureaucracies developed. The king and his staff required the compulsory service of the dependent classes; they in turn were dependent on that bureaucracy. The king also held a military monopoly. In the west, self-equipment and religious brotherhoods (eg, crusaders) meant kings did not have a military monopoly, and so cities could be formed in a western sense, based on mutual defense.

Also, ideas and institutions in the orient connected with magic, which supported such systems as caste systems, did not exist in such strength in the occident.

The Rational State

Modern capism can survive only in the modern rational state.

Characteristics of the Modern Rational State:

1) Expert officialdom and rational law. Key: rationalization of procedure... formal juristic thinking inherited from Roman law.
2) Economic policy that is continuous and consistent and not dependent on ritualistic/traditional considerations. The first appearance of a rational economic policy was mercantilism: external economic policy consists in taking every advantage of the opponent, to strengthen the hand of the government in its external relations. Mercantilism signifies the development of the state as a political power, this development is to be done directly by increasing the tax paying power of the population. However, mercantilism wasn't free market: the govt supported monopolies, gave colonial privileges, etc. It disappeared when free trade was established.

The Evolution of The Capitalistic Spirit

While several factors fed into the development of capitalism, "in the last resort the factor which produced capitalism is the rational permanent enterprise, rational accounting, rational technology and rational law, but not these alone. Necessary complementary factors were the rational spirit, the rationalization of the conduct of life in general, and a rationalistic economic ethic" (260).

In the middle ages, the position of the church on economic ethics was that it excluded "higgling" (cute word; he means haggling), overpricing and free competition and included the principle of a just price and the assurance to everyone of a chance to live.

Since Judaism made Christianity possible and gave it the character of a religion essentially free from magic, it rendered a service by removing one of the most serious obstructions to the rationalization of economic life (magic). Prophesies (rather than oracles by lot, etc.) have released the world from magic and in so doing have created the basis for our modern science and technology, and for capitalism.

Basically, then, Weber chats re: the spirit of capitalism, which you know all about from somewhere else. As noted earlier, the breakdown of the dual economic ethics was key.

A note on class conflict: "It was possible for the working class to accept its lot as long as the promise of eternal happiness could be held out to it. When this consolation fell away it was inevitable that those strains and stresses would appear in economic society which since then have been growing rapidly. This point had been reached at the end of the early period of capitalism, at the beginning of the age of iron, in the 19th century".

The Types of Authority and Imperative Control/The Types of Legitimate Domination (depends on your translation)

Basis of Legitimacy

Domination is defined as the probability that certain specific commands (or all commands) will be obeyed by a given group of people. A certain minimum of voluntary submission is necessary; thus on the part of the submitter there is an interest (whether based on ulterior motives or genuine acceptance) in obedience.

- Not every claim protected by custom or law involves a relation of authority. For instance, if I ask Charles to pay me for the work i do as fulfilment of our contract, I am not exercising authority over him.

- The legitimacy of a system of authority may be treated sociologically only as the probability that to a relevant degree the appropriate attitudes will exist and the corresponding conduct ensue.
- Obedience means the action of the person 'obeying' follows a course such that the content of the command can be taken as the reason for his/her action.

Pure Types of Legitimate Authority

1. Rational/legal grounds. belief in the legality of patterns of normative rules and the right of those elevated to authority under such rules to issue commands. Authority held by legally established impersonal order, extends to people only by virtue of offices they hold.
2. Traditional grounds. established belief in the sanctity of immemorial traditions and the legitimacy of the status of those exercising authority under them. Authority held by person of the chief who occupies the traditionally sanctioned position of authority; matter of personal obligation and loyalty within the scope of tradition.
3. Charismatic grounds. devotion to the specific and exceptional sanctity, heroism or exemplary character of an individual person, and of the normative pattern or order revealed by him. Leader obeyed by personal trust in him, his revelation, heroism, coolness, as far as those qualities fall within the scope of the obeyers belief in his charisma.

Rational Legal Authority with a Bureaucratic Administrative Staff

Typical person in authority occupies an office. Person who obeys authority does so only in his capacity as a member of the corporate group, and what he obeys is only the law. Fundamental Qualities:

1) continuous organization of official functions bound by rules

2) specified spheres of competence involving a) sphere of obligations as marked out by a specialized division of labour, b) provision to incumbent of necessary authority to do his sphere of thangs, c) necessary means of compulsion clearly defined and their use subject to definite conditions.
3) organization of offices follows principle of hierarchy.
4) rules which regulate conduct of an office can be either technical rules or norms. when their application is fully rational, specialized training is necessary.
5) office holder separated from ownership of means of production and administration (first of all, separation of house from workplace)
6) complete absence of appropriate of position by incumbent
7) acts, rules and decisions are formulated and recorded in writing

BUREAUCRACY, almost the same...

1) office holders personally free and subject to authority only within the scope of their impersonal official obligations
2) hierarchy of offices
3) sphere of competence
4) free selection into office; filled by free contractual relationship; always free to resign
5) candidates appointed, not elected, on basis of technical qualifications
6) remuneration is by fixed salaries of $$
7) office is sole or primary occupation of incumbent
8) constitutes a career; system of promotion
9) official can't own means or appropriate position
10) official subject to strict and systematic discipline and control in conduct of office.

Monocratic bureaucracy is capable of attaining the highest degrees of efficiency and is the most rational means known of carrying out imperative control over people. Makes possible a high degree of calculability.

Bureaucratic administration means fundamentally the exercise of control on the basis of knowledge.

General Social Consequences of bureaucratic control

1) tendency of levelling in the interest of broadest possible recruitment in terms of technical competence
2) tendency to plutocracy due to interest in greatest possible length of technical training
3) dominance of spirit of formalistic impersonality. Sine ira et studio, w/o anger or passion, and hence without affection or enthusiasm. All subject to formal equality of treatment.

Traditional Authority

Traditional authority is bound to the precedents handed down from the past and to this extent is oriented to rules.

Leaders' commands legitimated in one of two ways:

1) in terms of traditions which themselves directly determine the content of the command and the objects and intent of authority.
2) a matter of the chief's free personal decision, in that tradition leaves him some leeway.

When resistance occurs, the accusation is that the chief is not following the tradition. The system itself is not questioned.

A chief can have an administrative staff: patrimonial recruitment of staff comes from people who have a traditional tie of personal loyalty to the chief (children, slaves, clients, etc.). Extrapatrimonial recruitment comes from people in a purely personal relation of loyalty (vassals, etc.)

The staff lacks: clearly defined spheres of competence subject to impersonal rules; rational ordering of relations of superiority and inferiority; regular system of promotion and free contract; technical training as a requirement; fixed salaries in $$.

Gerontocracy and Patrimonialism are forms of traditional authority w/o a personal administrative staff of the chief. G is rule by elders, and P is where there's rule by someone designated by inheritance. There is still a general idea of everyone being a member of the group, though there is by no means equal distribution of power. With the development of a purely personal administrative staff, we get patrimonialism. Members of the group are now treated as subjects.

A patrimonial retainer can be supported by: maintenance at his lords table, by allowances from the chief (primarily in kind), by rights of land use in return for services, by appropriation of property income, fees, or taxes, by fifes.

Charismatic Authority

The basis for obedience lies in the conception that it is the duty of those who have been called to a charismatic mission to recognize its quality and to act accordingly... it's a matter of personal devotion to the possessor of the quality.

There is no legal wisdom oriented to judicial precedent. Charismatic authority is specifically irrational in the sense of being foreign to all rules. It repudiates the past, and is in this sense a revolutionary force.

It is hostile to everyday economic considerations. It can only tolerate irregular, unsystematic, acquisitive acts.

In traditional periods, it is the greatest revolutionary force. Reason is equally revolutionary, and works from without by altering the situations of action, or it intellectualizes the individual. Charisma may involve a subjective or internal reorientation which may result in a radical alteration of the central system of attitudes, a completely new orientation towards different problems and structures of the world.

The Routinization of Charisma

In pure form, charismatic authority exists only in the process of originating. It becomes either rationalize or traditionalized, or a combo of both for the following reasons:

1) ideal and material interests of the followers in the continual reactivation of the community

2) interests of the administrative staff, disciples or followers of the char'ic leader in continuing their positions, so that their own status is stable on a day to day basis.

As soon as the position of authority is well established, and above all as soon as control over large masses of people exists, it gives way to the forces of everyday routine. There is an objective necessity of patterns of order and organization of the administrative staff in order to meet the normal, everyday needs and conditions of carrying on administration. In addition, there is a striving for security, requiring legitimation of positions of authority and social prestige and economic advantages held by the followers.

The process of routinization is thus not confined to the problem of succession, and does not stop when it is solved. The most fundamental problem is the transition from the charismatic administrative staff and its mode of administration to one that can handle everyday conditions.

Possible Types of Solution

1) search for new charismatic leader on basis of criteria that will fit him for position of authority
2) revelation thorough oracles, lots, etc... legitimacy is then dependent on technique of selection, which means a form of legalization
3) by designation by leader of his successor
4) designation of successor by charismatically qualified staff, and successors recognition by the community... legitimacy can come to depend on technique of selection, again legalization
5) hereditary charisma... this may lead to either traditionalization or legalization (divine right, etc.)
6) charisma transmitted by ritual means from one bearer to another, or created in a new person... this may become charisma of office (eg, the Big Potato, the Pope himself).

Routinization also takes the form of the appropriation of powers of control and economic advantages by the disciples. Again, it can be either traditional or legal, depending on whether or not legislation of some sort is involved. This is how we get differences between, say, the clergy and the laity.

MAX WEBER: POLITICS AS A VOCATION

Politics is a strong and slow boring of hard boards. First, a general chat on states. Politics is any kind of leadership in action (Class, Status, Party: remember, social clubs and grad school cohorts can have parties, just as states can). For this lecture, we will understand politics as the leadership or influencing the leadership of a political association, today (1918) a state.

The decisive means of politics is violence. A state is defined by the specific means peculiar to it, the use of physical force. The state is a human community that successfully claims the monopoly of the legitimate use of physical force within a given territory. Politics, then, means striving to share power or striving to influence the distribution of power, either among states or among groups within a state. The state is a relation of men dominating men by means of legitimate violence (you already know the three ways it can get legitimated, so I'm not telling you). Leaders may arise on those three foundations as well.

How do the politically dominant powers maintain that dominance? Organized domination calls for continuous administration, requires that human conduct be conditioned to obedience to the power-bearers. It requires control over the material goods necessary for the use of physical violence. Thus, it requires control of the personal executive staff and the material implements of administration. All states may be classified by whether the staff of men themselves owns the administrative means, or whether they are separated from it (necesse. for bureaucracy).

Now to chatting about politics as a vocation. There are two ways to make politics your vocation: you can live for it or off it. It you live for it, you make it your life in an internal sense, either because you enjoy power or because you serve some cause. If you live off it, you strive to make it your permanent source of income (cf Dan Rostenkowski). All party struggles are struggles for the patronage of office, as well as struggles for objective goals. Setbacks in participating in offices are felt more severely by parties than is action against their objective goals. The development of politics into an organization which demanded training in the struggle for power, and int eh methods of this struggle as developed by modern party policies, determined the separation of public functionaries into two categories: administrative officials and political officials. Political officials can be transferred any time at will, and can be dismissed or at least temporarily withdrawn. Cabinet ministers often are much less in control of their areas than divisional heads, who are long-term, administrative appointees; a minister is simply the representative of a given political power constellation.

The genuine official, even a political official, conducts his business sine ira et studio (at least formally, as long as the vital interests of the ruling order are not in question). To be passionate, on the other hand, is the element of the politician and above all of the political leader. "Since the time of the constitutional state, and definitely since democracy has been established, the demagogue has been the typical political leader". The current state of affairs is a "dictatorship resting on the exploitation of mass emotionality". Next to the qualities of will, the force of demagogic speech has been above all decisive in the choice of strong leaders.

"What kind of man must one be if he is to be allowed to put his hand on the wheel of history?". He must have passion, a feeling of responsibility, and a sense of proportion. Passion in the sense of matter-of-factness, of passionate devotion to a cause, to the god or demon who is its overlord. Responsibility to the cause must be the guiding star of action. For this, a sense of proportion is needed Warm passion and a cool sense of proportion must be forged together in one and the same soul.

The politician must combat vanity, in order to be matter-of-factly devoted to his cause and preserve some distance, not least from himself. Lack of objectivity and irresponsibility are the two deadly sins of politics; vanity, the need to personally stand in the foreground, temps the politician to commit these sins. The final result of political action regularly stands in completely inadequate and often paradoxical relation to its original meaning (oh, cheery old Weber). Because of this fact, the serving of a cause must not be absent if action is to have inner strength. Exactly which cause looks like a matter of belief. Some kind of faith must exist in a politician, "otherwise it is absolutely true that the curse of the creature's worthlessness overshadows even the externally strongest political successes".

Then is a discussion of two ethics, the ethic of ultimate ends and the ethic of responsibility. They are fundamentally different and irreconcilably opposed. The ethic of ultimate ends, formulated in religious terms, is: "The Christian does rightly and leaves the results with the Lord." If an action of good intention leads to bad results, then, in the actor's eyes, not he, but the world, or the stupidity of other men, or God's will who made them thus, is responsible for the evil. The ethic of responsibility, on the other hand, requires one to give an account of the foreseeable results of one's action. The man who believes in an ethic of responsibility takes into account precisely the average deficiencies of people. He does not feel in a position to burden others with the results of his own actions so far as he was able to foresee them; he will say, these results are ascribed to my action. On the other hand, the ultimate ends dude feels a "responsibility" only to keep his intentions good.

In many cases, the attainment of good ends is bound up with the price of using morally dubious or dangerous means, and must face the possibility of evil ramifications. From no ethics in the world can it be concluded when and to what extent a good ends justifies ethically dangerous means and ramifications. The ethics of absolutism goes to pieces on the problem of justification of means by ends. Everything that is striven for through political action operating with violent means and following an ethic of responsibility endangers the salvation of the soul. If, however, on chases after the ultimate good in a war of beliefs, following a pure ethic of absolute ends, then the goals may be damaged and discredited for generations because responsibility for consequences is lacking. A man following an ethic of responsibility will arise at a place where he must say, Here I stand; I can do no other. Here, the ethic of ultimate ends and the ethic of responsibility are supplements, which only in unison constitute a genuine man, a man who can have the calling for politics.

DEFINITION OF SOCIOLOGY

Sociology (in the sense in which this highly ambiguous word is used here) is a science which attempts the interpretive understanding of social action in order thereby to arrive at a causal explanation of its course and effects. In "action" is included all human behaviour when and insofar as the acting individual attaches a subjective meaning to it. Action in this sense may be either overt or purely inward or subjective; it may consist of positive intervention in a situation, or of deliberately refraining from such intervention or passively acquiescing in the situation. Action is social insofar as, by virtue of the subjective meaning attached to it by the acting individual (or individuals), it takes account of the behaviour of others and is thereby oriented in its course.

The Methodological Foundations of Sociology

"Meaning" may be of two kinds. The term may refer first to the actual existing meaning in the given concrete case of a particular actor, or to the average or approximate meaning attributable to a given plurality of actors; or secondly to the theoretically conceived pure type of subjective meaning attributed to the hypothetical actor or actors in a given type of action. In no case does it refer to an objectively "correct" meaning or one which is "true" in some metaphysical sense. It is this which distinguishes the empirical sciences of action, such as sociology and history, from the dogmatic disciplines in that area, such as jurisprudence, logic, ethics, and aesthetics, which seek to ascertain the "true" and "valid" meanings associated with the objects of their investigation.

The line between meaningful action and merely reactive behaviour to which no subjective meaning is attached, cannot be sharply drawn empirically. A very considerable part of all sociologically relevant behaviour, especially purely traditional behaviour, is marginal between the two. In the case of many psychophysical processes, meaningful (i.e., subjectively understandable) action is not to be found at all; in others it is discernible only by the expert psychologist. Many mystical experiences which cannot be adequately communicated in words are, for a person who is not susceptible to such experiences, not fully understandable. At the same time the ability to imagine one's self performing a similar action is not a necessary prerequisite to understanding; "one need not have been Caesar in order to understand Caesar." For the verifiable accuracy of interpretation of the meaning of a phenomenon, it is a great help to be able to put one's self imaginatively in the place of the actor and thus sympathetically to participate in his experiences, but this is not an essential condition of meaningful interpretation. Understandable and non-understandable components of a process are often intermingled and bound up together.

All interpretation of meaning, like all scientific observation, strives for clarity and verifiable accuracy of insight and comprehension. The basis for certainty in understanding can be either rational, which can be further subdivided into logical and mathematical, or it can be of an emotionally empathic or artistically appreciative quality. In the sphere of action things are rationally evident chiefly when we attain a completely clear intellectual grasp of the action-elements in their intended context of meaning. Empathic or appreciative accuracy is attained when, through sympathetic participation, we can adequately grasp the emotional context in which the action took place. The highest degree of rational understanding is attained in cases involving the meanings of logically or mathematically related propositions; their meaning may be immediately and unambiguously intelligible. We have a perfectly clear understanding of what it means when somebody employs the proposition $2 \times 2 = 4$ or the Pythagorean theorem in reasoning or argument, or when someone correctly carries out a logical train of reasoning according to our accepted modes of thinking. In the same way we also understand what a person is doing when he tries to achieve certain ends by choosing appropriate means on the basis of the facts of the situation as experience has accustomed us to interpret them. Such an interpretation of this type of rationally purposeful action possesses, for the understanding of the choice of means, the highest degree of verifiable certainty. With a lower degree of certainty, which is, however, adequate for most purposes of explanation, we are able to understand errors, including confusion of problems of the sort that we ourselves are liable to, or the origin of which we can detect by sympathetic self-analysis.

On the other hand, many ultimate ends or values toward which experience shows that human action may be oriented, often cannot be understood completely, though sometimes we are able to grasp them intellectually. The more radically they differ from our own ultimate values, however, the more difficult it is for us to make them understandable by imaginatively participating in them. Depending upon the circumstances of the particular case we must be content either with a purely intellectual understanding of such values or when even that fails, sometimes we must simply accept them as given data. Then we can try to understand the action motivated by them on the basis of whatever opportunities for approximate emotional and intellectual interpretation seem to be available at different points in its course. These difficulties apply, for instance, for people not susceptible to the relevant values, to many unusual acts of religious and charitable zeal; also certain kinds of extreme rationalistic fanaticism of the type involved in some forms of the ideology of the "rights of man" are in a similar position for people who radically repudiate such points of view.

The more we ourselves are susceptible to them the more readily can we imaginatively participate in such emotional reactions as anxiety, anger, ambition, envy, jealousy, love, enthusiasm, pride, vengefulness, loyalty, devotion, and appetites of all sorts, and thereby understand the irrational conduct which grows out of them. Such conduct is "irrational," that is, from the point of view of the rational pursuit of a given end. Even when such emotions are found in a degree of intensity of which the observer himself is completely incapable, he can still have a significant degree of emotional understanding of their meaning and can interpret intellectually their influence on the course of action and the selection of means.

For the purposes of a typological scientific analysis it is convenient to treat all irrational, affectually determined elements of behaviour as factors of deviation from a conceptually pure type of rational action. For example, a panic on the stock exchange can be most conveniently analysed by attempting to determine first what the course of action would have been if it had not been influenced by irrational affects; it is then possible to introduce the irrational components as accounting for the observed deviations from this hypothetical course. Similarly, in analysing a political or military campaign it is convenient to determine in the first place what would have been a rational course, given the ends of the participants and adequate knowledge of all the circumstances. Only in this way is it possible to assess the causal significance of irrational factors as accounting for the deviations from this type. The construction of a purely rational course of action in such cases serves the sociologist as a type ("ideal type") which has the merit of clear understandability and lack of ambiguity. By comparison with this it is possible to understand the ways in which actual action is influenced by irrational factors of all sorts, such as affects and errors, in that they account for the deviation from the line of conduct which would be expected on the hypothesis that the action were purely rational.

Only in this respect and for these reasons of methodological convenience, is the method of sociology "rationalistic." It is naturally not legitimate to interpret this procedure as involving a "rationalistic bias" of sociology, but only as a methodological device. It certainly does not involve a belief in the actual predominance of rational elements in human life, for on the question of how far this predominance does or does not exist, nothing whatever has been said. That there is, however, a danger of rationalistic interpretations where they are out of place naturally cannot be denied. All experience unfortunately confirms the existence of this danger.

In all the sciences of human action, account must be taken of processes and phenomena which are devoid of subjective meaning, in the role of stimuli, results, favouring or hindering circumstances. To be devoid of meaning is not identical with being lifeless or non-human; every artefact, such as for example a machine, can be understood only in terms of the meaning which its production and use have had or will have for human action; a meaning which may derive from a relation to exceedingly various purposes. Without reference to this meaning such an object remains wholly unintelligible. That which is intelligible or understandable about it is thus its relation to human action in the role either of means or of end; a relation of which the actor or actors can be said to have been aware and to which their action has been oriented. Only in terms of such categories is it possible to "understand" objects of this kind. On the other hand, processes or conditions, whether they are animate or inanimate, human or non-human, are in the present sense devoid of meaning insofar as they cannot be related to an intended purpose. That is to say they are devoid of meaning if they cannot be related to action in the role of means or ends but constitute only the stimulus, the favouring or hindering circumstances. It may be that the incursion of the Dollart at the beginning of the twelfth century had historical significance as a stimulus to the beginning of certain migrations of considerable importance. Human mortality, indeed the organic life cycle generally from the helplessness of infancy to that of old age, is naturally of the very greatest sociological importance through the various ways in which human action has been oriented to these facts. To still another category of facts devoid of meaning belong certain psychic or psycho-physical phenomena such as fatigue, habituation, memory, etc.; also certain typical states of euphoria under some conditions of ascetic mortification; finally, typical variations in the reactions of individuals according to reaction-time, precision, and other modes. But in the last analysis the same principle applies to these as to other phenomena which are devoid of meaning. Both the actor and the sociologist must accept them as data to be taken into account.

It is altogether possible that future research may be able to discover non-understandable uniformities underlying what has appeared to be specifically meaningful action, though little has been accomplished in this direction thus far. Thus, for example, differences in hereditary biological constitution, as of "races," would have to be treated by sociology as given data in the same way as the physiological facts of the need of nutrition or the effect of senescence on action. This would be the case if, and insofar as, we had statistically conclusive proof of their influence on sociologically relevant behaviour. The recognition of the causal significance of such factors would naturally not in the least alter the specific task of sociological analysis or of that of the other sciences of action, which is the interpretation of action in terms of its subjective meaning. The effect would be only to introduce certain non-understandable data of the same order as others which, it has been noted above, are already present, into the complex of subjectively understandable motivation at certain points. Thus it may come to be known that there are typical relations between the frequency of certain types of teleological orientation of action or of the degree of certain kinds of rationality and the cephalic index or skin colour or any other biologically inherited characteristic.

Understanding may be of two kinds: the first is the direct observational understanding of the subjective meaning of a given act as such, including verbal utterances. We thus understand by direct observation, in this sense, the meaning of the proposition 2 × 2 =4 when we hear or read it. This is a case of the direct rational understanding of ideas. We also understand an outbreak of anger as manifested by facial expression, exclamations or irrational movements. This is direct observational understanding of irrational emotional reactions. We can understand in a similar observational way the action of a woodcutter or of somebody who reaches for the knob to shut a door or who aims a gun at an animal. This is rational observational understanding of actions.

Understanding may, however, be of another sort, namely explanatory understanding. Thus we understand in terms of motive the meaning an actor attaches to the proposition twice two equals four, when he states it or writes it down, in that we understand what makes him do this at precisely this moment and in these circumstances. Understanding in this sense is attained if we know that he is engaged in balancing a ledger or in making a scientific demonstration, or is engaged in some other task of which this particular act would be an appropriate part. This is rational understanding of motivation, which consists in placing the act in an intelligible and more inclusive context of meaning. Thus we understand the chopping of wood or aiming of a gun in terms of motive in addition to direct observation if we know that the wood-chopper is working for a wage, or is chopping a supply of firewood for his own use, or possibly is doing it for recreation. But he might also be "working off" a fit of rage, an irrational case. Similarly we understand the motive of a person aiming a gun if we know that he has been commanded to shoot as a member of a firing squad, that he is fighting against an enemy, or that he is doing it for revenge. The last is affectually determined and thus in a certain sense irrational. Finally we have a motivational understanding of the outburst of anger if we know that it has been provoked by jealousy, injured pride, or an insult. The last examples are all affectually determined and hence derived from irrational motives. In all the above cases the particular act has been placed in an understandable sequence of motivation, the understanding of which can be treated as an explanation of the actual course of behaviour. Thus for a science which is concerned with the subjective meaning of action, explanation requires a grasp of the complex of meaning in which an actual course of understandable action thus interpreted belongs. In all such cases, even where the processes are largely affectual, the subjective meaning of the action, including that also of the relevant meaning complexes, will be called the "intended" meaning. This involves a departure from ordinary usage, which speaks of intention in this sense only in the case of rationally purposive action.

In all these cases understanding involves the interpretive grasp of the meaning present in one of the following contexts: (a) as in the historical approach, the actually intended meaning for concrete individual action; or (b) as in cases of sociological mass phenomena the average of, or an approximation to, the actually intended meaning; or (c) the meaning appropriate to a scientifically formulated pure type (an ideal type) of a common phenomenon. The concepts and "laws" of pure economic theory are examples of this kind of ideal type. They state what course a given type of human action would take if it were strictly rational, unaffected by errors or emotional factors and if, furthermore, it were completely and unequivocally directed to a single end, the maximisation of economic advantage. In reality, action takes exactly this course only in unusual cases, as sometimes on the stock exchange; and even then there is usually only an approximation to the ideal type. Every interpretation attempts to attain clarity and certainty, but no matter how clear an interpretation as such appears to be from the point of view of meaning, it cannot on this account alone claim to be the causally valid interpretation.

On this level it must remain only a peculiarly plausible hypothesis. In the first place the "conscious motives" may well, even to the actor himself, conceal the various "motives" and "repressions" which constitute the real driving force of his action. Thus in such cases even subjectively honest self-analysis has only a relative value. Then it is the task of the sociologist to be aware of this motivational situation and to describe and analyse it, even though it has not actually been concretely part of the conscious "intention" of the actor; possibly not at all, at least not fully. This is a borderline case of the interpretation of meaning. Secondly, processes of action which seem to an observer to be the same or similar may fit into exceedingly various complexes of motive in the case of the actual actor. Then even though the situations appear superficially to be very similar we must actually understand them or interpret them as very different; perhaps, in terms of meaning, directly opposed. Third, the actors in any given situation are often subject to opposing and conflicting impulses, all of which we are able to understand. In a large number of cases we know from experience it is not possible to arrive at even an approximate estimate of the relative strength of conflicting motives and very often we cannot be certain of our interpretation. Only the actual outcome of the conflict gives a solid basis of judgment.

More generally, verification of subjective interpretation by comparison with the concrete course of events is, as in the case of all hypotheses, indispensable. Unfortunately this type of verification is feasible with relative accuracy only in the few very special cases susceptible of psychological experimentation. The approach to a satisfactory degree of accuracy is exceedingly various, even in the limited number of cases of mass phenomena which can be statistically described and unambiguously interpreted. For the rest there remains only the possibility of comparing the largest possible number of historical or contemporary processes which, while otherwise similar, differ in the one decisive point of their relation to the particular motive or factor the role of which is being investigated. This is a fundamental task of comparative sociology. Often, unfortunately there is available only the dangerous and uncertain procedure of the "imaginary experiment" which consists in thinking away certain elements of a chain of motivation and working out the course of action which would then probably ensue, thus arriving at a causal judgment.

For example, the generalisation called Gresham's Law is a rationally clear interpretation of human action under certain conditions and under the assumption that it will follow a purely rational course. How far any actual course of action corresponds to this can be verified only by the available statistical evidence for the actual disappearance of undervalued monetary units from circulation. In this case our information serves to demonstrate a high degree of accuracy. The facts of experience were known before the generalisation, which was formulated afterward; but without this successful interpretation our need for causal understanding would evidently be left unsatisfied. On the other hand, without the demonstration that what can here be assumed to be a theoretically adequate interpretation also is in some degree relevant to an actual course of action, a "law," no matter how fully demonstrated theoretically, would be worthless for the understanding of action in the real world. In this case the correspondence between the theoretical interpretation of motivation and its empirical verification is entirely satisfactory and the cases are numerous enough so that verification can be considered established. But to take another example, Eduard Meyer has advanced an ingenious theory of the causal significance of the battles of Marathon, Salamis, and Platea for the development of the cultural peculiarities of Greek, and hence, more generally, Western, civilisation. This is derived from a meaningful interpretation of certain symptomatic facts having to do with the attitudes of the Greek oracles and prophets toward the Persians. It can only be directly verified by reference to the examples of the conduct of the Persians in cases where they were victorious, as in Jerusalem, Egypt, and Asia Minor, and even this verification must necessarily remain unsatisfactory in certain respects. The striking rational plausibility of the hypothesis must here necessarily be relied on as a support. In very many cases of historical interpretation which seem highly plausible, however, there is not even a possibility of the order of verification which was feasible in this case. Where this is true the interpretation must necessarily remain a hypothesis.

A motive is a complex of subjective meaning which seems to the actor himself or to the observer an adequate ground for the conduct in question. We apply the term "adequacy on the level of meaning" to the subjective interpretation of a coherent course of conduct when and insofar as, according to our habitual modes of thought and feeling, its component parts taken in their mutual relation are recognised to constitute a "typical" complex of meaning. It is more common to say "correct." The interpretation of a sequence of events will on the other hand be called causally adequate insofar as, according to established generalisations from experience, there is a probability that it will always actually occur in the same way. An example of adequacy on the level of meaning in this sense is what is, according to our current norms of calculation or thinking, the correct solution of an arithmetical problem. On the other hand, a causally adequate interpretation of the same phenomenon would concern the statistical probability that, according to verified generalisations from experience, there would be a correct or an erroneous solution of the same problem. This also refers to currently accepted norms but includes taking account of typical errors or of typical confusions. Thus causal explanation depends on being able to determine that there is a probability, which in the rare ideal case can be numerically stated, but is always in some sense calculable, that a given observable event (overt or subjective) will be followed or accompanied by another event.

A correct causal interpretation of a concrete course of action is arrived at when the overt action and the motives have both been correctly apprehended and at the same time their relation has become meaningfully comprehensible. A correct causal interpretation of typical action means that the process which is claimed to be typical is shown to be both adequately grasped on the level of meaning and at the same time the interpretation is to some degree causally adequate. If adequacy in respect to meaning is lacking, then no matter how high the degree of uniformity and how precisely its probability can be numerically determined, it is still an incomprehensible statistical probability, whether dealing with overt or subjective processes. On the other hand, even the most perfect adequacy on the level of meaning has causal significance from a sociological point of view only insofar as there is some kind of proof for the existence of a probability that action in fact normally takes the course which has been held to be meaningful. For this there must be some degree of determinable frequency of approximation to an average or a pure type.

Statistical uniformities constitute understandable types of action in the sense of this discussion, and thus constitute "sociological generalisations," only when they can be regarded as manifestations of the understandable subjective meaning of a course of social action. Conversely, formulations of a rational course of subjectively understandable action constitute sociological types of empirical process only when they can be empirically observed with a significant degree of approximation. It is unfortunately by no means the case that the actual likelihood of the occurrence of a given course of overt action is always directly proportional to the clarity of subjective interpretation. There are statistics of processes devoid of meaning such as death rates, phenomena of fatigue, the production rate of machines, the amount of rainfall, in exactly the same sense as there are statistics of meaningful phenomena. But only when the phenomena are meaningful is it convenient to speak of sociological statistics. Examples are such cases as crime rates, occupational distributions, price statistics, and statistics of crop acreage. Naturally there are many cases where both components are involved, as in crop statistics.

Processes and uniformities which it has here seemed convenient not to designate as (in the present case) sociological phenomena or uniformities because they are not "understandable," are naturally not on that account any the less important. This is true even for sociology in the present sense which restricts it to subjectively understandable phenomena – a usage which there is no intention of attempting to impose on anyone else. Such phenomena, however important, are simply treated by a different method from the others; they become conditions, stimuli, furthering or hindering circumstances of action.

Action in the sense of a subjectively understandable orientation of behaviour exists only as the behaviour of one or more individual human beings. For other cognitive purposes it may be convenient or necessary to consider the individual, for instance, as a collection of cells, as a complex of biochemical reactions, or to conceive his "psychic" life as made up of a variety of different elements, however these may be defined. Undoubtedly such procedures yield valuable knowledge of causal relationships. But the behaviour of these elements, as expressed in such uniformities, is not subjectively understandable. This is true even of psychic elements because the more precisely they are formulated from a point of view of natural science, the less they are accessible to subjective understanding. This is never the road to interpretation in terms of subjective meaning. On the contrary, both for sociology in the present sense, and for history, the object of cognition is the subjective meaning-complex of action. The behaviour of physiological entities such as cells, or of any sort of psychic elements may at least in principle be observed and an attempt made to derive uniformities from such observations. It is further possible to attempt, with their help, to obtain a causal explanation of individual phenomena; that is, to subsume them under uniformities. But the subjective understanding of action takes the same account of this type of fact and uniformity as of any others not capable of subjective interpretation. This is true, for example, of physical, astronomical, geological, meteorological, geographical, botanical, zoological, and anatomical facts and of such facts as those aspects of psychopathology which are devoid of subjective meaning or the facts of the natural conditions of technological processes.

For still other cognitive purposes as, for instance, juristic, or for practical ends, it may on the other hand be convenient or even indispensable to treat social collectivities, such as states, associations, business corporations, foundations, as if they were individual persons. Thus they may be treated as the subjects of rights and duties or as the performers of legally significant actions. But for the subjective interpretation of action in sociological work these collectivities must be treated as solely the resultants and modes of organisation of the particular acts of individual persons, since these alone can be treated as agents in a course of subjectively understandable action. Nevertheless, the sociologist cannot for his purposes afford to ignore these collective concepts derived from other disciplines. For the subjective interpretation of action has at least two important relations to these concepts. In the first place it is often necessary to employ very similar collective concepts, indeed often using the same terms, in order to obtain an understandable terminology. Thus both in legal terminology and in everyday speech the term "state" is used both for the legal concept of the state and for the phenomena of social action to which its legal rules are relevant. For sociological purposes, however, the phenomenon "the state" does not consist necessarily or even primarily of the elements which are relevant to legal analysis; and for sociological purposes there is no such thing as a collective personality which "acts." When reference is made in a sociological context to a "state," a "nation," a "corporation," a "family," or an "army corps," or to similar collectivities, what is meant is, on the contrary, only a certain kind of development of actual or possible social actions of individual persons. Both because of its precision and because it is established in general usage the juristic concept is taken over, but is used in an entirely different meaning.

Secondly, the subjective interpretation of action must take account of a fundamentally important fact. These concepts of collective entities which are found both in common sense and in juristic and other technical forms of thought, have a meaning in the minds of individual persons, partly as of something actually existing, partly as something with normative authority. This is true not only of judges and officials, but of ordinary private individuals as well. Actors thus in part orient their action to them, and in this role such ideas have a powerful, often a decisive, causal influence on the course of action of real individuals. This is above all true where the ideas concern a recognised positive or negative normative pattern. Thus, for instance, one of the important aspects of the "existence" of a modern state, precisely as a complex of social interaction of individual persons, consists in the fact that the action of various individuals is oriented to the belief that it exists or should exist, thus that its acts and laws are valid in the legal sense. This will be further discussed below. Though extremely pedantic and cumbersome it would be possible, if purposes of sociological terminology alone were involved, to eliminate such terms entirely, and substitute newly-coined words. This would be possible even though the word "state" is used ordinarily not only to designate the legal concept but also the real process of action. But in the above important connection, at least, this would naturally be impossible.

Thirdly, it is the method of the so-called "organic" school of sociology to attempt to understand social interaction by using as a point of departure the "whole" within which the individual acts. His action and behaviour are then interpreted somewhat in the way that a physiologist would treat the role of an organ of the body in the "economy" of the organism, that is from the point of view of the survival of the latter. How far in other disciplines this type of functional analysis of the relation of "parts" to a "whole" can be regarded as definitive, cannot be discussed here; but it is well known that the biochemical and biophysical modes of analysis of the organism are in principle opposed to stopping there. For purposes of sociological analysis two things can be said. First, this functional frame of reference is convenient for purposes of practical illustration and for provisional orientation. In these respects it is not only useful but indispensable. But at the same time if its cognitive value is overestimated and its concepts illegitimately "reified," it can be highly dangerous. Secondly, in certain circumstances this is the only available way of determining just what processes of social action it is important to understand in order to explain a given phenomenon. But this is only the beginning of sociological analysis as here understood. In the case of social collectivities, precisely as distinguished from organisms, we are in a position to go beyond merely demonstrating functional relationships and uniformities. We can accomplish something which is never attainable in the natural sciences, namely the subjective understanding of the action of the component individuals. The natural sciences on the other hand cannot do this, being limited to the formulation of causal uniformities in objects and events, and the explanation of individual facts by applying them. We do not "understand" the behaviour of cells, but can only observe the relevant functional relationships and generalise on the basis of these observations. This additional achievement of explanation by interpretive understanding, as distinguished from external observation, is of course attained only at a price-the more hypothetical and fragmentary character of its results. Nevertheless, subjective understanding is the specific characteristic of sociological knowledge.

It would lead too far afield even to attempt to discuss how far the behaviour of animals is subjectively understandable to us and vice versa; in both cases the meaning of the term understanding and its extent of application would be highly problematical. But insofar as such understanding existed it would be theoretically possible to formulate a sociology of the relations of men to animals, both domestic and wild. Thus many animals "understand" commands, anger, love, hostility, and react to them in ways which are evidently often by no means purely instinctive and mechanical and in some sense both consciously meaningful and affected by experience. There is no *a priori* reason to suppose that our ability to share the feelings of primitive men is very much greater. Unfortunately we either do not have any reliable means of determining the subjective state of mind of an animal or what we have is at best very unsatisfactory. It is well known that the problems of animal psychology, however interesting, are very thorny ones. There are in particular various forms of social organisation among animals: "monogamous and polygamous families," herds, flocks, and finally "state," with a functional division of labour. The extent of functional differentiation found in these animal societies is by no means, however, entirely a matter of the degree of organic or morphological differentiation of the individual members of the species. Thus, the functional differentiation found among the termites, and in consequence that of the products of their social activities, is much more advanced than in the case of the bees and ants. In this field it goes without saying that a purely functional point of view is often the best that can, at least for the present, be attained, and the investigator must be content with it. Thus it is possible to study the ways in which the species provides for its survival; that is, for nutrition, defence, reproduction, and reconstruction of the social units. As the principal bearers of these functions, differentiated types of individuals can be identified: "kings," "queens," "workers," "soldiers," "drones," "propagators," "queen's substitutes," and so on. Anything more than that was for a long time merely a matter of speculation or of an attempt to determine the extent to which heredity on the one hand and environment on the other would be involved in the development of these "social" proclivities. This was particularly true of the controversies between Gotte and Weisman. The latter's conception of the omnipotence of natural selection was largely based on wholly non-empirical deductions. But all serious authorities are naturally fully agreed that the limitation of analysis to the functional level is only a necessity imposed by our present ignorance which it is hoped will only be temporary.

It is relatively easy to grasp the significance of the functions of these various differentiated types for survival. It is also not difficult to work out the bearing of the hypothesis of the inheritance of acquired characteristics or its reverse on the problem of explaining how these differentiations have come about, and further, what is the bearing of different variants of the theory of heredity. But this is not enough. We would like especially to know first what factors account for the original differentiation of specialised types from the still neutral undifferentiated species-type. Secondly, it would be important to know what leads the differentiated individual in the typical case to behave in a way which actually serves the survival value of the organised group. Wherever research has made any progress in the solution of these problems it has been through the experimental demonstration of the probability or possibility of the role of chemical stimuli or physiological processes, such as nutritional states, the effects of parasitic castration, etc., in the case of the individual organism. How far there is even a hope that the existence of "subjective" or "meaningful" orientation could be made experimentally probable, even the specialist today would hardly be in a position to say. A verifiable conception of the state of mind of these social animals, accessible to meaningful understanding, would seem to be attainable even as an ideal goal only within narrow limits. However that may be, a contribution to the understanding of human social action is hardly to be expected from this quarter. On the contrary, in the field of animal psychology, human analogies are and must be continually employed. The most that can be hoped for is, then, that these biological analogies may some day be useful in suggesting significant problems. For instance they may throw light on the question of the relative role in the early stages of human social differentiation of mechanical and instinctive factors, as compared with that of the factors which are accessible to subjective interpretation generally, and more particularly to the role of consciously rational action. It is necessary for the sociologist to be thoroughly aware of the fact that in the early stages even of human development, the first set of factors is completely predominant. Even in the later stages he must take account of their continual interaction with the others in a role which is often of decisive importance. This is particularly true of all "traditional" action and of many aspects of charisma. In the latter field of phenomena lie the seeds of certain types of psychic "contagion" and it is thus the bearer of many dynamic tendencies of social processes. These types of action are very closely related to phenomena which are understandable either only in biological terms or are subject to interpretation in terms of subjective motives only in fragments and with an almost imperceptible transition to the biological. But all these facts do not discharge sociology from the obligation, in full awareness of the narrow limits to which it is confined, to accomplish what it alone can do.

The various works of Othmar Spann are often full of suggestive ideas, though at the same time he is guilty of occasional misunderstandings, and above all, of arguing on the basis of pure value judgments which have no place in an empirical investigation. But he is undoubtedly correct in doing something to which, however, no one seriously objects, namely, emphasising the sociological significance of the functional point of view for preliminary orientation to problems. This is what he calls the "universalistic method." We certainly need to know what kind of action is functionally necessary for "survival," but further and above all for the maintenance of a cultural type and the continuity of the corresponding modes of social action, before it is possible even to inquire how this action has come about and what motives determine it. It is necessary to know what a "king," an "official," an "entrepreneur," a "procurer," or a "magician" does; that is, what kind of typical action, which justifies classifying an individual in one of these categories, is important and relevant for an analysis, before it is possible to undertake the analysis itself. But it is only this analysis itself which can achieve the sociological understanding of the actions of typically differentiated human (and only human) individuals, and which hence constitutes the specific function of sociology. It is a monstrous misunderstanding to think that an "individualistic" method should involve what is in any conceivable sense an individualistic system of values. It is as important to avoid this error as the related one which confuses the unavoidable tendency of sociological concepts to assume a rationalistic character with a belief in the predominance of rational motives, or even a positive valuation of "rationalism." Even a socialistic economy would have to be understood sociologically in exactly the same kind of "individualistic" terms; that is, in terms of the action of individuals, the types of "officials" found in it, as would be the case with a system of free exchange analysed in terms of the theory of marginal utility. It might be possible to find a better method, but in this respect it would be similar. The real empirical sociological investigation begins with the question: What motives determine and lead the individual members and participants in this socialistic community to behave in such a way that the community came into being in the first place, and that it continues to exist? Any form of functional analysis which proceeds from the whole to the parts can accomplish only a preliminary preparation for this investigation – a preparation, the utility and indispensability of which, if properly carried out, is naturally beyond question.

It is customary to designate various sociological generalisations, as for example "Gresham's Law," as scientific "laws." These are in fact typical probabilities confirmed by observation to the effect that under certain given conditions an expected course of social action will occur, which is understandable in terms of the typical motives and typical subjective intentions of the actors. These generalisations are both understandable and define in the highest degree insofar as the typically observed course of action can be understood in terms of the purely rational pursuit of an end, or where for reasons of methodological convenience such a theoretical type can be heuristically employed.

In such cases the relations of means and end will be clearly understandable on grounds of experience, particularly where the choice of means was "inevitable." In such cases it is legitimate to assert that insofar as the action was rigorously rational it could not have taken any other course because for technical reasons, given their clearly defined ends, no other means were available to the actors. This very case demonstrates how erroneous it is to regard any kind of "psychology" as the ultimate foundation of the sociological interpretation of action. The term "psychology," to be sure, is today understood in a wide variety of senses. For certain quite specific methodological purposes the type of treatment which attempts to follow the procedures of the natural sciences employs a distinction between "physical" and "psychic" phenomena which is entirely foreign to the disciplines concerned with human action, at least in the present sense.

The results of a type of psychological investigation which employs the methods of the natural sciences in any one of various possible ways may naturally, like the results of any other science, have, in specific contexts, outstanding significance for sociological problems; indeed this has often happened. But this use of the results of psychology is something quite different from the investigation of human behaviour in terms of its subjective meaning. Hence sociology has no closer logical relationship on a general analytical level to this type of psychology than to any other science. The source of error lies in the concept of the "psychic." It is held that everything which is not physical is *ipso facto* psychic, but that the meaning of a train of mathematical reasoning which a person carries out is not in the relevant sense "psychic." Similarly the rational deliberation of an actor as to whether the results of a given proposed course of action will or will not promote certain specific interests, and the corresponding decision, do not become one bit more understandable by taking "psychological" considerations into account. But it is precisely on the basis of such rational assumptions that most of the laws of sociology, including those of economics, are built up. On the other hand, in explaining the irrationalities of action sociologically, that form of psychology which employs the method of subjective understanding undoubtedly can make decisively important contributions. But this does not alter the fundamental methodological situation.

It has continually been assumed as obvious that the science of sociology seeks to formulate type concepts and generalised uniformities of empirical process. This distinguishes it from history, which is oriented to the causal analysis and explanation of individual actions, structures, and personalities possessing cultural significance. The empirical material which underlies the concepts of sociology consists to a very large extent, though by no means exclusively, of the same concrete processes of action which are dealt with by historians. Among the various bases on which its concepts are formulated and its generalisations worked out, is an attempt to justify its important claim to be able to make a contribution to the causal explanation of some historically and culturally important phenomenon. As in the case of every generalising science, the abstract character of the concepts of sociology is responsible for the fact that, compared with actual historical reality, they are relatively lacking in fullness of concrete content. To compensate for this disadvantage, sociological analysis can offer a greater precision of concepts. This precision is obtained by striving for the highest possible degree of adequacy on the level of meaning in accordance with the definition of that concept put forward above. It has already been repeatedly stressed that this aim can be realised in a particularly high degree in the case of concepts and generalisations which formulate rational processes. But sociological investigation attempts to include in its scope various irrational phenomena, as well as prophetic, mystic, and affectual modes of action, formulated in terms of theoretical concepts which are adequate on the level of meaning. In all cases, rational or irrational, sociological analysis both abstracts from reality and at the same time helps us to understand it, in that it shows with what degree of approximation a concrete historical phenomenon can be subsumed under one or more of these concepts. For example, the same historical phenomenon may be in one aspect "feudal," in another "patrimonial," in another "bureaucratic," and in still another "charismatic." In order to give a precise meaning to these terms, it is necessary for the sociologist to formulate pure ideal types of the corresponding forms of action which in each case involve the highest possible degree of logical integration by virtue of their complete adequacy on the level of meaning. But precisely because this is true, it is probably seldom if ever that a real phenomenon can be found which corresponds exactly to one of these ideally constructed pure types. The case is similar to a physical reaction which has been calculated on the assumption of an absolute vacuum. Theoretical analysis in the field of sociology is possible only in terms of such pure types. It goes without saying that in addition it is convenient for the sociologist from time to time to employ average types of an empirical statistical character. These are concepts which do not require methodological discussion at this point. But when reference is made to "typical" cases, the term should always be understood, unless otherwise stated, as meaning ideal-types, which may in turn be rational or irrational as the case may be (thus in economic theory they are always rational), but in any case are always constructed with a view to adequacy on the level of meaning.

It is important to realise that in the sociological field as elsewhere, averages, and hence average types, can be formulated with a relative degree of precision only where they are concerned with differences of degree in respect to action which remains qualitatively the same. Such cases do occur, but in the majority of cases of action important to history or sociology the motives which determine it are qualitatively heterogeneous. Then it is quite impossible to speak of an "average" in the true sense. The ideal-types of social action which for instance are used in economic theory are thus "unrealistic" or abstract in that they always ask what course of action would take place if it were purely rational and oriented to economic ends alone. But this construction can be used to aid in the understanding of action not purely economically determined but which involves deviations arising from traditional restraints, affects, errors, and the intrusion of other than economic purposes or considerations. This can take place in two ways. First, in analysing the extent to which in the concrete case, or on the average for a class of cases, the action was in part economically determined along with the other factors. Secondly, by throwing the discrepancy between the actual course of events and the ideal-type into relief, the analysis of the non-economic motives actually involved is facilitated. The procedure would be very similar in employing an ideal-type of mystical orientation with its appropriate attitude of indifference to worldly things, as a tool for analysing its consequences for the actor's relation to ordinary life; for instance, to political or economic affairs. The more sharply and precisely the ideal-type has been constructed, thus the more abstract and unrealistic in this sense it is, the better it is able to perform its methodological functions in formulating the clarification of terminology, and in the formulation of classifications, and of hypotheses. In working out a concrete causal explanation of individual events, the procedure of the historian is essentially the same. Thus in attempting to explain the campaign of 1866, it is indispensable both in the case of Moltke and of Benedek to attempt to construct imaginatively how each, given fully adequate knowledge both of his own situation and of that of his opponent, would have acted. Then it is possible to compare with this the actual course of action and to arrive at a causal explanation of the observed deviations, which will be attributed to such factors as misinformation, strategical errors, logical fallacies, personal temperament, or considerations outside the realm of strategy. Here, too, an ideal-typical construction of rational action is actually employed even though it is not made explicit.

The theoretical concepts of sociology are ideal-types not only from the objective point of view, but also in their application to subjective processes. In the great majority of cases actual action goes on in a state of inarticulate half-consciousness or actual unconsciousness of its subjective meaning. The actor is more likely to "be aware" of it in a vague sense than he is to "know" what he is doing or be explicitly self-conscious about it. In most cases his action is governed by impulse or habit. Only occasionally and, in the uniform action of large numbers often only in the case of a few individuals, is the subjective meaning of the action, whether rational or irrational, brought clearly into consciousness. The ideal-type of meaningful action where the meaning is fully conscious and explicit is a marginal case. Every sociological or historical investigation, in applying its analysis to the empirical facts, must take this fact into account. But the difficulty need not prevent the sociologist from systematising his concepts by the classification of possible types of subjective meaning. That is, he may reason as if action actually proceeded on the basis of clearly self-conscious meaning. The resulting deviation from the concrete facts must continually be kept in mind whenever it is a question of this level of concreteness, and must be carefully studied with reference both to degree and kind. It is often necessary to choose between terms which are either clear or unclear. Those which are clear will, to be sure, have the abstractness of ideal types, but they are nonetheless preferable for scientific purposes.

"Objectivity" in Social Science

There is no absolutely "objective" scientific analysis of culture – or put perhaps more narrowly but certainly not essentially differently for our purposes – of "social phenomena" independent of special and "one-sided" viewpoints according to which – expressly or tacitly, consciously or unconsciously – they are selected, analysed and organised for expository purposes. The reasons for this lie in the character of the cognitive goal of all research in social science which seeks to transcend the purely formal treatment of the legal or conventional norms regulating social life.

The type of social science in which we are interested is an empirical science of concrete reality. Our aim is the understanding of the characteristic uniqueness of the reality in which we move. We wish to understand on the one hand the relationships and the cultural significance of individual events in their contemporary manifestations and on the other the causes of their being historically so and not otherwise. Now, as soon as we attempt to reflect about the way in which life confronts us in immediate concrete situations, it presents an infinite multiplicity of successively and coexistently emerging and disappearing events, both "within" and "outside" ourselves. The absolute infinitude of this multiplicity is seen to remain undiminished even when our attention is focused on a single "object," for instance, a concrete act of exchange, as soon as we seriously attempt an exhaustive description of all the individual components of this "individual phenomenon," to say nothing of explaining it causally.

All the analysis of infinite reality which the finite human mind can conduct rests on the tacit assumption that only a finite portion of this reality constitutes the object of scientific investigation, and that only it is "important" in the sense of being "worthy of being known." But what are the criteria by which this segment is selected? It has often been thought that the decisive criterion in the cultural sciences, too, was in the last analysis, the "regular" recurrence of certain causal relationships.

The "laws" which we are able to perceive in the infinitely manifold stream of events must – according to this conception – contain the scientifically "essential" aspect of reality. As soon as we have shown some causal relationship to be a "law," (i.e., if we have shown it to be universally valid by means of comprehensive historical induction, or have made it immediately and tangibly plausible according to our subjective experience), a great number of similar cases order themselves under the formula thus attained. Those elements in each individual event which are left unaccounted for by the selection of their elements subsumable under the "law" are considered as scientifically unintegrated residues which will be taken care of in the further perfection of the system of "laws." Alternatively they will be viewed as "accidental" and therefore scientifically unimportant because they do not fit into the structure of the "law;" in other words, they are not typical of the event and hence can only be the objects of "idle curiosity." Accordingly, even among the followers of the Historical School we continually find the attitude which declares that the ideal, which all the sciences, including the cultural sciences, serve and toward which they should strive even in the remote future, is a system of propositions from which reality can be "deduced." As is well known, a leading natural scientist believed that he could designate the (factually unattainable) ideal goal of such a treatment of cultural reality as a sort of "astronomical" knowledge.

Let us not, for our part, spare ourselves the trouble of examining these matters more closely – however often they have already been discussed. The first thing that impresses one is that the "astronomical" knowledge which was referred to is not a system of laws at all. On the contrary, the laws which it presupposes have been taken from other disciplines like mechanics. But it too concerns itself with the question of the individual consequence which the working of these laws in a unique configuration produces, since it is these individual configurations which are significant for us.

Every individual constellation which it "explains" or predicts is causally explicable only as the consequence of another equally individual constellation which has preceded it. As far back as we may go into the grey mist of the far-off past, the reality to which the laws apply always remains equally individual, equally undeducible from laws. A cosmic "primeval state" which had no individual character or less individual character than the cosmic reality of the present would naturally be a meaningless notion. But is there not some trace of similar ideas in our field in those propositions sometimes derived from natural law and sometimes verified by the observation of "primitives," concerning an economic-social "primeval state" free from historical "accidents," and characterised by phenomena such as "primitive agrarian communism," sexual "promiscuity," etc., from which individual historical development emerges by a sort of fall from grace into concreteness?

The social-scientific interest has its point of departure, of course, in the real, i.e., concrete, individually-structured configuration of our cultural life in its universal relationships which are themselves no less individually structured, and in its development out of other social cultural conditions, which themselves are obviously likewise individually structured. It is clear here that the situation which we illustrated by reference to astronomy as a limiting case (which is regularly drawn on by logicians for the same purpose) appears in a more accentuated form. Whereas in astronomy, the heavenly bodies are of interest to us only in their quantitative and exact aspects, the qualitative aspect of phenomena concerns us in the social sciences. To this should be added that in the social sciences we are concerned with psychological and intellectual phenomena the empathic understanding of which is naturally a problem of a specifically different type from those which the schemes of the exact natural sciences in general can or seek to solve.

Despite that, this distinction in itself is not a distinction in principle, as it seems at first glance. Aside from pure mechanics, even the exact natural sciences do not proceed without qualitative categories. Furthermore, in our own field we encounter the idea (which is obviously distorted) that at least the phenomena characteristic of a money-economy – which are basic to our culture – are quantifiable and on that account subject to formulation as "laws." Finally it depends on the breadth or narrowness of one's definition of "law" as to whether one will also include regularities which because they are not quantifiable are not subject to numerical analysis. Especially insofar as the influence of psychological and intellectual factors is concerned, it does not in any case exclude the establishment of rules governing rational conduct. Above all, the point of view still persists which claims that the task of psychology is to play a role comparable to mathematics for the *Geisteswissenschaften* in the sense that it analyses the complicated phenomena of social life into their psychic conditions and effects, reduces them to their most elementary possible psychic factors and then analyses their functional interdependences.

Thereby a sort of "chemistry," if not "mechanics," of the psychic foundations of social life would be created. Whether such investigations can produce valuable and – what is something else – useful results for the cultural sciences, we cannot decide here. But this would be irrelevant to the question as to whether the aim of socioeconomic knowledge in our sense, i.e., knowledge of reality with respect to its cultural significance and its causal relationships, can be attained through the quest for recurrent sequences. Let us assume that we have succeeded by means of psychology or otherwise in analysing all the observed and imaginable relationships, of social phenomena into some ultimate elementary "factors," that we have made an exhaustive analysis and classification of them and then formulated rigorously exact laws covering their behaviour. – What would be the significance of these results for our knowledge of the historically given culture or any individual phase thereof, such as capitalism, in its development and cultural significance?

As an analytical tool, it would be as useful as a textbook of organic chemical combinations would be for our knowledge of the biogenetic aspect of the animal and plant world. In each case, certainly an important and useful preliminary step would have been taken. In neither case can concrete reality be deduced from "laws" and "factors." This is not because some higher mysterious powers reside in living phenomena (such as "dominants," "entelechies," or whatever they might be called). This, however, presents a problem in its own right. The real reason is that the analysis of reality is concerned with the configuration into which those (hypothetical!) "factors" are arranged to form a cultural phenomenon which is historically significant to us. Furthermore, if we wish to "explain" this individual configuration "causally" we must invoke other equally individual configurations on the basis of which we will explain it with the aid of those (hypothetical!) "laws."

The determination of those (hypothetical) "laws" and "factors" would in any case only be the first of the many operations which would lead us to the desired type of knowledge. The analysis of the historically given individual configuration of those "factors" and their significant concrete interaction, conditioned by their historical context and especially the rendering intelligible of the basis and type of this significance would be the next task to be achieved. This task must be achieved, it is true, by the utilisation of the preliminary analysis, but it is nonetheless an entirely new and distinct task. The tracing as far into the past as possible of the individual features of these historically evolved configurations which are contemporaneously significant, and their historical explanation by antecedent and equally individual configurations would be the third task. Finally the prediction of possible future constellations would be a conceivable fourth task.

For all these purposes, clear concepts and the knowledge of those (hypothetical) "laws" are obviously of great value as heuristic means – but only as such. Indeed they are quite indispensable for this purpose. But even in this function their limitations become evident at a decisive point. In stating this, we arrive at the decisive feature of the method of the cultural sciences. We have designated as "cultural sciences" those disciplines which analyse the phenomena of life in terms of their cultural significance. The significance of a configuration of cultural phenomena and the basis of this significance cannot however be derived and rendered intelligible by a system of analytical laws, however perfect it may be, since the significance of cultural events presupposes a value-orientation toward these events. The concept of culture is a value-concept. Empirical reality becomes "culture" to us because and insofar as we relate it to value ideas. It includes those segments and only those segments of reality which have become significant to us because of this value-relevance. Only a small portion of existing concrete reality is coloured by our value-conditioned interest and it alone is significant to us. It is significant because it reveals relationships which are important to us due to their connection with our values. Only because and to the extent that this is the case is it worthwhile for us to know it in its individual features. We cannot discover, however, what is meaningful to us by means of a "presuppositionless" investigation of empirical data. Rather, perception of its meaningfulness to us is the presupposition of its becoming an object of investigation. Meaningfulness naturally does not coincide with laws as such, and the more general the law the less the coincidence. For the specific meaning which a phenomenon has for us is naturally not to be found in those relationships which it shares with many other phenomena.

The focus of attention on reality under the guidance of values which lend it significance and the selection and ordering of the phenomena which are thus affected in the light of their cultural significance is entirely different from the analysis of reality in terms of laws and general concepts. Neither of these two types of the analysis of reality has any necessary logical relationship with the other. They can coincide in individual instances but it would be most disastrous if their occasional coincidence caused us to think that they were not distinct in principle. The cultural significance of a phenomenon, e.g., the significance of exchange in a money economy, can be the fact that it exists on a mass scale as a fundamental component of modern culture.

But the historical fact that it plays this role must be causally explained in order to render its cultural significance understandable. The analysis of the general aspects of exchange and the technique of the market is a – highly important and indispensable – preliminary task. For not only does this type of analysis leave unanswered the question as to how exchange historically acquired its fundamental significance in the modern world; but above all else, the fact with which we are primarily concerned, namely, the cultural significance of the money-economy – for the sake of which we are interested in the description of exchange technique, and for the sake of which alone a science exists which deals with that technique – is not derivable from any "law." The generic features of exchange, purchase, etc., interest the jurist – but we are concerned with the analysis of the cultural significance of the concrete historical fact that today exchange exists on a mass scale. When we require an explanation, when we wish to understand what distinguishes the social-economic aspects of our culture, for instance, from that of Antiquity, in which exchange showed precisely the same generic traits as it does today, and when we raise the question as to where the significance of "money economy" lies, logical principles of quite heterogenous derivation enter into the investigation.

We will apply those concepts with which we are provided by the investigation of the general features of economic mass phenomena – indeed, insofar as they are relevant to the meaningful aspects of our culture, we shall use them as means of exposition. The goal of our investigation is not reached through the exposition of those laws and concepts, precise as it may be. The question as to what should be the object of universal conceptualisation cannot be decided "presuppositionlessly" but only with reference to the significance which certain segments of that infinite multiplicity which we call "commerce" have for culture. We seek knowledge of an historical phenomenon, meaning by historical: significant in its individuality. And the decisive element in this is that only through the presupposition that a finite part alone of the infinite variety of phenomena is significant, does the knowledge of an individual phenomenon become logically meaningful.

Even with the widest imaginable knowledge of "laws," we are helpless in the face of the question: how is the causal explanation of an individual fact possible – since a description of even the smallest slice of reality can never be exhaustive? The number and type of causes which have influenced any given event are always infinite and there is nothing in the things themselves to set some of them apart as alone meriting attention. A chaos of "existential judgments" about countless individual events would be the only result of a serious attempt to analyse reality "without presuppositions." And even this result is only seemingly possible, since every single perception discloses on closer examination an infinite number of constituent perceptions which can never be exhaustively expressed in a judgment. Order is brought into this chaos only on the condition that in every case only a part of concrete reality is interesting and significant to us, because only it is related to the cultural values with which we approach reality. Only certain sides of the infinitely complex concrete phenomenon, namely those to which we attribute a general cultural significance, are therefore worthwhile knowing.

They alone are objects of causal explanation. And even this causal explanation evinces the same character; an exhaustive causal investigation of any concrete phenomena in its full reality is not only practically impossible – it is simply nonsense. We select only those causes to which are to be imputed in the individual case, the "essential" feature of an event. Where the individuality of a phenomenon is concerned, the question of causality is not a question of laws but of concrete causal relationships; it is not a question of the subsumption of the event under some general rubric as a representative case but of its imputation as a consequence of some constellation. It is in brief a question of imputation. Wherever the causal explanation of a "cultural phenomenon" – a "historical individual" is under consideration, the knowledge of causal laws is not the end of the investigation but only a means. It facilitates and renders possible the causal imputation to their concrete causes of those components of a phenomenon the individuality of which is culturally significant. So far and only so far as it achieves this, is it valuable for our knowledge of concrete relationships. And the more "general" (i.e., the more abstract) the laws, the less they can contribute to the causal imputation of individual phenomena and, more indirectly, to the understanding of the significance of cultural events.

What is the Consequence of all This?

Naturally, it does not imply that the knowledge of universal propositions, the construction of abstract concepts, the knowledge of regularities and the attempt to formulate "laws" have no scientific justification in the cultural sciences. Quite the contrary, if the causal knowledge of the historians consists of the imputation of concrete effects to concrete causes, a valid imputation of any individual effect without the application of "nomological" knowledge – i.e., the knowledge of recurrent causal sequences-would in general be impossible. Whether a single individual component of a relationship is, in a concrete case, to be assigned causal responsibility for an effect, the causal explanation of which is at issue, can in doubtful cases be determined only by estimating the effects which we generally expect from it and from the other components of the same complex which are relevant to the explanation. In other words, the "adequate" effects of the causal elements involved must be considered in arriving at any such conclusion. The extent to which the historian (in the widest sense of the word) can perform this imputation in a reasonably certain manner, with his imagination sharpened by personal experience and trained in analytic methods, and the extent to which he must have recourse to the aid of special disciplines which make it possible, varies with the individual case. Everywhere, however, and hence also in the sphere of complicated economic processes, the more certain and the more comprehensive our general knowledge the greater is the certainty of imputation. This proposition is not in the least affected by the fact that even in the case of all so-called "economic laws" without exception, we are concerned here not with "laws" in the narrower exact natural-science sense, but with adequate causal relationships expressed in rules and with the application of the category of "objective possibility." The establishment of such regularities is not the end but rather the means of knowledge. It is entirely a question of expediency, to be settled separately for each individual case, whether a regularly recurrent causal relationship of everyday experience should be formulated into a "law." Laws are important and valuable in the exact natural sciences, in the measure that those sciences are universally valid. For the knowledge of historical phenomena in their concreteness, the most general laws, because they are most devoid of content, are also the least valuable. The more comprehensive the validity – or scope – of a term, the more it leads us away from the richness of reality since in order to include the common elements of the largest possible number of phenomena, it must necessarily be as abstract as possible and hence devoid of content. In the cultural sciences, the knowledge of the universal or general is never valuable in itself.

The conclusion which follows from the above is that an "objective" analysis of cultural events, which proceeds according to the thesis that the ideal of science is the reduction of empirical reality to "laws," is meaningless. It is not meaningless, as is often maintained, because cultural or psychic events for instance are "objectively" less governed by laws. It is meaningless for a number of other reasons. Firstly, because the knowledge of social laws is not knowledge of social reality but is rather one of the various aids used by our minds for attaining this end; secondly, because knowledge of cultural events is inconceivable except on a basis of the significance which the concrete constellations of reality have for us in certain individual concrete situations. In which sense and in which situations this is the case is not revealed to us by any law; it is decided according to the value-ideas in the light of which we view "culture" in each individual case. "Culture" is a finite segment of the meaningless infinity of the world process, a segment on which human beings confer meaning and significance. This is true even for the human being who views a particular culture as a mortal enemy and who seeks to "return to nature." He can attain this point of view only after viewing the culture in which he lives from the standpoint of his values, and finding it "too soft." This is the purely logical-formal fact which is involved when we speak of the logically necessary rootedness of all historical entities in "evaluative ideas." The transcendental presupposition of every cultural science lies not in our finding a certain culture or any "culture" in general to be valuable but rather in the fact that we are cultural beings, endowed with the capacity and the will to take a deliberate attitude toward the world and to lend it significance. Whatever this significance may be, it will lead us to judge certain phenomena of human existence in its light and to respond to them as being (positively or negatively) meaningful. Whatever may be the content of this attitude, these phenomena have cultural significance for us and on this significance alone rests its scientific interest. Thus when we speak here of the conditioning of cultural knowledge through evaluative ideas (following the terminology of modern logic), it is done in the hope that we will not be subject to crude misunderstandings such as the opinion that cultural significance should be attributed only to valuable phenomena. Prostitution is a cultural phenomenon just as much as religion or money. All three are cultural phenomena only because, and only insofar as, their existence and the form which they historically assume touch directly or indirectly on our cultural interests and arouse our striving for knowledge concerning problems brought into focus by the evaluative ideas which give significance to the fragment of reality analysed by those concepts.

All knowledge of cultural reality, as may be seen, is always knowledge from particular points of view. When we require from the historian and social research worker as an elementary presupposition that they distinguish the important from the trivial and that they should have the necessary "point of view" for this distinction, we mean that they must understand how to relate the events of the real world consciously or unconsciously to universal "cultural values," and to select out those relationships which are significant for us. If the notion that those standpoints can be derived from the "facts themselves" continually recurs, it is due to the naive self-deception of the specialist, who is unaware that it is due to the evaluative ideas with which he unconsciously approaches his subject matter, that he has selected from an absolute infinity a tiny portion with the study of which he concerns himself In connection with this selection of individual special "aspects" of the event, which always and everywhere occurs, consciously or unconsciously, there also occurs that element of cultural-scientific work which is referred to by the often-heard assertion that the "personal" element of a scientific work is what is really valuable in it, and that personality must be expressed in every work if its existence is to be justified. To be sure, without the investigator's evaluative ideas, there would be no principle of selection of subject-matter and no meaningful knowledge of the concrete reality. Just as without the investigator's conviction regarding the significance of particular cultural facts, every attempt to analyse concrete reality is absolutely meaningless, so the direction of his personal belief, the refraction of values in the prism of his mind, gives direction to his work. And the values to which the scientific genius relates the object of his inquiry may determine (i.e., decide) the "conception" of a whole epoch, not only concerning what is regarded as "valuable," but also concerning what is significant or insignificant, "important" or "unimportant" in the phenomena.

Accordingly, cultural science in our sense involves "subjective" presuppositions insofar as it concerns itself only with those components of reality which have some relationship, however indirect, to events to which we attach cultural significance. Nonetheless, it is entirely causal knowledge exactly in the same sense as the knowledge of significant concrete natural events which have a qualitative character. Among the many confusions which the overreaching tendency of a formal-juristic outlook has brought about in the cultural sciences, there has recently appeared the attempt to "refute" the "materialistic conception of history" by a series of clever but fallacious arguments which state that since all economic life must take place in legally or conventionally regulated forms, all economic "development" must take the form of striving for the creation of new legal forms. Hence it is said to be intelligible only through ethical maxims, and is on this account essentially different from every type of "natural" development. Accordingly the knowledge of economic development is said to be "teleological" in character. Without wishing to discuss the meaning of the ambiguous term "development," or the logically no-less-ambiguous term "teleology" in the social sciences, it should be stated that such knowledge need not be "teleological" in the sense assumed by this point of view. The cultural significance of normatively regulated legal relations and even norms themselves can undergo fundamental revolutionary changes even under conditions of the formal identity of the prevailing legal norms. Indeed, if one wishes to lose one's self for a moment in fantasies about the future, one might theoretically imagine, let us say, the "socialisation of the means of production" unaccompanied by any conscious "striving" toward this result, and without even the disappearance or addition of a single paragraph of our legal code; the statistical frequency of certain legally regulated relationships might be changed fundamentally, and in many cases, even disappear entirely; a great number of legal norms might become practically meaningless and their whole cultural significance changed beyond identification. *De lege ferenda* discussions may be justifiably disregarded by the "materialistic conception of history," since its central proposition is the indeed inevitable change in the significance of legal institutions. Those who view the painstaking labour of causally understanding historical reality as of secondary importance can disregard it, but it is impossible to supplant it by any type of a "teleology." From our viewpoint, "purpose" is the conception of an effect which becomes a cause of an action. Since we take into account every cause which produces or can produce a significant effect, we also consider this one. Its specific significance consists only in the fact that we not only observe human conduct but can and desire to understand it.

Undoubtedly, all evaluative ideas are "subjective." Between the "historical" interest in a family chronicle and that in the development of the greatest conceivable cultural phenomena which were and are common to a nation or to mankind over long epochs, there exists an infinite gradation of "significance" arranged into an order which differs for each of us. And they are, naturally, historically variable in accordance with the character of the culture and the ideas which rule men's minds. But it obviously does not follow from this that research in the cultural sciences can only have results which are "subjective" in the sense that they are valid for one person and not for others. Only the degree to which they interest different persons varies. In other words, the choice of the object of investigation and the extent or depth to which this investigation attempts to penetrate into the infinite causal web, are determined by the evaluative ideas which dominate the investigator and his age. In the method of investigation, the guiding "point of view" is of great importance for the construction of the conceptual scheme which will be used in the investigation. In the mode of their use, however, the investigator is obviously bound by the norms of our thought just as much here as elsewhere. For scientific truth is precisely what is valid for all who seek the truth.

5

Max Weber: Religion and Social Stratification

Max Weber's (1864-1920) sociology is the foundation of scientific sociology of religion in a sense of typological and objective understanding. Rejecting Karl Marx's evolutionary law of class society, or Emile Durkheim's sustained law of moral society, Weber established the understanding sociology of the subjective meaning of religious action or inaction. To make such knowledge of the understanding objective, he founded the methodology of the ideal type and the elective affinity of causal relationships. Weber "elabourated a set of categories, such as types of prophecy, the idea of charisma (spiritual power), routinization, and other categories, which became tools to deal with the comparative material; he was thus the real founder of comparative sociology." Weber holds that there is no universal law of society as supposed in natural science, or the law of history which determines the course of the dynamic mechanically. The goal of Weber's sociology of religion is to understand religious action from the subjective meaning of the actor rationally and also emphatically; it is not to establish the laws of religion and society, or to extract the essence of religious action. Or the goal is not even to formulate and evaluate the social function of religion as Marx did that religion was the opium of the mass or as Durkheim did that religion was what made moral society hold together.

Typological and comparative understanding of religious action depends on the theoretical construction of the ideal type through thinking or empathic experiments. Objective understanding of religious action, on the other hand, depends on the value-judgement free analysis of the subjective meaning of social action from the viewpoint of ideas as well as material and mental interests. To avoid the injunction of value-judgments, one has to distinguish the empirical recognition of "what is" from the normative judgment of "what should be." The validity of an ethical claim is not the matter of social analysis, but the matter of conscience and belief. The criteria of value-judgment is imperative, and does not depend on empirical reality. The understanding of "what is," on the other hand, involves not just empirical facts of social action, but also the subjective meaning of the social action. Social action is not mechanical reaction of the law of material interests, but the dynamic of ideas and interests which give the actor the conscious or unconscious meaning of life and the world. In order to understand sociological reality of religion, Weber holds the importance of religious idea which cannot be reduced to the component of material interests (Marx) or to the social nexus and function (Durkheim). Weber says:

> Not ideas, but material and ideal [ideological] interests, directly govern men's conduct. Yet very frequently the world images that have been created by ideas, like a switchman, have determined the tracks along which action has been pushed by the dynamic of interest.

RELIGIOUS AFFILIATION AND SOCIAL STRATIFICATION

A glance at the occupational statistics of any country of mixed religious composition brings to light with remarkable frequency a situation which has several times provoked discussion in the Catholic press and literature, and in Catholic congresses in Germany, namely, the fact that business leaders and owners of capital, as well as the higher grades of skilled labour, and even more the higher technically and commercially trained personnel of modern enterprises, are overwhelmingly Protestant. This is true not only in cases where the difference in religion coincides with one of nationality, and thus of cultural development, as in Eastern Germany between Germans and Poles. The same thing is shown in the figures of religious affiliation almost wherever capitalism, at the time of its great expansion, has had a free hand to alter the social distribution of the population in accordance with its needs, and to determine its occupational structure. The more freedom it has had, the more clearly is the effect shown. It is true that the greater relative participation of Protestants in the ownership of capital, in management, and the upper ranks of labour in great modern industrial and commercial enterprises, may in part be explained in terms of historical circumstances which extend far back into the past, and in which religious affiliation is not a cause of the economic conditions, but to a certain extent appears to be a result of them. Participation in the above economic functions usually involves some previous ownership of capital, and generally an expensive education; often both. These are today largely dependent on the possession of inherited wealth, or at least on a certain degree of material well-being. A number of those sections of the old Empire which were most highly developed economically and most favoured by natural resources and situation, in particular a majority of the wealthy towns, went over to Protestantism in the sixteenth century. The results of that circumstance favour the Protestants even today in their struggle for economic existence. There arises thus the historical question: why were the districts of highest economic development at the same time particularly favourable to a revolution in the Church? The answer is by no means so simple as one might think.

The emancipation from economic traditionalism appears, no doubt, to be a factor which would greatly strengthen the tendency to doubt the sanctity of the religious tradition, as of all traditional authorities. But it is necessary to note, what has often been forgotten, that the Reformation meant not the elimination of the Church's control over everyday life, but rather the substitution of a new form of control for the previous one. It meant the repudiation of a control which was very lax, at that time scarcely perceptible in practice, and hardly more than formal, in favour of a regulation of the whole of conduct which, penetrating to all departments of private and public life, was infinitely burdensome and earnestly enforced. The rule of the Catholic Church, "punishing the heretic, but indulgent to the sinner", as it was in the past even more than today, is now tolerated by peoples of thoroughly modern economic character, and was borne by the richest and economically most advanced peoples on earth at about the turn of the fifteenth century. The rule of Calvinism, on the other hand, as it was enforced in the sixteenth century in Geneva and in Scotland, at the turn of the sixteenth and seventeenth centuries in large parts of the Netherlands, in the seventeenth in New England, and for a time in England itself, would be for us the most absolutely unbearable form of ecclesiastical control of the individual which could possibly exist. That was exactly what large numbers of the old commercial aristocracy of those times, in Geneva as well as in Holland and England, felt about it. And what the reformers complained of in those areas of high economic development was not too much supervision of life on the part of the Church, but too little. Now how does it happen that at that time those countries which were most advanced economically, and within them the rising citizen middle classes, not only failed to resist this unexampled tyranny of Puritanism, but even developed a heroism in its defence? For citizen classes as such have seldom before and never since displayed heroism. It was "the last of our heroisms", as Carlyle, not without reason, has said.

But further, and especially important: it may be, as has been claimed, that the greater participation of Protestants in the positions of ownership and management in modern economic life may today be understood, in part at least, simply as a result of the greater material wealth they have inherited. But there are certain other phenomena which cannot be explained in the same way. Thus, to mention only a few facts: there is a great difference discoverable in Baden, in Bavaria, in Hungary, in the type of higher education which Catholic parents, as opposed to Protestant, give their children. That the percentage of Catholics among the students and graduates of higher educational institutions in general lags behind their proportion of the total population, may, to be sure, be largely explicable in terms of inherited differences of wealth. But among the Catholic graduates themselves the percentage of those graduating from the institutions preparing, in particular, for technical studies and industrial and commercial occupations, but in general from those preparing for middle-class business life, lags still farther behind the percentage of Protestants. On the other hand, Catholics prefer the sort of training which the humanistic Gymnasium affords. That is a circumstance to which the above explanation does not apply, but which, on the contrary, is one reason why so few Catholics are engaged in capitalistic enterprise.

Even more striking is a fact which partly explains the smaller proportion of Catholics among the skilled labourers of modern industry. It is well known that the factory has taken its skilled labour to a large extent from young men in the handicrafts; but this is much more true of Protestant than of Catholic journeymen. Among journeymen, in other words, the Catholics show a stronger propensity to remain in their crafts, that is they more often become master craftsmen, whereas the Protestants are attracted to a larger extent into the factories in order to fill the upper ranks of skilled labour and administrative positions. The explanation of these cases is undoubtedly that the mental and spiritual peculiarities acquired from the environment, here the type of education favoured by the religious atmosphere of the home community and the parental home, have determined the choice of occupation, and through it the professional career.

The smaller participation of Catholics in the modern business life of Germany is all the more striking because it runs counter to a tendency which has been observed at all times including the present. National or religious minorities which are in a position of subordination to a group of rulers are likely, through their voluntary or involuntary exclusion from positions of political influence, to be driven with peculiar force into economic activity. Their ablest members seek to satisfy the desire for recognition of their abilities in this field since there is no opportunity in the service of the State. This has undoubtedly been true of the Poles in Russia and Eastern Prussia, who have without question been undergoing a more rapid economic advance than in Galicia, where they have been in the ascendant. It has in earlier times been true of the Huguenots in France under Louis XIV, the Nonconformists and Quakers in England, and, last but not least, the Jew for two thousand years. But the Catholics in Germany have shown no striking evidence of such a result of their position. In the past they have, unlike the Protestants, undergone no particularly prominent economic development in the times when they were persecuted or only tolerated, either in Holland or in England. On the other hand, it is a fact that the Protestants (especially certain branches of the movement to be fully discussed later) both as ruling classes and as ruled, both as majority and as minority, have shown a special tendency to develop economic rationalism which cannot be observed to the same extent among Catholics either in the one situation or in the other. Thus the principal explanation of this difference must be sought in the permanent intrinsic character of their religious beliefs, and not only in their temporary external historico-political situations.

It will be our task to investigate these religions with a view to finding out what peculiarities they have or have had which might have resulted in the behaviour we have described. On superficial analysis, and on the basis of certain current impressions, one might be tempted to express the difference by saying that the greater other-worldliness of Catholicism, the ascetic character of its highest ideals, must have brought up its adherents to a greater indifference toward the good things of this world. Such an explanation fits the popular tendency in the judgment of both religions. On the Protestant side it is used as a basis of criticism of those (real or imagined) ascetic ideals of the Catholic way of life, while the Catholics answer with the accusation that materialism results from the secularization of all ideals through Protestantism. One recent writer has attempted to formulate the difference of their attitudes toward economic life in the following manner: "The Catholic is quieter, having less of the acquisitive impulse; he prefers a life of the greatest possible security, even with a smaller income, to a life of risk and excitement, even though it may bring the chance of gaining honour and riches. The proverb says jokingly, 'either eat well or sleep well'. In the present case the Protestant prefers to eat well, the Catholic to sleep undisturbed."

In fact, this desire to eat well may be a correct though incomplete characterization of the motives of many nominal Protestants in Germany at the present time. But things were very different in the past: the English, Dutch, and American Puritans were characterized by the exact opposite of the joy of living, a fact which is indeed, as we shall see, most important for our present study. Moreover, the French Protestants, among others, long retained, and retain to a certain extent up to the present, the characteristics which were impressed upon the Calvinistic Churches everywhere, especially under the cross in the time of the religious struggles.

Nevertheless (or was it, perhaps, as we shall ask later, precisely on that account?) it is well known that these characteristics were one of the most important factors in the industrial and capitalistic development of France, and on the small scale permitted them by their persecution remained so. If we may call this seriousness and the strong predominance of religious interests in the whole conduct of life otherworldliness, then the French Calvinists were and still are at least as other-worldly as, for instance, the North German Catholics, to whom their Catholicism is undoubtedly as vital a matter as religion is to any other people in the world. Both differ from the predominant religious trends in their respective countries in much the same way.

The Catholics of France are, in their lower ranks, greatly interested in the enjoyment of life, in the upper directly hostile to religion. Similarly, the Protestants of Germany are today absorbed in worldly economic life, and their upper ranks are most indifferent to religion. Hardly anything shows so clearly as this parallel that, with such vague ideas as that of the alleged other-worldliness of Catholicism, and the alleged materialistic joy of living of Protestantism, and others like them, nothing can be accomplished for our purpose. In such general terms the distinction does not even adequately fit the facts of today, and certainly not of the past. If, however, one wishes to make use of it at all, several other observations present themselves at once which, combined with the above remarks, suggest that the supposed conflict between other-worldliness, asceticism, and ecclesiastical piety on the one side, and participation in capitalistic acquisition on the other, might actually turn out to be an intimate relationship.

As a matter of fact it is surely remarkable, to begin with quite a superficial observation, how large is the number of representatives of the most spiritual forms of Christian piety who have sprung from commercial circles. In particular, very many of the most zealous adherents of Pietism are of this origin. It might be explained as a sort of reaction against mammonism on the part of sensitive natures not adapted to commercial life, and, as in the case of Francis of Assisi, many Pietists have themselves interpreted the process of their conversion in these terms. Similarly, the remarkable circumstance that so many of the greatest capitalistic entrepreneurs—down to Cecil Rhodes—hav come from clergymen's families might be explained as a reaction against their ascetic upbringing. But this form of explanation fails where an extraordinary capitalistic business sense is combined in the same persons and groups with the most intensive forms of a piety which penetrates and dominates their whole lives. Such cases are not isolated, but these traits are characteristic of many of the most important Churches and sects in the history of Protestantism.

Especially Calvinism, wherever it has appeared, has shown this combination. However little, in the time of the expansion of the Reformation, it (or any other Protestant belief) was bound up with any particular social class, it is characteristic and in a certain sense typical that in French Huguenot Churches monks and business men (merchants, craftsmen) were particularly numerous among the proselytes, especially at the time of the persecution. Even the Spaniards knew that heresy (i.e. the Calvinism of the Dutch) promoted trade, and this coincides with the opinions which Sir William Petty expressed in his discussion of the reasons for the capitalistic development of the Netherlands. Gothein rightly calls the Calvinistic diaspora the seedbed of capitalistic economy. Even in this case one might consider the decisive factor to be the superiority of the French and Dutch economic cultures from which these communities sprang, or perhaps the immense influence of exile in the breakdown of traditional relationships. But in France the situation was, as we know from Colbert's struggles, the same even in the seventeenth century. Even Austria, not to speak of other countries, directly imported Protestant craftsmen.

But not all the Protestant denominations seem to have had an equally strong influence in this direction. That of Calvinism, even in Germany, was among the strongest, it seems, and the reformed faith more than the others seems to have promoted the development of the spirit of capitalism, in the Wupperthal as well as elsewhere. Much more so than Lutheranism, as comparison both in general and in particular instances, especially in the Wupperthal, seems to prove. For Scotland, Buckle, and among English poets, Keats, have emphasized these same relationships. Even more striking, as it is only necessary to mention, is the connection of a religious way of life with the most intensive development of business acumen among those sects whose other-worldliness is as proverbial as their wealth, especially the Quakers and the Mennonites. The part which the former have played in England and North America fell to the latter in Germany and the Netherlands. That in East Prussia Frederick William I tolerated the Mennonites as indispensable to industry, in spite of their absolute refusal to perform military service, is only one of the numerous well-known cases which illustrates the fact, though, considering the character of that monarch, it is one of the most striking. Finally, that this combination of intense piety with just as strong a development of business acumen, was also characteristic of the Pietists, is common knowledge.

It is only necessary to think of the Rhine country and of Calw. In this purely introductory discussion it is unnecessary to pile up more examples. For these few already all show one thing: that the spirit of hard work, of progress, or whatever else it may be called, the awakening of which one is inclined to ascribe to Protestantism, must not be understood, as there is a tendency to do, as joy of living nor in any other sense as connected with the Enlightenment. The old Protestantism of Luther, Calvin, Knox, Voet, had precious little to do with what today is called progress. To whole aspects of modern life which the most extreme religionist would not wish to suppress today, it was directly hostile. If any inner relationship between certain expressions of the old Protestant spirit and modern capitalistic culture is to be found, we must attempt to find it, for better or worse, not in its alleged more or less materialistic or at least anti-ascetic joy of living, but in its purely religious characteristics. Montesquieu says *(The Spirit of Law,* Book XX, chap. 7) of the English that they "had progressed the farthest of all peoples of the world in three important things: in piety, in commerce, and in freedom". Is it not possible that their commercial superiority and their adaptation to free political institutions are connected in some way with that record of piety which Montesquieu ascribes to them?

A large number of possible relationships, vaguely perceived, occur to us when we put the question in this way. It will now be our task to formulate what occurs to us confusedly as clearly as is possible, considering the inexhaustible diversity to be found in all historical material. But in order to do this it is necessary to leave behind the vague and general concepts with which we have dealt up to this point, and attempt to penetrate into the peculiar characteristics of and the differences between those great worlds of religious thought which have existed historically in the various branches of Christianity. Before we can proceed to that, however, a few remarks are necessary, first on the peculiarities of the phenomenon of which we are seeking an historical explanation, then concerning the sense in which such an explanation is possible at all within the limits of these investigations.

SOCIOLOGY OF THE WORLD RELIGIONS

By 'world religions,' we understand the five religions or religiously determined systems of life-regulation which have known how to gather multitudes of confessors around them. The term is used here in a completely value-neutral sense. The Confucian, Hinduist, Buddhist, Christian, and Islamist religious ethics all belong to the category of world religion. A sixth religion, Judaism, will also be dealt with. It is included because it contains historical preconditions decisive for understanding Christianity and Islamism, and because of its historic and autonomous significance for the development of the modern economic ethic of the Occident—a significance, partly real and partly alleged, which has been discussed several times recently. References to other religions will be made only when they are indispensable for historical connections.

What is meant by the 'economic ethic' of a religion will become increasingly clear during the course of our presentation. This term does not bring into focus the ethical theories of theological compendia; for however important such compendia may be under certain circumstances, they merely serve as tools of knowledge. The term 'economic ethic' points to the practical impulses for action which are founded in the psychological and pragmatic contexts of religions. The following presentation may be sketchy, but it will make obvious how complicated the structures and how manysided the conditions of a concrete economic ethic usually are. Furthermore, it will show that externally similar forms of economic organization may agree with very different economic ethics and, according to the unique character of their economic ethics, how such forms of economic organization may produce very different historical results. An economic ethic is not a simple 'function' of a form of economic organization; and just as little does the reverse hold, namely, that economic ethics unambiguously stamp the form of the economic organization.

No economic ethic has ever been determined solely by religion. In the face of man's attitudes towards the world—as determined by religious or other (in our sense) 'inner' factors—an economic ethic has, of course, a high measure of autonomy. Given factors of economic geography and history determine this measure of autonomy in the highest degree. The religious determination of life-conduct, however, is also one—note this—only one, of the determinants of the economic ethic. Of course, the religiously determined way of life is itself profoundly influenced by economic and political factors operating within given geographical, political, social, and national boundaries. We should lose ourselves in these discussions if we tried to demonstrate these dependencies in all their singularities. Here we can only attempt to peel off the directive elements in the life-conduct of those social *strata* which have most strongly influenced the practical ethic of their respective religions. These elements have stamped the most characteristic features upon practical ethics, the features that distinguish one ethic from others; *and,* at the same time, they have been important for the respective economic ethics.

By no means must we focus upon only one stratum. Those strata which are decisive in stamping the characteristic features of an economic ethic may change in the course of history. And the influence of a single stratum is never an exclusive one. Nevertheless, as a rule one may determine the strata whose styles of life have been at least predominantly decisive for certain religions. Here are some examples, if one may anticipate:

Confucianism was the status ethic of prebendaries, of men with literary educations who were characterized by a secular rationalism. If one did not belong to this *cultured* stratum he did not count. The religious (or if one wishes, irreligious) status ethic of this stratum has determined the Chinese way of life far beyond the stratum itself.

Earlier Hinduism was borne by a hereditary caste of cultured literati, who, being remote from any office, functioned as a kind of ritualist and spiritual advisers for individuals and communities. They formed a stable center for the orientation of the status stratification, and they placed their stamp upon the social order. Only Brahmans, *educated* in the Veda, formed, as bearers of tradition, the fully recognized religious status group. And only later a non-Brahman status group of ascetics emerged by the side of the Brahmans and competed with them. Still later, during the Indian Middle Ages, Hinduism entered the plain. It represented the ardent sacramental religiosity of the saviour, and was borne by the lower strata with their plebeian mystagogues.

Buddhism was propagated by strictly contemplative, mendicant monks, who rejected the world and, having no homes, migrated. Only these were full members of the religious community; all others remained religious laymen of inferior value: objects, not subjects, of religiosity.

During its first period, Islamism was a religion of world-conquering warriors, a knight order of disciplined crusaders. They lacked only the sexual asceticism of their Christian copies of the age of the Crusades. But during the Islamic Middle Ages, contemplative and mystical Sufism attained at least an equal standing under the leadership of plebeian technicians of orgiastics. The brotherhoods of the petty bourgeoisie grew out of Sufism in a manner similar to the Christian Tertiarians, except they were far more universally developed.

Since the Exile, Judaism has been the religion of a civic 'pariah people.' We shall in time become acquainted with the precise meaning of the term. During the Middle Ages Judaism fell under the leadership of a stratum of intellectuals who were trained in literature and ritual, a peculiarity of Judaism. This stratum has represented an increasingly quasi-proletarian and rationalist petty-bourgeois intelligentsia.

Christianity, finally, began its course as a doctrine of itinerant artisan journeymen. During all periods of its mighty external and internal development it has been a quite specifically urban, and above all a civic, religion. This was true during Antiquity, during the Middle Ages, and in Puritanism. The city of the Occident, unique among all other cities of the world—and citizenship, in the sense in which it has emerged only in the Occident—has been the major theatre for Christianity. This holds for the pneumatic piety of the ancient religious community, for the mendicant monk orders of the high Middle Ages, and for the [Protestant] sects of the reformation up to Pietism and Methodism.

It is not our thesis that the specific nature of a religion is a simple 'function' of the social situation of the stratum which appears as its characteristic bearer, or that it represents the stratum's 'ideology,' or that it is a 'reflection' of a stratum's material or ideal interest-situation. On the contrary, a more basic misunderstanding of the standpoint of these discussions would hardly be possible.

However incisive the social influences, economically and politically determined, may have been upon a religious ethic in a particular case, it receives its stamp primarily from religious sources, and, first of all, from the content of its annunciation and its promise. Frequently the very next generation reinterprets these annunciations and promises in a fundamental fashion. Such reinterpretations adjust the revelations to the needs of the religious community. If this occurs, then it is at least usual that religious doctrines are adjusted to *religious needs.* Other spheres of interest could have only a secondary influence; often, however, such influence is very obvious and sometimes it is decisive.

For every religion we shall find that a change in the socially decisive strata has usually been of profound importance. On the other hand, the type of a religion, once stamped, has usually exerted a rather far-reaching influence upon the life-conduct of very heterogeneous strata. In various ways people have sought to interpret the connection between religious ethics and interest-situations in such a way that the former appear as mere 'functions' of the latter. Such interpretation occurs in so-called historical materialism—which we shall not here discuss—as well as in a purely psychological sense.

A quite general and abstract class-determination of religious ethics might be deduced from the theory of 'resentment,' known since Friedrich Nietzsche's brilliant essay and since then spiritedly treated by psychologists. As is known, this theory regards the moral glorification of mercy and brotherliness as a 'slave revolt in morals' among those who are disadvantaged, either in their natural endowments or in their opportunities as determined by life-fate. The ethic of 'duty' is thus considered a product of 'repressed' sentiments for vengeance on the part of banausic men who 'displace' their sentiments because they are powerless, and condemned to work and to money-making. They resent the way of life of the lordly stratum who live free of duties. A very simple solution of the most important problems in the typology of religious ethics would obviously result if this were the case. However fortunate and fruitful the disclosure of the psychological significance of resentment as such has been, great caution is necessary in estimating its bearing for social ethics.

Later we shall have to discuss the motives that have determined the different forms of ethical 'rationalization' of life conduct, *per se.* In the main, these have had nothing whatsoever to do with resentment. But that the evaluation of *suffering* in religious ethics has been subject to a typical change is beyond doubt. If properly understood, this change carries a certain justification for the theory first worked out by Nietzsche. The primeval attitude towards suffering has been thrown into relief most drastically during the religious festivities of the community, especially in the treatment of those haunted by disease or other cases of obstinate misfortune. Men, permanently suffering, mourning, diseased, or otherwise unfortunate, were, according to the nature of their suffering, believed either to be possessed by a demon or burdened with the wrath of a god whom they had insulted. To tolerate such men in the midst of the cultic community could result in disadvantages for it. In any case, they were not allowed to participate in cultic feasts and sacrifices, for the gods did not enjoy the sight of them and could be incited to wrath by it. The sacrificial feasts were occasions for rejoicing—even in Jerusalem during times of siege.

In treating suffering as a symptom of odiousness in the eyes of the gods and as a sign of secret guilt, religion has psychologically met a very general need. The fortunate is seldom satisfied with the fact of being fortunate. Beyond this, he needs to know that he has a *right* to his good fortune. He wants to be convinced that he 'deserves' it, and above all, that he deserves it in comparison with others. He wishes to be allowed the belief that the less fortunate also merely experience his due. Good fortune thus wants to be 'legitimate' fortune.

If the general term 'fortune' covers all the 'good' of honour, power, possession, and pleasure, it is the most general formula for the service of legitimation, which religion has had to accomplish for the external and the inner interests of all ruling men, the propertied, the victorious, and the healthy. In short, religion provides the theodicy of good fortune for those who are fortunate. This theodicy is anchored in highly robust ('pharisaical') needs of man and is therefore easily understood, even if sufficient attention is often not paid to its effects.

In contrast, the way in which this negative evaluation of suffering has led to its religious glorification is more complicated. Numerous forms of chastisement and of abstinences from normal diet and sleep, as well as from sexual intercourse, awaken, or at least facilitate, the charisma of ecstatic, visionary, hysterical, in short, of all extraordinary states that are evaluated as 'holy.' Their production therefore forms the object of magical asceticism. The prestige of these chastisements has resulted from the notion that certain kinds of suffering and abnormal states provoked through chastisement are avenues to the attainment of superhuman, that is magical, powers. The ancient prescriptions of taboo and abstinences in the interest of cultic purity, which follow from a belief in demons, has worked in the same direction. The development of cults of 'salvation' has been added to these prescriptions, abstinences, and interests. In principle, these cults have occupied an independent and new position in the face of individual suffering. The primeval cult, and above all, the cult of the political associations, have left all individual interests out of consideration. The tribal and local god, the gods of the city and of the empire, have taken care only of interests that have concerned the collectivity as a whole. They have been concerned with rain and with sunshine, with the booty of the hunt and with victory over enemies. Thus, in the community cult, the collectivity as such turned to its god.

The individual, in order to avoid or remove evils that concerned himself—above all, sickness—has not turned to the cult of the community, but as an individual he has approached the sorcerer as the oldest personal and 'spiritual adviser.' The prestige of particular magicians, and of those spirits or divinities in whose names they have performed their miracles, has brought them patronage, irrespective of local or of tribal affiliation. Under favourable conditions this has led to the formation of a religious 'community,' which has been independent of ethnic associations. Some, though not all, 'mysteries' have taken this course. They have promised the salvation of individuals *qua* individuals from sickness, poverty, and from all sorts of distress and danger. Thus the magician has transformed himself into the mystagogue; that is, hereditary dynasties of mystagogues or organizations of trained personnel under a head determined in accordance with some sort of rules have developed. This head has either been recognized as the incarnation of a superhuman being or merely as a prophet, that is, as the mouthpiece and agent of his god. Collective religious arrangements for individual 'suffering' *per se,* and for 'salvation' from it, have originated in this fashion.

The annunciation and the promise of religion have naturally been addressed to the masses of those who were in need of salvation. They and their interests have moved into the center of the professional organization for the 'cure of the soul,' which, indeed, only therewith originated. The typical service of magicians and priests becomes the determination of the factors to be blamed for suffering, that is, the confession of 'sins.' At first, these sins were offenses against ritual commandments. The magician and priest also give counsel for behaviour fit to remove the suffering. The material and ideal interests of magicians and priests could thereby actually and increasingly enter the service of specifically *plebeian* motives.

A further step along this course was signified when, under the pressure of typical and ever-recurrent distress, the religiosity of a 'redeemer' evolved. This religiosity presupposed the myth of a saviour, hence (at least relatively) of a *rational* view of the world. Again, suffering became the most important topic. The primitive mythology of nature frequently offered a point of departure for this religiosity. The spirits who governed the coming and going of vegetation and the paths of celestial bodies important for the seasons of the year became the preferred carriers of the myths of the suffering, dying, and resurrecting god to needful men. The resurrected god guaranteed the return of good fortune in this world or the security of happiness in the world beyond. Or, a popularized figure from heroic sagas—like Krishna in India—is embellished with the myths of childhood, love, and struggle; and such figures became the object of an ardent cult of the saviour. Among people under political pressure, like the Israelites, the title of 'saviour' (Joshua) was originally attached to the saviors from political distress, as transmitted by hero sagas (Gideon, Jephthah). The 'Messianic' promises were determined by these sagas. With this people, and in this clear-cut fashion only among them and under other very particular conditions, the suffering of a people's *community,* rather than the suffering of an individual, became the object of hope for religious salvation. The rule was that the saviour bore an individual and universal character at the same time that he was ready to guarantee salvation for the *individual* and to every individual who would turn to him. The figure of the saviour has been of varying stamp. In the late form of Zoroastrianism with its numerous abstractions, a purely constructed figure assumed the role of the mediator and saviour in the economy of salvation. The reverse has also occurred: a historical person, legitimized through miracles and visionary reappearances, ascends to the rank of saviour. Purely historical factors have been decisive for the realization of these very different possibilities. Almost always, however, some kind of theodicy of suffering has originated from the hope for salvation.

The promises of the religions of salvation at first remained tied to ritualist rather than to ethical preconditions. Thus, for instance, both the worldly and the other worldly advantages of the Eleusinian mysteries were tied to ritual purity and to attendance at the Eleusinian mass. When law gained in significance, these special deities played an increasing role, and the task of protecting the traditional order, of punishing the unjust and rewarding the righteous, was transferred to them as guardians of juridical procedure.

Where religious development was decisively influenced by a prophecy, naturally 'sin' was no longer a mere magical offense. Above all, it was a sign of disbelief in the prophet and in his commandments. Sin figured as the basic cause of all sorts of misfortunes. The prophet has not regularly been a descendant or a representative of depressed classes. The reverse, as we shall see, has almost always been the rule. Neither has the content of the prophet's doctrine been derived preponderantly from the intellectual horizon of the depressed classes. As a rule, however, the oppressed, or at least those threatened by distress, were in need of a redeemer and prophet; the fortunate, the propertied, the ruling strata were not in such need. Therefore, in the great majority of cases, a prophetically announced religion of salvation has had *its* permanent locus among the less-favoured social strata. Among these, such religiosity has either been a substitute for, or a rational supplement to, magic. Wherever the promises of the prophet or the redeemer have not sufficiently met the needs of the socially less-favoured strata, a secondary salvation religion of the masses has regularly developed beneath the official doctrine. The rational conception of the world is contained in germ within the myth of the redeemer. A rational theodicy of misfortune has, therefore, as a rule, been a development of this conception of the world. At the same time, this rational view of the world has often furnished suffering as such with a 'plus' sign, which was originally quite foreign to it.

Suffering, voluntarily created through mortification, changed its meaning with the development of ethical divinities who punish and reward. Originally, the magical coercion of spirits by the formula of prayer was increased through mortification as a source of charismatic states. Such coercion was preserved in mortification by prayer as well as in cultic prescriptions of abstinence. This has remained the case, even after the magical formula for coercing spirits became a supplication to be heard by a deity. Penances were added as a means of cooling the wrath of deities by repentance, and of avoiding through self-punishment the sanctions that have been incurred. The numerous abstinences were originally attached to the mourning for the dead (with special clarity in China) in order to turn away their jealousy and wrath. These abstinences were easily transferred to relations with the appropriate divinities; they made self-mortification, and finally, unintentional deprivation as such, appear more pleasing to the gods than the naive enjoyment of the goods of this earth. Such enjoyment, indeed, made the pleasure-seeking man less accessible to the influence of the prophet or the priest. The force of all these individual factors was tremendously enhanced under certain conditions.

The need for an ethical interpretation of the 'meaning' of the distribution of fortunes among men increased with the growing rationality of conceptions of the world. As the religious and ethical reflections upon the world were increasingly rationalized and primitive, and magical notions were eliminated, the theodicy of suffering encountered increasing difficulties. Individually 'undeserved' woe was all too frequent; not 'good' but 'bad' men succeeded—even when 'good' and 'bad' were measured by the yardstick of the master stratum and not by that of a 'slave morality.'

One can explain suffering and injustice by referring to individual sin committed in a former life (the migration of souls), to the guilt of ancestors, which is avenged down to the third and fourth generation, or— the most principled—to the wickedness of all creatures *per se.* As compensatory promises, one can refer to hopes of the individual for a better life in the future in this world (transmigration of souls) or to hopes for the successors (Messianic realm), or to a better life in the hereafter (paradise).

The metaphysical conception of God and of the world, which the ineradicable demand for a theodicy called forth, could produce only a few systems of ideas on the whole—as we shall see, only three. These three gave rationally satisfactory answers to the questioning for the basis of the incongruity between destiny and merit: the Indian doctrine of Kharma, Zoroastrian dualism, and the predestination decree of the *deus abscondidus.* These solutions are rationally closed; in pure form, they are found only as exceptions.

The rational need for a theodicy of suffering and of dying has had extremely strong effects. As a matter of fact, this need has moulded important traits of such religions as Hinduism, Zoroastrism, and Judaism, and, to a certain extent, Paulinian and later Christianity. Even as late as 1906, a mere minority among a rather considerable number of proletarians gave as reasons for their disbelief in Christianity conclusions derived from modern theories of natural sciences. The majority, however, referred to the 'injustice' of the order of this world—to be sure, essentially because they believed in a revolutionary compensation in this world.

The theodicy of suffering can be coloured by resentment. But the need of compensation for the insufficiency of one's fate in this world has not, as a rule, had resentment as a basic and decisive colour. Certainly, the need for vengeance has had a special affinity with the belief that the unjust are well off in this world only because hell is reserved for them later. Eternal bliss is reserved for the pious; occasional sins, which, after all, the pious also commit, ought therefore to be expiated in this world. Yet one can readily be convinced that even this way of thinking, which occasionally appears, is not always determined by resentment, and that it is by no means always the product of socially oppressed strata. We shall see that there have been only a few examples of religion to which resentment contributed essential features. Among these examples only one is a fully developed case. All that can be said is that resentment *could* be, and often and everywhere has been, significant as one factor, among others, in influencing the religiously determined rationalism of socially disadvantaged strata. It has gained such significance, in highly diverse and often minute degrees, in accordance with the nature of the promises held out by different religions. In any case, it would be quite wrong to attempt to deduce 'asceticism' in general from these sources.

The distrust of wealth and power, which as a rule exists in genuine religions of salvation, has had its natural basis primarily in the experience of redeemers, prophets, and priests. They understood that those strata which were 'satiated' and favoured in this world had only a small urge to be saved, regardless of the kind of salvation offered. Hence, these master strata have been less 'devout' in the sense of salvation religions. The development of a rational religious ethic has had positive and primary roots in the inner conditions of those social strata which were less socially valued.

Strata in solid possession of social honour and power usually tend to fashion their status-legend in such a way as to claim a special and intrinsic quality of their own, usually a quality of blood; their sense of dignity feeds on their actual or alleged being. The sense of dignity of socially repressed strata or of strata whose status is negatively (or at least not positively) valued is nourished most easily on the belief that a special 'mission' is entrusted to them; their worth is guaranteed or constituted by an *ethical imperative,* or by their own functional *achievement.* Their value is thus moved into something beyond themselves, into a 'task' placed before them by God. One source of the ideal power of ethical prophecies among socially disadvantaged strata lies in this fact. Resentment has not been required as a leverage; the rational interest in material and ideal compensations as such has been perfectly sufficient. There can be no doubt that prophets and priests through intentional or unintentional propaganda have taken the resentment of the masses into their service. But this is by no means always the case. This essentially negative force of resentment, so far as is known, has never been the source of those essentially metaphysical conceptions which have lent uniqueness to every salvation religion.

Moreover, in general, the nature of a religious promise has by no means necessarily or even predominantly been the mere mouthpiece of a class interest, either of an external or internal nature. By themselves, the masses, as we shall see, have everywhere remained engulfed in the massive and archaic growth of magic—unless a prophecy that holds out specific promises has swept them into a religious movement of an ethical character. For the rest, the specific nature of the great religious and ethical systems has been determined by social conditions of a far more particular nature than by the mere contrast of ruling and ruled strata. In order to avoid repetition, some further comments about these relationships may be stated in advance.

For the empirical student, the sacred values, differing among themselves, are by no means only, nor even preferably, to be interpreted as 'other-worldly.' This is so quite apart from the fact that not every religion, nor every world religion, knows of a 'beyond' as a locus of definite promises. At first the sacred values of primitive as well as of cultured, prophetic or non-prophetic, religions were quite solid goods of this world. With the only partial exception of Christianity and a few other specifically ascetic creeds, they have consisted of health, a long life, and wealth. These were offered by the promises of the Chinese, Vedic, Zoroastrian, ancient Hebrew, and Islamite religions; and in the same manner by the Phoenician, Egyptian, Babylonian, and ancient Germanic religions, as well as by the promises of Hinduism and Buddhism for the devout laymen. Only the religious virtuoso, the ascetic, the monk, the Sufi, the Dervish strove for sacred values, which were 'other-worldly' as compared with such solid goods of this world, as health, wealth, and long life. And these other-worldly sacred values were by no means only values of the *beyond*. This was not the case even where it was understood to be so by the participants.

Psychologically considered, man in quest of salvation has been primarily preoccupied by attitudes of the here and now. The puritan *certitudo salutis,* the permanent state of grace that rests in the feeling of 'having proved oneself,' was psychologically the only concrete object among the sacred values of this ascetic religion. The Buddhist monk, certain to enter Nirvana, seeks the sentiment of a cosmic love; the devout Hindu seeks either Bhakti (fervent love in the possession of God) or apathetic ecstasy. The Chlyst with his radjeny, as well as the dancing Dervish, strives for orgiastic ecstasy. Others seek to be possessed by God and to possess God, to be a bridegroom of the Virgin Mary, or to be the bride of the Saviour. The Jesuit's cult of the heart of Jesus, quietistic edification, the pietists' tender love for the child Jesus and its 'running sore,' the sexual and semi-sexual orgies at the wooing of Krishna, the sophisticated cultic dinners of the Vallabhacharis, the gnostic onanist cult activities, the various forms of the *unïo mystica,* and the contemplative submersion in the All-one—these states undoubtedly have been sought, first of all, for the sake of such emotional value as they directly offered the devout. In this respect, they have in fact been absolutely equal to the religious and alcoholic intoxication of the Dionysian or the soma cult; to totemic meat-orgies, the cannibalistic feasts, the ancient and religiously consecrated use of hashish, opium, and nicotine; and, in general, to all sorts of magical intoxication. They have been considered specifically consecrated and divine because of their psychic extraordinariness and because of the intrinsic value of the respective states conditioned by them.

Even the most primitive orgy has not entirely lacked a meaningful interpretation, although only the rationalized religions have imputed a metaphysical meaning into such specifically religious actions, in addition to the direct appropriation of sacred values. Rationalized religions have thus sublimated the orgy into the 'sacrament.' The orgy, however, has had a pure animist and magical character; it has contained only small or, indeed, no beginnings of the universalist, cosmic pragmatism of the holy. And such pragmatism is peculiar to all religious rationalism. Yet even after such a sublimation of orgy into sacrament has occurred, the fact remains, of course, that for the devout the sacred value, first and above all, has been a psychological state in the *here and now.* Primarily this state consists in the emotional attitude *per se,* which was directly called forth by the specifically religious (or magical) act, by methodical asceticism, or by contemplation.

As extraordinary attitudes, religious states can be only transient in character and in external appearance. Originally this, of course, was everywhere the case. The only way of distinguishing between 'religious' and 'profane' states is by referring to the extraordinary character of the religious states. A special state, attained by religious means, can be striven for as a 'holy state' which is meant to take possession of the entire man and of his lasting fate. The transition from a passing to a permanent holy state has been fluid.

The two highest conceptions of sublimated religious doctrines of salvation are 'rebirth' and 'salvation.' Rebirth, a primeval magical value, has meant the acquisition of a new soul by means of an orgiastic act or through methodically planned asceticism. Man transitorily acquired a new soul in ecstasy; but by means of magical asceticism, he could seek to gain it permanently. The youth who wished to enter the community of warriors as a hero, or to participate in its magical dances or orgies, or who wished to commune with the divinities in cultic feasts, had to have a new soul. The heroic and magical asceticism, the initiation rites of youths, and the sacramental customs of rebirth at important phases of private and collective life are thus quite ancient. The means used in these activities varied, as did their ends: that is, the answers to the question, 'For what should I be reborn?'

The various religious or magical states that have given their psychological stamp to religions may be systematized according to very different points of view. Here we shall not attempt such a systematization. In connection with what we have said, we merely wish to indicate quite generally the following.

The kind of empirical state of bliss or experience of rebirth that is sought after as the supreme value by a religion has obviously and necessarily varied according to the character of the stratum which was foremost in adopting it. The chivalrous warrior class, peasants, business classes, and intellectuals with literary education have naturally pursued different religious tendencies. As will become evident, these tendencies have not by themselves determined the psychological character of religion; they have, however, exerted a very lasting influence upon it. The contrast between warrior and peasant classes, and intellectual and business classes, is of special importance. Of these groups, the intellectuals have always been the exponents of a rationalism which in their case has been relatively theoretical. The business classes (merchants and artisans) have been at least possible exponents of rationalism of a more practical sort. Rationalism of either kind has borne very different stamps, but has always exerted a great influence upon the religious attitude. Above all, the peculiarity of the intellectual strata in this matter has been in the past of the greatest importance for religion. At the present time, it matters little in the development of a religion whether or not modern intellectuals feel the need of enjoying a 'religious' state as an 'experience,' in addition to all sorts of other sensations, in order to decorate their internal and stylish furnishings with paraphernalia guaranteed to be genuine and old. A religious revival has never sprung from such a source.

In the past, it was the work of the intellectuals to sublimate the possession of sacred values into a belief in 'salvation.' The conception of the idea of salvation, as such, is very old, if one understands by it a liberation from distress, hunger, drought, sickness, and ultimately from suffering and death. Yet salvation attained a specific significance only where it expressed a systematic and rationalized 'image of the world' and represented a stand in the face of the world. For the meaning as well as the intended and actual psychological quality of salvation has depended upon such a world image and such a stand.

Not ideas, but material and ideal interests, directly govern men's conduct. Yet very frequently the 'world images' that have been created by 'ideas' have, like switchmen, determined the tracks along which action has been pushed by the dynamic of interest. 'From what' and 'for what' one wished to be redeemed and, let us not forget, 'could be' redeemed, depended upon one's image of the world. There have been very different possibilities in this connection: One could wish to be saved from political and social servitude and lifted into a Messianic realm in the future of this world; or one could wish to be saved from being defiled by ritual impurity and hope for the pure beauty of psychic and bodily existence.

One could wish to escape being incarcerated in an impure body and hope for a purely spiritual existence. One could wish to be saved from the eternal and senseless play of human passions and desires and hope for the quietude of the pure beholding of the divine. One could wish to be saved from radical evil and the servitude of sin and hope for the eternal and free benevolence in the lap of a fatherly god. One could wish to be saved from peonage under the astrologically conceived determination of stellar constellations and long for the dignity of freedom and partaking of the substance of the hidden deity. One could wish to be redeemed from the barriers to the finite, which express themselves in suffering, misery and death, and the threatening punishment of hell, and hope for an eternal bliss in an earthly or paradisical future existence. One could wish to be saved from the cycle of rebirths with their inexorable compensations for the deeds of the times past and hope for eternal rest. One could wish to be saved from senseless brooding and events and long for the dreamless sleep. Many more varieties of belief have, of course, existed. Behind them always lies a stand towards something in the actual world which is experienced as specifically 'senseless.' Thus, the demand has been implied: that the world order in its totality is, could, and should somehow be a meaningful 'cosmos.' This quest, the core of genuine religious rationalism, has been borne precisely by strata of intellectuals. The avenues, the results, and the efficacy of this metaphysical need for a meaningful cosmos have varied widely. Nevertheless, some general comments may be made.

The general result of the modern form of thoroughly rationalizing the conception of the world and of the way of life, theoretically and practically, in a purposive manner, has been that religion has been shifted into the realm of the irrational. This has been the more the case the further the purposive type of rationalization has progressed, if one takes the standpoint of an intellectual articulation of an image of the world. This shift of religion into the irrational realm has occurred for several reasons. On the one hand, the calculation of consistent rationalism has not easily come out even with nothing left over. In music, the Pythagorean 'comma' resisted complete rationalization oriented to tonal physics. The various great systems of music of all peoples and ages have differed in the manner in which they have either covered up or bypassed this inescapable irrationality or, on the other hand, put irrationality into the service of the richness of tonalities. The same has seemed to happen to the theoretical conception of the world, only far more so; and above all, it has seemed to happen to the rationalization of practical life. The various great ways of leading a rational and methodical life have been characterized by irrational presuppositions, which have been accepted simply as 'given' and which have been incorporated into such ways of life. What these presuppositions have been is historically and socially determined, at least to a very large extent, through the peculiarity of those strata that have been the carriers of the ways of life during its formative and decisive period. The *interest* situation of these strata, as determined socially and psychologically, has made for their peculiarity, as we here understand it.

Furthermore, the irrational elements in the rationalization of reality have been the *loci* to which the irrepressible quest of intellectualism for the possession of supernatural values has been compelled to retreat. That is the more so the more denuded of irrationality the world appears to be. The unity of the primitive image of the world, in which everything was concrete magic, has tended to split into rational cognition and mastery of nature, on the one hand, and into 'mystic' experiences, on the other. The inexpressible contents of such experiences remain the only possible 'beyond,' added to the mechanism of a world robbed of gods. In fact, the beyond remains an incorporeal and metaphysical realm in which individuals intimately possess the holy. Where this conclusion has been drawn without any residue, the individual can pursue his quest for salvation only as an individual. This phenomenon appears in some form, with progressive intellectualist rationalism, wherever men have ventured to rationalize the image of the world as being a cosmos governed by impersonal rules. Naturally it has occurred most strongly among religions and religious ethics which have been quite strongly determined by genteel strata of intellectuals devoted to the purely cognitive comprehension of the world and of its 'meaning.' This was the case with Asiatic and, above all, Indian world religions.

For all of them, contemplation became the supreme and ultimate religious value accessible to man. Contemplation offered them entrance into the profound and blissful tranquillity and immobility of the All-one. All other forms of religious states, however, have been at best considered a relatively valuable *Ersatz* for contemplation. This has had far-reaching consequences for the relation of religion to life, including economic life, as we shall repeatedly see. Such consequences flow from the general character of 'mystic' experiences, in the contemplative sense, and from the psychological preconditions of the search for them.

The situation in which strata decisive for the development of a religion were active in practical life has been entirely different. Where they were chivalrous warrior heroes, political officials, economically acquisitive classes, or, finally, where an organized hierocracy dominated religion, the results were different than where genteel intellectuals were decisive.

The rationalism of hierocracy grew out of the professional preoccupation with cult and myth or—to a far higher degree—out of the cure of souls, that is, the confession of sin and counsel to sinners. Everywhere hierocracy has sought to monopolize the administration of religious values. They have also sought to bring and to temper the bestowal of religious goods into the form of 'sacramental' or 'corporate grace,' which could be ritually bestowed only by the priesthood and could not be attained by the individual. The individual's quest for salvation or the quest of free communities by means of contemplation, orgies, or asceticism, has been considered highly suspect and has had to be regulated ritually and, above all, controlled hierocratically. From the standpoint of the interests of the priesthood in power, this is only natural.

Every body of *political* officials, on the other hand, has been suspicious of all sorts of individual pursuits of salvation and of the free formation of communities as sources of emancipation from domestication at the hands of the institution of the state. Political officials have distrusted the competing priestly corporation of grace and, above all, at bottom they have despised the very quest for these impractical values lying beyond utilitarian and worldly ends. For all political bureaucracies, religious duties have ultimately been simply official or social obligations of the citizenry and of status groups. Ritual has corresponded to rules and regulations, and, therefore, wherever a bureaucracy has determined its nature, religion has assumed a ritualist character. It is also usual for a stratum of *chivalrous* warriors to pursue absolutely worldly interests and to be remote from all 'mysticism.' Such strata, however, have lacked—and this is characteristic of heroism in general— the desire as well as the capacity for a rational mastery of reality. The irrationality of 'fate' and, under certain conditions, the idea of a vague and deterministically conceived 'destiny' (the Homeric *Moira)* has stood above and behind the divinities and demons who were conceived of as passionate and strong heroes, measuring out assistance and hostility, glory and booty, or death to the human heroes.

Peasants have been inclined towards magic. Their whole economic existence has been specifically bound to nature and has made them dependent upon elemental forces. They readily believe in a compelling Sorcery directed against spirits who rule over or through natural forces, or they believe in simply buying divine benevolence. Only tremendous transformations of life-orientation have succeeded in tearing them away from this universal and primeval form of religiosity. Such transformations have been derived either from other strata or from mighty prophets, who, through the power of miracles, legitimize themselves as sorcerers. Orgiastic and ecstatic states of 'possession,' produced by means of toxics or by the dance, are strange to the status honour of knights because they are considered undignified. Among the peasants, however, such states have taken the place that 'mysticism' holds among the intellectuals.

Finally, we may consider the strata that in the western European sense are called 'civic,' as well as those which elsewhere correspond to them: artisans, traders, enterprisers engaged in cottage industry, and their derivatives existing only in the modern Occident. Apparently these strata have been the most ambiguous with regard to the religious stands open to them. And this is especially important to us.

Among these 'civic' strata the following religious phenomena have had especially strong roots: the institutional and sacramental grace of the Roman church in the medieval cities—the pillars of the popes; the mystagogic and sacramental grace in the ancient cities and in India; the orgiastic and contemplative Sufi, and Dervish religion of the Middle Eastern Orient; the Taoist magic; the Buddhist contemplation; the ritualist appropriation of grace under the direction of souls by mystagogues in Asia; all the forms of love for a saviour; the beliefs in salvation the world over, from the cult of Krishna to the cult of Christ; the rational ritualism of the law and the sermon of the synagogue denuded of all magic among Jewry; the pneumatic and ancient as well as the asceticist medieval sects; the grace of predestination and the ethical regeneration of the Puritan and the Methodist; as well as all sorts of individual pursuits of salvation. All of these have been more firmly rooted among 'civic' strata than among any other.

Of course, the religions of all strata are certainly far from being unambiguously dependent upon the character of the strata we have presented as having special affinities with them. Yet, at first sight, civic strata appear, in this respect and on the whole, to lend themselves to a more varied determination. Yet it is precisely among these strata that elective affinities for special types of religion stand out. The tendency towards a *practical* rationalism in conduct is common to all civic strata; it is conditioned by the nature of their way of life, which is greatly detached from economic bonds to nature. Their whole existence has been based upon technological or economic calculations and upon the mastery of nature and of man, however primitive the means at their disposal. The technique of living handed down among them may, of course, be frozen in traditionalism, as has occurred repeatedly and everywhere.

But precisely for these, there has always existed the possibility—even though in greatly varying measure—of letting an *ethical* and rational regulation of life arise. This may occur by the linkage of such an ethic to the tendency of technological and economic rationalism. Such regulation has not always been able to make headway against traditions which, in the main, were magically stereotyped. But where prophecy has provided a religious basis.

Prophecy can be one of two fundamental types of prophecy which we shall repeatedly discuss: 'exemplary' prophecy, and 'emissary' prophecy. Exemplary prophecy points out the path to salvation by exemplary living, usually by a contemplative and apathetic-ecstatic life. The emissary type of prophecy addresses its *demands* to the world in the name of a god. Naturally these demands are ethical; and they are often of an active ascetic character.

It is quite understandable that the more weighty the civic strata as such have been, and the more they have been torn from bonds of taboo and from divisions into sibs and castes, the more favourable has been the soil for religions that call for action in this world. Under these conditions, the preferred religious attitude could become the attitude of active asceticism, of God-willed *action* nourished by the sentiment of being God's 'tool,' rather than the possession of the deity or the inward and contemplative surrender to God, which has appeared as the supreme value to religions influenced by strata of genteel intellectuals. In the Occident the attitude of active asceticism has repeatedly retained supremacy over contemplative mysticism and orgiastic or apathetic ecstasy, even though these latter types have been well known in the Occident. Active asceticism, however, has not been confined to civic strata. Such an unambiguous social determination has not in any way existed. The prophecy of Zoroaster was directed at the nobility and the peasantry; the prophecy of Islam was directed to warriors. These prophecies, like the Israelite and the early Christian prophecy and preaching, have had an active character, which stands in contrast with the propaganda of Buddhism, Taoism, Neo-Pythagorism, Gnosticism, and Sufism. Certain specific conclusions of emissary prophecies, however, have been drawn precisely on 'civic' grounds. In the missionary prophecy the devout have not experienced themselves as vessels of the divine but rather as instruments of a god.

This emissary prophecy has had a profound elective affinity to a special conception of God: the conception of a supra-mundane, personal, wrathful, forgiving, loving, demanding, punishing Lord of Creation. Such a conception stands in contrast to the supreme being of exemplary prophecy. As a rule, though by no means without exception, the supreme being of an exemplary prophecy is an impersonal being because, as a static state, he is accessible only by means of contemplation. The conception of an active God, held by emissary prophecy, has dominated the Iranian and Mideastern religions and those Occidental religion which are derived from them. The conception of a supreme and static being, held by exemplary prophecy, has come to dominate Indian and Chinese religiosity.

These differences are not primitive in nature. On the contrary, they have come into existence only by means of a far-reaching sublimation of primitive conceptions of animist spirits and of heroic deities which are everywhere similar in nature. Certainly the connection of conceptions of God with religious states, which are evaluated and desired as sacred values, have also been strongly influential in this process of sublimation. These religious states have simply been interpreted in the direction of a different conception of God, according to whether the holy states, evaluated as supreme, were contemplative mystic experiences or apathetic ecstasy, or whether they were the orgiastic possession of god, or visionary inspirations and 'commands.'

At the present time, it is widely held that one should consider emotional content as primary, with thoughts being merely its secondary expression. Of course, this point of view is to a great extent justified. From such a standpoint one might be inclined to consider the primacy of 'psychological' as over against 'rational' connections as the only decisive causal nexus, hence to view these rational connections as *mere* interpretations of the psychological ones. This, however, would be going much too far, according to factual evidence. A whole series of purely historical motives have determined the development toward the supra-mundane or the immanent conception of God. These conceptions, in turn, have decisively influenced the way in which experiences of salvation have been articulated. This definitely holds for the conception of the supra-mundane God, as we shall see again and again. If even Meister Eckhart occasionally and expressly placed Martha above Mary, he did so ultimately because he could not realize the pantheist experience of God, which is peculiar to the mystic, without entirely sacrificing all the decisive elements of Occidental belief in God and creation. The rational elements of a religion, its 'doctrine,' also have an autonomy: for instance, the Indian doctrine of Kharma, the Calvinist belief in predestination, the Lutheran justification through faith, and the Catholic doctrine of sacrament. The rational religious pragmatism of salvation, flowing from the nature of the images of God and of the world, have under certain conditions had far-reaching results for the fashioning of a practical way of life.

These comments presuppose that the nature of the desired sacred values has been strongly influenced by the nature of the external interest-situation and the corresponding way of life of the ruling strata and thus by the social stratification itself. But the reverse also holds: wherever the direction of the whole way of life has been methodically rationalized, it has been profoundly determined by the ultimate values toward which this rationalization has been directed. These values and positions were thus *religiously* determined. Certainly they have not always, or exclusively, been decisive; however, they have been decisive in so far as an *ethical* rationalization held sway, at least so far as its influence reached. As a rule, these religious values have been also, and frequently absolutely, decisive. One factor has been very important in determining the nature of the mutual inter-relations between external and internal interest-situations. The 'supreme' sacred values, which are promised by religion and have been discussed above, have not necessarily been the most universal ones. Not everybody had entree to Nirvana, to the contemplative union with the divine, the orgiastic or the ascetic possession of God. In a weakened form, the transposition of persons into religious states of frenzy or into the trance may become the object of a universal cult of the people. But even in this form such psychic states have not been elements of everyday life.

The empirical fact, important for us, that men are *differently qualified* in a religious way stands at the beginning of the history of religion. This fact had been dogmatized in the sharpest rationalist form in the 'particularism of grace,' embodied in the doctrine of predestination by the Calvinists. The sacred values that have been most cherished, the ecstatic and visionary capacities of shamans, sorcerers, ascetics, and pneumatics of all sorts, could not be attained by everyone. The possession of such faculties is a 'charisma,' which, to be sure, might be awakened in some but not in all. It follows from this that all intensive religiosity has a tendency toward a sort of *status stratification,* in accordance with differences in the charismatic qualifications. 'Heroic' or 'virtuoso' religiosity is opposed to mass religiosity. By 'mass' we understand those who are religiously 'unmusical'; we do not, of course, mean those who occupy an inferior position in the secular status order. In this sense, the status carriers of a virtuoso religion have been the leagues of sorcerers and sacred dancers; the religious status group of the Indian Sramana and of the early Christian 'ascetics,' who were expressly recognized in the congregation as a special 'estate'; the Paulinian, and still more the Gnostic, 'pneumatics,' the pietist *ecclesiola;* all genuine 'sects'—that is, sociologically speaking, associations that accept only religiously qualified persons in their midst; and finally, monk communities all over the world.

Now, every hierocratic and official authority of a 'church'—that is, a community organized by officials into an institution which bestows gifts of grace—fights principally against all virtuoso-religion and against its autonomous development. For the church, being the holder of institutionalized grace, seeks to organize the religiosity of the masses and to put its own officially monopolized and mediated sacred values in the place of the autonomous and religious status qualifications of the religious virtuosos. By its nature, that is, according to the interest-situation of its officeholders, the church must be 'democratic' in the sense of making the sacred values generally accessible. This means that the church stands for a universalism of grace and for the ethical sufficiency of all those who are enrolled under its institutional authority. Sociologically, the process of leveling constitutes a complete parallel with the political struggles of the bureaucracy against the political privileges of the aristocratic estates. As with hierocracy, every full-grown political bureaucracy is necessarily and in a quite similar sense 'democratic'—namely, in the sense of leveling and of fighting against status privileges that compete with its power.

The most varied compromises have resulted from this struggle between officialdoms and the virtuosos. These struggles have not always been official but they have always existed at least covertly. Thus, the religiosity of the Ulema stood against the religiosity of the Dervishes; the early Christian bishops against the pneumatics and heroist sectaries as well as against the power of The Key of asceticist charisma; the Lutheran preacher's office and the Anglican and priestly church stood against asceticism in general; the Russian state church was opposed to the sects; and the official management of the Confucian cult stood against Buddhist, Taoist, and sectarian pursuits of salvation of all sorts.

The religious virtuosos saw themselves compelled to adjust their demands to the possibilities of the religiosity of everyday life in order to gain and to maintain ideal and material mass-patronage. The nature of their concessions have naturally been of primary significance for the way in which they have religiously influenced everyday life. In almost all Oriental religions, the virtuosos allowed the masses to remain stuck in magical tradition. Thus, the influence of religious virtuosos has been infinitely smaller than was the case where religion has undertaken ethically and generally to rationalize everyday life. This has been the case even when religion has aimed precisely at the masses and has cancelled however many of its ideal demands. Besides the relations between the religiosity of the virtuosos and the religion of the masses, which finally resulted from this struggle, the peculiar nature of the concrete religiosity of the virtuosos has been of decisive importance for the development of the way of life of the masses. This virtuoso religiosity has therefore also been important for the economic ethic of the respective religion. The religion of the virtuoso has been the genuinely 'exemplary' and practical religion. According to the way of life his religion prescribed to the virtuoso, there have been various possibilities of establishing a rational ethic of everyday life. The relation of virtuoso religion to *workaday life* in the locus of the economy has varied, especially according to the peculiarity of the sacred values desired by such religions.

Wherever the sacred values and the redemptory means of a virtuoso religion bore a contemplative or orgiastic-ecstatic character, there has been no bridge between religion and the practical action of the workaday world. In such cases, the economy and all other action in the world has been considered religiously inferior, and no psychological motives for worldly action could be derived from the attitude cherished as the supreme value. In their innermost beings, contemplative and ecstatic religions have been rather specifically hostile to economic life. Mystic, orgiastic, and ecstatic experiences are extraordinary psychic states; they lead away from everyday life and from all expedient conduct. Such experiences are, therefore, deemed to be 'holy.'

With such religions, a deep abyss separates the way of life of the laymen from that of the community of virtuosos. The rule of the status groups of religious virtuosos over the religious community readily shifts into a magical anthropolatry; the virtuoso is directly worshipped as a Saint, or at least laymen buy his blessing and his magical powers as a means of promoting mundane success or religious salvation. As the peasant was to the landlord, so the layman was to the Buddhist and Jainist bhikshu: ultimately, mere sources of tribute. Such tribute allowed the virtuosos to live entirely for religious salvation without themselves performing profane work, which always would endanger their salvation. Yet the conduct of the layman could still undergo a certain ethical regulation, for the virtuoso was the layman's spiritual adviser, his father confessor and *directeur de l'ame.* Hence, the virtuoso frequently exercises a powerful influence over the religiously 'unmusical' laymen; this influence might not be in the direction of his (the virtuoso's) own religious way of life; it might be an influence in merely ceremonious, ritualist, and conventional particulars. For action in this world remained in principle religiously insignificant; and compared with the desire for the religious end, action lay in the very opposite direction. In the end, the charisma of the pure 'mystic' serves only himself. The charisma of the genuine magician serves others.

Things have been quite different where the religiously qualified virtuosos have combined into an ascetic sect, striving to mould life in this world according to the will of a god. To be sure, two things were necessary before this could happen in a genuine way. First, the supreme and sacred value must not be of a contemplative nature; it must not consist of a union with a supra-mundane being who, in contrast to the world, lasts forever; nor in a *unio mystica* to be grasped orgiastically or apathetic-ecstatically. For these ways always lie apart from everyday life and beyond the real world and lead away from it. Second, such a religion must, so far as possible, have given up the purely magical or sacramental character of the *means* of grace. For these means always devalue action in this world as, at best, merely relative in their religious significance, and they link the decision about salvation to the success of processes which are *not* of a rational everyday nature.

When religious virtuosos have combined into an active asceticist sect, two aims are completely attained: the disenchantment of the world and the blockage of the path to salvation by a flight from the world. The path to salvation is turned away from a contemplative 'flight from the world' and towards an active ascetic 'work in this world.' If one disregards the small rationalist sects, such as are found all over the world, this has been attained only in the great church and sect organizations of Occidental and asceticist Protestantism. The quite distinct and the purely historically determined destinies of Occidental religions have co-operated in this matter. Partly, the social environment exerted an influence, above all, the environment of the stratum that was decisive for the development of such religion. Partly, however—and just as strongly—the intrinsic character of Christianity exerted an influence: the supra-mundane God and the specificity of the means and paths of salvation as determined historically, first by Israelite prophecy and the Thora doctrine. The religious virtuoso can be placed in the world as the instrument of a God and cut off from all magical means of salvation.

At the same time, it is imperative for the virtuoso that he 'prove' himself before God, as being called *solely* through the ethical quality of his conduct in this world: This actually means that he 'prove' himself to himself as well. No matter how much the 'world' as such is religiously devalued and rejected as being creatural and a vessel of sin, yet psychologically the world is all the more affirmed as the theatre of God-willed activity in one's worldly 'calling.' For this inner-worldly asceticism rejects the world in the sense that it despises and taboos the values of dignity and beauty, of the beautiful frenzy and the dream, purely secular power, and the purely worldly pride of the hero. Asceticism outlawed these values as competitors of the kingdom of God. Yet precisely because of this rejection, asceticism did not fly from the world, as did contemplation. Instead, asceticism has wished to rationalize the world ethically in accordance with God's commandments. It has therefore remained oriented towards the world in a more specific and thoroughgoing sense than did the naive 'affirmation of the world' of unbroken humanity, for instance, in Antiquity and in lay-Catholicism. In inner-worldly asceticism, the grace and the chosen state of the religiously qualified man prove themselves in everyday life. To be sure, they do so not in the everyday life as it is given, but in methodical and rationalized routine activities of workaday life in the service of the Lord. Rationally raised into a vocation, everyday conduct becomes the locus for proving one's state of grace. The Occidental sects of the religious virtuosos have fermented the methodical rationalization of conduct, including economic conduct. These sects have not constituted valves for the longing to escape from the senselessness of work in this world, as did the Asiatic communities of the ecstatics: contemplative, orgiastic, or apathetic.

The most varied transitions and combinations are found between the polar opposites of 'exemplary' and 'emissary' prophecy. Neither religions nor men are open books. They have been historical rather than logical or even psychological constructions without contradiction. Often they have borne within themselves a series of motives, each of which, if separately and consistently followed through, would have stood in the way of the others or run against them head-on. In religious matters 'consistency has been the exception and not the rule. The ways and means of salvation are also psychologically ambiguous. The search for God of the early Christian monk as well as of the Quaker contained very strong contemplative elements. Yet the total content of their religions and, above all, their supramundane God of creation and their way of making sure of their states of grace again and again directed them to the course of action. On the other hand, the Buddhist monk was also active, but his activities were withdrawn from any consistent rationalization *in this world;* his quest for salvation was ultimately oriented to the flight from the 'wheel' of the rebirths. The sectarians and other brotherhoods of the Occidental Middle Ages spearheaded the religious penetration of everyday life. They found their counter-image in the brotherhoods of Islam, which were even more widely developed. The stratum typical of such brotherhoods in the Occident and in Islam were identical: petty bourgeois and especially artisans. Yet the spirit of their respective religions were very different. Viewed externally, numerous Hinduist religious communities appear to be 'sects' just as do those of the Occident. The sacred value, however, and the manner in which values were mediated pointed in radically different directions.

We shall not accumulate more examples here, as we wish to consider the great religions separately. In no respect can one simply integrate various world religions into a chain of types, each of them signifying a new 'stage.' All the great religions are historical individualities of a highly complex nature; taken all together, they exhaust only a few of the possible combinations that could conceivably be formed from the very numerous individual factors to be considered in such historical combinations.

Thus, the following presentations do not in any way constitute a systematic 'typology' of religion. On the other hand, they do not constitute a purely historical work. They are 'typological' in the sense that they consider what is typically important in the historical realizations of the religious ethics.

This is important for the connection of religions with the great contrasts of the *economic* mentalities. Other aspects will be neglected; these presentations do not claim to offer a well-rounded picture of world religions. Those features peculiar to the individual religions, in contrast to other religions, but which at the same time are important for our interest, must be brought out strongly. A presentation that disregards these special accents of importance would often have to tone down the special features in which we are interested. Such a balanced presentation would almost always have to add other features and occasionally would have to give greater emphasis to the fact that, of course, all qualitative contrasts in reality, in the last resort, can somehow be comprehended as purely quantitative differences in the combinations of single factors. However, it would be extremely unfruitful to emphasize and repeat here what goes without saying.

The features of religions that are important for economic ethics shall interest us primarily from a definite point of view: we shall be interested in the way in which they are related to economic rationalism. More precisely, we mean the economic rationalism of the type which, since the sixteenth and seventeenth centuries, has come to dominate the Occident as part of the particular rationalization of civic life, and which has become familiar in this part of the world.

We have to remind ourselves in advance that 'rationalism' may mean very different things. It means one thing if we think of the kind of rationalization the systematic thinker performs on the image of the world: an increasing theoretical mastery of reality by means of increasingly precise and abstract concepts. Rationalism means another thing if we think of the methodical attainment of a definitely given and practical end by means of an increasingly precise calculation of adequate means. These types of rationalism are very different, in spite of the fact that ultimately they belong inseparately together. Similar types may be distinguished even within the intellectual comprehension of reality; for instance, the differences between English Physics and Continental Physics has been traced back to such a type difference within the comprehension of reality. The rationalization of life conduct with which we have to deal here can assume unusually varied forms. In the sense of the absence of all metaphysics and almost all residues of religious anchorage, Confucianism is rationalist to such a far-going extent that it stands at the extreme boundary of what one might possibly call a 'religious' ethic. At the same time, Confucianism is more rationalist and sober, in the sense of the absence and the rejection of all non-utilitarian yardsticks, than any other ethical system, with the possible exception of J. Bentham's. Yet Confucianism, in spite of constantly actual and apparent analogies, nevertheless differs extraordinarily from Bentham's as well as from all other Occidental types of practical rationalism. The supreme artistic ideal of the Renaissance was 'rational' in the sense of a belief in a valid 'canon,' and the view of life of the Renaissance was rational in the sense of rejecting traditionalist bonds and of having faith in the power of the *naturalis ratio.* This type of rationalism prevailed in spite of certain elements of Platonizing mysticism.

'Rational' may also mean a 'systematic arrangement.' In this sense, the following methods are rational: methods of mortificatory or of magical asceticism, of contemplation in its most consistent forms—for instance, in *yoga*— or in the manipulations of the prayer machines of later Buddhism.

In general, all kinds of practical ethics that are systematically and unambiguously oriented to fixed goals of salvation are 'rational,' partly in the same sense as formal method is rational, and partly in the sense that they distinguish between 'valid' norms and what is empirically given. These types of rationalization processes are of interest to us in the following presentations. It would be senseless to try to anticipate the typologies of these presentations here, for they aim to make a contribution to such typology.

In order to make this attempt, the author must take the liberty of being 'unhistorical,' in the sense that the ethics of individual religions are presented systematically and essentially in greater unity than has ever been the case in the flux of their actual development. Rich contrasts which have been alive in individual religions, as well as incipient developments and ramifications, must be left aside; and the features that to the author are important must often be presented in greater logical consistency and less historical development than was actually the case. If it were done arbitrarily, this simplification would be a historical 'falsification.' This, however, is not the case, at least not intentionally. The author has always underscored those features in the total picture of a religion which have been decisive for the fashioning of the *practical* way of life, as well as those which distinguish one religion from another.

Finally, before going into the subject matter, some remarks by way of explaining terminological peculiarities which frequently recur in the presentation may be advanced. When fully developed, religious associations and communities belong to a type of corporate authority. They represent 'hierocratic' associations, that is, their power to rule is supported by their monopoly in the bestowal or denial of sacred values.

All ruling powers, profane and religious, political and apolitical, may be considered as variations of, or approximations to, certain pure types. These types are constructed by searching for the basis of *legitimacy,* which the ruling power claims. Our modern 'associations,' above all the political ones, are of the type of 'legal' authority. That is, the legitimacy of the power-holder to give commands rests upon rules that are rationally established by enactment, by agreement, or by imposition. The legitimation for establishing these rules rests, in turn, upon a rationally enacted or interpreted 'constitution.' Orders are given in the name of the impersonal norm, rather than in the name of a personal authority; and even the giving of a command constitutes obedience toward a norm rather than an arbitrary freedom, favour, or privilege.

The 'official' is the holder of the power to command; he never exercises this power in his own right; he holds it as a trustee of the impersonal and 'compulsory institution.' This institution is made up of the specific patterns of life of a plurality of men, definite or indefinite, yet specified according to rules. Their joint pattern of life is normatively governed by statutory regulations.

The 'area of jurisdiction' is a functionally delimited realm of possible objects for command and thus delimits the sphere of the official's legitimate power. A hierarchy of superiors, to which officials may appeal and complain in an order of rank, stands opposite the citizen or member of the association. Today this situation also holds for the hierocratic association that is the church. The pastor or priest has his definitely limited 'jurisdiction,' which is fixed by rules. This also holds for the supreme head of the church. The present concept of [papal] 'infallibility' is a jurisdictional concept. Its inner meaning differs from that which preceded it, even up to the time of Innocent III.

The separation of the 'private sphere' from the 'official sphere' (in the case of infallibility: the *ex cathedra* definition) is carried through in the church in the same way as in political, or other, officialdoms. The legal separation of the official from the means of administration (either in natural or in pecuniary form) is carried through in the sphere of political and hierocratic associations in the same way as is the separation of the worker from the means of production in capitalist economy: it runs fully parallel to them.

No matter how many beginnings may be found in the remote past, in its full development all this is specifically modern. The past has known other bases for authority, bases which, incidentally, extend as survivals into the present. Here we wish merely to outline these bases of authority in a terminological way.

In the following discussions the term 'charisma' shall be understood to refer to an *extraordinary* quality of a person, regardless of whether this quality is actual, alleged, or presumed. 'Charismatic authority,' hence, shall refer to a rule over men, whether predominantly external or predominantly internal, to which the governed submit because of their belief in the extraordinary quality of the specific *person*. The magical sorcerer, the prophet, the leader of hunting and booty expeditions, the warrior chieftain, the so-called 'Caesarist' ruler, and, under certain conditions, the personal head of a party are such types of rulers for their disciples, followings, enlisted troops, parties, et cetera. The legitimacy of their rule rests on the belief in and the devotion to the extraordinary, which is valued because it goes beyond the normal human qualities, and which was originally valued as supernatural. The legitimacy of charismatic rule thus rests upon the belief in magical powers, revelations and hero worship. The source of these beliefs is the 'proving' of the charismatic quality through miracles, through victories and other successes, that is, through the welfare of the governed. Such beliefs and the claimed authority resting on them therefore disappear, or threaten to disappear, as soon as proof is lacking and as soon as the charismatically qualified person appears to be devoid of his magical power or forsaken by his god. Charismatic rule is not managed according to general norms, either traditional or rational, but, in principle, according to concrete revelations and inspirations, and in this sense, charismatic authority is 'irrational.' It is 'revolutionary' in the sense of not being bound to the existing order: 'It is written— but I say unto you... !'

'Traditionalism' in the following discussions shall refer to the psychic attitude-set for the habitual workaday and to the belief in the everyday routine as an inviolable norm of conduct. Domination that rests upon this basis, that is, upon piety for what actually, allegedly, or presumably has always existed, will be called 'traditionalist authority.'

Patriarchalism is by far the most important type of domination the legitimacy of which rests upon tradition. Patriarchalism means the authority of the father, the husband, the senior of the house, the sib elder over the members of the household and sib; the rule of the master and patron over bondsmen, serfs, freed men; of the lord over the domestic servants and household officials; of the prince over house-and court-officials, nobles of office, clients, vassals; of the patrimonial lord and sovereign prince *(Landesvater)* over the 'subjects.'

It is characteristic of patriarchal and of patrimonial authority, which represents a variety of the former, that the system of inviolable norms is considered sacred; an infraction of them would result in magical or religious evils. Side by side with this system there is a realm of free arbitrariness and favour of the lord, who in principle judges only in terms of 'personal,' not 'functional,' relations. In this sense, traditionalist authority is irrational.

Throughout early history, charismatic authority, which rests upon a belief in the sanctity or the value of the extraordinary, and traditionalist (patriarchal) domination, which rests upon a belief in the sanctity of everyday routines, divided the most important authoritative relations between them. The bearers of charisma, the oracles of prophets, or the edicts of charismatic war lords alone could integrate 'new' laws into the circle of what was upheld by tradition. Just as revelation and the sword were the two extraordinary powers, so were they the two typical innovators. In typical fashion, however, both succumbed to routinization as soon as their work was done.

With the death of the prophet or the war lord the question of successorship arises. This question can be solved by nomination which was originally not an 'election' but a selection in terms of charismatic qualification; or the question can be solved by the sacramental substantiation of charisma, the successor being designated by consecration, as is the case in hierocratic or apostolic succession; or the belief in the charismatic qualification of the charismatic leader's sib can lead to a belief in hereditary charisma, as represented by hereditary kingship and hereditary hierocracy. With these routinizations, *rules* in some form always come to govern. The prince or the hierocrat no longer rules by virtue of purely personal qualities, but by virtue of acquired or inherited qualities, or because he has been legitimized by an act of charismatic election. The process of routinization, and thus traditionalization, has set in.

Perhaps it is even more important that when the organization of authority becomes permanent, the staff supporting the charismatic ruler becomes routinized. The ruler's disciples, apostles, and followers became priests, feudal vassals and, above all, officials. The original charismatic community lived communistically off donations, alms, and the booty of war: they were thus specifically alienated from the economic order. The community was transformed into a stratum of aids to the ruler and depended upon him for maintenance through the usufruct of land, office fees, income in kind, salaries, and hence, through prebends. The staff derived its legitimate power in greatly varying stages of appropriation, infeudation, conferment, and appointment. As a rule, this meant that princely prerogatives became *patrimonial* in nature. Patrimonialism can also develop from pure patriarchalism through the disintegration of the patriarchal master's strict authority. By virtue of conferment, the prebendary or the vassal has as a rule had a personal *right* to the office bestowed upon him. Like the artisan who possessed the economic means of production, the prebendary possessed the means of administration. He had to bear the costs of administration out of his office fees or other income, or he passed on to the lord only part of the taxes gathered from the subjects, retaining the rest. In the extreme case he could bequeath and alienate his office like other possession. We wish to speak of *status* patrimonialism when the development by appropriation of prerogatory power has reached this stage, without regard to whether it developed from charismatic or patriarchal beginnings.

The development, however, has seldom stopped at this stage. We always meet with a *struggle* between the political or hierocratic lord and the owners or usurpers of prerogatives, which they have appropriated as status groups. The ruler attempts to expropriate the estates, and the estates attempt to expropriate the ruler. The more the ruler succeeds in attaching to himself a staff of officials who depend solely on him and whose interests are linked to his, the more this struggle is decided in favour of the ruler and the more the privilege-holding estates are gradually expropriated. In this connection, the prince acquires administrative means of his own and he keeps them firmly in his own hands. Thus we find political rulers in the Occident, and progressively from Innocent III to Johann XXII, also hierocratic rulers who have finances of their own, as well as secular rulers who have magazines and arsenals of their own for the provisioning of the army and the officials.

The *character* of the stratum of officials upon whose support the ruler has relied in the struggle for the expropriation of status prerogatives has varied greatly in history. In Asia and in the Occident during the early Middle Ages they were typically clerics; during the Oriental Middle Ages they were typically slaves and clients; for the Roman Principate, freed slaves to a limited extent were typical; humanist literati were typical for

China; and finally, jurists have been typical for the modern Occident, in ecclesiastical as well as in political associations.

The triumph of princely power and the expropriation of particular prerogatives has everywhere signified at least the possibility, and often the actual introduction, of a rational administration. As we shall see, however, this rationalization has varied greatly in extent and meaning. One must, above all, distinguish between the *substantive* rationalization of administration and of judiciary by a patrimonial prince, and the *formal* rationalization carried out by trained jurists. The former bestows utilitarian and social ethical blessings upon his subjects, in the manner of the master of a large house upon the members of his household. The trained jurists have carried out the rule of general laws applying to all 'citizens of the state.' However fluid the difference has been—for instance, in Babylon or Byzantium, in the Sicily of the Hohenstaufen, or the England of the Stuarts, or the France of the Bourbons—in the final analysis, the difference between substantive and formal rationality has persisted. And, in the main, it has been the work of *jurists* to give birth to the modern Occidental 'state' as well as to the Occidental 'churches.' We shall not discuss at this point the source of their strength, the substantive ideas, and the technical means for this work.

With the triumph of *formalist* juristic rationalism, the legal type of domination appeared in the Occident at the side of the transmitted types of domination. Bureaucratic rule was not and is not the only variety of legal authority, but it is the purest. The modern state and municipal official, the modern Catholic priest and chaplain, the officials and employees of modern banks and of large capitalist enterprises represent, as we have already mentioned, the most important types of this structure of domination.

The following characteristic must be considered decisive for our terminology: in legal authority, submission does not rest upon the belief and devotion to charismatically gifted persons, like prophets and heroes, or upon sacred tradition, or upon piety toward a personal lord and master who is defined by an ordered tradition, or upon piety toward the possible incumbents of office fiefs and office prebends who are legitimized in their own right through privilege and conferment. Rather, submission under legal authority is based upon an *impersonal* bond to the generally defined and functional 'duty of office.' The official duty—like the corresponding right to exercise authority: the 'jurisdictional competency'—is fixed by *rationally established* norms, by enactments, decrees, and regulations, in such a manner that the legitimacy of the authority becomes the legality of the general rule, which is purposely thought out, enacted, and announced with formal correctness.

The differences between the types of authority we have sketched pertain to all particulars of their social structure and of their economic significance. Only a systematic presentation could demonstrate how far the distinctions and terminology chosen here are expedient. Here we may emphasize merely that by approaching in this way, we do not claim to use the only possible approach nor do we claim that all empirical structures of domination must correspond to one of these 'pure' types. On the contrary, the great majority of empirical cases represent a combination or a state of transition among several such pure types. We shall be compelled again and again to form expressions like 'patrimonial bureaucracy' in order to make the point that the characteristic traits of the respective phenomenon belong in part to the rational form of domination, whereas other traits belong to a traditionalist form of domination, in this case to that of estates. We also recognize highly important forms that have been universally diffused throughout history, such as the feudal structure of domination. Important aspects of these structures, however, cannot be classified smoothly under any one of the three forms we have distinguished. They can be understood only as combinations involving several concepts, in this case the concepts of 'status group' and 'status honour.' There are also forms that have to be understood partly in terms of principles other than those of 'domination,' partly in terms of peculiar variations of the concept of charisma. Examples are: the functionaries of *pure* democracy with rotations of honorific offices and similar forms, on the one hand, and plebiscitarian domination, on the other hand, or certain forms of notable rule that are special forms of traditional domination.

Such forms, however, have certainly belonged to the most important ferments for the delivery of political rationalism. By the terminology suggested here, we do not wish to force schematically the infinite and multifarious historical life, but simply to create concepts useful for special purposes and for orientation. The same qualifications hold for a final terminological distinction. We understand by 'status' the probability that certain social groups receive positive or negative social *honour*. The chances of attaining social honour are primarily determined by differences in the *styles of life* of these groups, hence chiefly by differences of *education*. Referring to the preceding terminology of forms of authority, we may say that, secondarily, social honour very frequently and typically is associated with the respective status group's legally guaranteed and monopolized claim to sovereign rights or to income and profit opportunities of a certain kind. Thus, if all these characteristics are found, which, of course, is not always the case, a 'status group' is a social group through its special styles of life, its conventional and specific notions of honour, and the economic opportunities it legally monopolizes. A status relationship is always somehow a social group, but it is not always organized into an association. Social intercourse and marriage among status groups are the typical characteristics of the *mutual esteem* among status equals; their absence signifies status differences.

By 'class,' in contrast, we shall understand the opportunities to gain sustenance and income that are primarily determined by typical, *economically* relevant, situations; property of a certain kind, or acquired skill in the execution of services that are in demand, is decisive for income opportunities. 'Class' also comprises the ensuing general and typical living conditions, for instance, the necessity of complying with the discipline of a capitalist proprietor's workshop.

A 'status' can be the cause as well as the result of a 'class relationship,' but it need be neither. Class relationship, in turn, can be primarily *determined by markets*, by the labour market and the commodity market. The specific and typical cases of class relationship today are ones determined by markets. But such is not necessarily the case: class relationship of landlord and small peasant may depend upon market relations only in a negligible way. In their differing relationship, the various categories of 'rentiers' depend on the market in greatly varying senses and extents, according to whether they derive their rents as landlords, slave-holders, or as owners of bonds and effects.

One must therefore distinguish between 'propertied classes' and primarily market-determined 'income classes.' Present-day society is predominantly stratified in classes, and to an especially high degree in income classes. But in the special *status* prestige of the 'educated' group, our society contains a very tangible element of status relationship. Externally, this status relationship is most obviously represented by economic monopolies and the preferential social opportunities of the holders of degrees.

In the past the significance of status groups was far more decisive, above all, for the economic structure of the societies. For, on the one hand, status stratification influences the economic structure by barriers or regulations of consumption, and by status monopolies which from the viewpoint of economic rationality are irrational, and on the other hand, status stratification influences the economy very strongly through carrying the status *conventions* of the respective ruling group who set the example. These conventions may be in the nature of *ritualist* stereotyped forms, which to a large extent has been the case with the status stratification of Asia.

MAX WEBER AND WORLD RELIGION

Durkheim based his arguments on a very small range of examples even though he claimed that his ideas apply to religion in general. Max Weber by contrast embarked on a massive study of religions world wide. Weber made detailed studies of Hinduism, Buddhism, Taoism and ancient Judaism and in The Protestant Ethic and the Spirit of Capitalism wrote extensively about the impact of Christianity on the history of the west. Weber concentrated on a connection between religion and social change something to which Durkheim gave little attention. Unlike Marx Weber argues that religion is not necessarily a conservative force on the contrary religiously inspired movements have produced dramatic social transformation. Protestantism particularly Puritanism was the source of capitalist outlook found in the modern west.

The early entrepreneurs were mostly Calvinists. Their drive to succeed which helped initiate western economic development was originally prompted by a desire to serve God. Material success was for them a sign of divine favour. Analysing the eastern religions Weber concludes that they provided inseparable barriers to the development of industrial capitalism of the kind that took place in the west. For example Hinduism is what Weber calls an 'other-worldly' religion that is its highest value stress escape from the toils of the material world to a higher plane of spiritual existence.

Max Weber and World Religion

Durkheim based his arguments on a very small range of examples even though he claimed that his ideas apply to religion in general. Max Weber by contrast embarked on a massive study of religions world wide. Weber made detailed studies of Hinduism, Buddhism, Taoism and ancient Judaism and in The Protestant Ethic and the Spirit of Capitalism wrote extensively about the impact of Christianity on the history of the west. Weber concentrated on a connection between religion and social change something to which Durkheim gave little attention. Unlike Marx Weber argues that religion is not necessarily a conservative force on the contrary religiously inspired movements have produced dramatic social transformation. Protestantism particularly Puritanism was the source of capitalist outlook found in the modern west.

The early entrepreneurs were mostly Calvinists. Their drive to succeed which helped initiate western economic development was originally prompted by a desire to serve God. Material success was for them a sign of divine favour. Analysing the eastern religions Weber concludes that they provided inseparable barriers to the development of industrial capitalism of the kind that took place in the west. For example Hinduism is what Weber calls an 'other-worldly' religion that is its highest value stress escape from the toils of the material world to a higher plane of spiritual existence.

Social Functions and Dysfunctions of Religion

Social scientists have analysed religion in terms of what it does for the individual, community or society through its functions and dysfunctions. Many of these social scientists are known to belong to the tradition of functionalist thought. A famous social anthropologist of early twentieth century, Malinowski, saw religion and magic as assisting the individual to cope with situations of stress or anxiety. Religious ritual, according to him, may enable the bereaved to reassert their collective solidarity, to express their common norms and values upon which the proper functioning of the community depends. Religion can also supplement practical, empirical knowledge, offering some sense of understanding and control in areas to which such knowledge does not extent.

A more influential tradition of functionalist thought on religion derives from Durkheim, whose Elementary Forms of the Religious Life presents a theory of religion identifying religion with social cohesion: religious beliefs and rituals are understood in terms of the role they play in promoting and maintaining social solidarity. Radcliffe-Brown argues that religious ceremonies, for example in the form of communal dancing, promoted unity and harmony and functioned to enhance social solidarity and the survival of the society. Religious beliefs contained in myths and legends, he observes, express the social values of the different objects which have a major influence on social life such as food, weapons, day and night etc. They form the value consensus around which society is integrated.

Recent functionalism while retaining his notion that religion has a central role in maintaining social solidarity has rejected Durkheim's view that religious beliefs are merely symbolic representations of society. Kingsley Davis argues that religious beliefs form the basis for socially valued goals and a justification of them. Religion provides a common focus for identity and an unlimited source of rewards and punishments for behaviour. Functionalist theories of religion face a problem in the apparent decline in religious belief and participation. What is viewed as secularization in other theories is seen as simply religious change in functionalist terms. Functionalist theorists argue that religion takes different forms in apparently secular societies: it is more individualized, less tied to religious institutions. The character of modern industrial capitalist society, particularly its rampant individualism, is thus seen to be expressed in the differentiated character of religion in a society like the USA. Although seemingly having little basis for integration, the celebration of individualism is itself an integrating feature of such diverse religious forms. Moreover, new and distinctive forms of religion may perform latent functions for the system by deflecting adherents from critical appraisal of their society and its distribution of rewards.

In anti-religious societies such as some communist States this argument cannot hold, but here it is claimed that functional alternatives to traditional religion operate. Other systems of belief such as communism itself fulfil the same role as religion elsewhere. National ceremonial, ritual celebration of communist victories, heroes, etc., meets the same need for collective rites, which reaffirm common sentiments and promote enhanced commitment to common goals. Finally, even in highly secularized Western societies civil religion exists. This consists in abstract beliefs and rituals, which relate society to ultimate things and provide a rationale for national history, a transcendental basis for national goals and purposes. Robert King Merton, a twentieth century functionalist, introduced the concept of dysfunction. Talking about religion, for instance, he pointed out the dysfunctional features of religion in a multi-religious society. In such a society religion, instead of bringing about solidarity, could become the cause of disorganization and disunity.

Apart from Merton, many other social thinkers have highlighted the dysfunctions of religion. Marx regarded religion as a source of false consciousness among the proletariat, which prevents the 'class for itself' from developing. It prevents them from developing their real powers and potentialities

Sect and Cult

The classification of churches or religious groups into cults, sects, denominations and ecclesias indicates different methods of relating to the society. The chief feature of a religious sect is that it is a voluntary association. A sect is a small religious group that has branched off of a larger established religion. Sects have many beliefs and practices in common with the religion that they have broken off from, but are differentiated by a number of doctrinal differences.

The word sect comes from the latin secta, meaning an organized religious body or organization, from Latin, meaning a course of action or way of life. Sociologists use the word sect to refer to a religious group with a high degree of tension with the surrounding society, but whose beliefs are (within the context of that society) largely traditional. A sect seeks to impose a rigid pattern of ideal conduct on its members but seeks toleration rather than change from the larger society.

Sects are concerned with purity of doctrine and with the depth of genuineness of religions feeling. As a result, demands are made upon the member to be an active participant, even a leader or missionary, as a warrant of his faith. The emphasis on purity of belief tends to create intolerance toward other groups and moves the sect toward critical assessment of the secular world in accordance with the ideals of the gospel. A cult, by contrast, also has a high degree of tension with the surrounding society, but its beliefs are (within the context of that society) new and innovative. It may seek to transform society but more often concentrate upon creating satisfying group experience.

The denomination is a major religious group which hopes that a separation of church and state will enable it to be influential even though not dominant. The ecclesia is a church claiming to be the spiritual expression of the total society.

PLURALISTIC RELIGION

Religious pluralism is the belief that one can overcome religious differences between different religions and denominational conflicts within the same religion. For most religious traditions, religious pluralism is essentially based on a non-literal view of one's religious traditions, hence allowing for respect to be engendered between different traditions on core principles rather than more marginal issues. It is perhaps summarized as an attitude, which rejects focus on immaterial differences, and instead gives respect to those beliefs held in common.

The existence of religious pluralism depends on the existence of freedom of religion. Freedom of religion is when different religions of a particular region possess the same rights of worship and public expression. Freedom of religion is consequently weakened when one religion is given rights or privileges denied to others, as in certain European countries where Roman Catholicism or regional forms of Protestantism have special status. Religious freedom has not existed at all in some communist countries where the state restricts or prevents the public expression of religious belief and may even actively persecute individual religions.

Religious pluralism has existed in the Indian Subcontinent since the rise of Buddhism around 500 BC and has widened in the course of several Muslim settlements (Delhi Sultanate 1276-1526 AD and the Mughal Empire 1526-1857 AD). In the 8th century, Zoroastrianism established in India as Zoroastrians fled from Persia to India in large numbers, where they were given refuge. The colonial phase ushered in by the British lasted until 1947 and furthered conversions to Christianity among low caste Hindus. The rise of religious pluralism in the modern West is closely associated with the Reformation and the Enlightenment.

Religions like Judaism and Islam had existed alongside Christianity in many parts of Europe, but they were not allowed the same freedoms as the established form of Christianity. Freedom of religion encompasses all religions acting within the law in a particular region, whether or not an individual religion accepts that other religions are legitimate or that freedom of religious choice and religious plurality in general are good things.

MONISTIC RELIGION

Monism is the metaphysical view that all is of one essential essence, substance or energy. Monism is to be distinguished from dualism, which holds that ultimately there are two kinds of substance, and from pluralism, which holds that ultimately there are many kinds of substance. Monism is often seen in relation to pantheism, panentheism, and an immanent God. Monism is often seen as partitioned into three different kinds:

1. Physicalism or materialism, which holds that only the physical is real, and that the mental can be reduced to the physical
2. Idealism or phenomenalism, which holds the converse
3. Neutral monism, which holds that both the mental and the physical can be reduced to some sort of third substance, or energy.

Functionalism, like materialism, holds that the mental can ultimately be reduced to the physical, but also holds that all critical aspects of the mind are also reducible to some substrate-neutral "functional" level. Thus something need not be made out of neurons to have mental states. This is a popular stance in cognitive science and artificial intelligence. Eliminativism, which holds that talk of the mental will eventually be proved as unscientific and completely discarded.

Just as we no longer follow the ancient Greeks in saying that all matter is composed of earth, air, water, and fire, people of the future will no longer speak of "beliefs", "desires", and other mental states. A subcategory of eliminativism is radical behaviourism, a view held by B. F. Skinner.) Anomalous monism, a position proposed by Donald Davidson in the 1970s as a way to resolve the Mind-body problem. It could be considered (by the above definitions) either physicalism or neutral monism.

Davidson holds that here is only physical matter, but that all mental objects and events are perfectly real and are identical with (some) physical matter.

But physicalism retains a certain priority, inasmuch as:

1. All mental things are physical, but not all physical things are mental
2. (As John Haugeland puts it) Once you take away all the atoms, there's nothing left.

This monism was widely considered an advance over previous identity theories of mind and body, because it does not entail that one must be able to provide an actual method for redescribing any particular kind of mental entity in purely physical terms.

For some, monism may also have religious/spiritual implications. Recognizing this, some inveigh against the 'dangers of monism, ' asserting that in order to resolve all things to a single substrate, one dissolves God in the process.

Others say that the "single substrate is God. Theological arguments can be made for this within Christianity for example the Roman Catholic doctrine of "divine simplicity", as well as in many other religions (Hinduism, Ayyavazhi and Judaism in particular). Historically, monism has been promoted in spiritual terms on several occasions, notably by Ernst Haeckel. To the dismay of most modern observers, Haeckel's various ideas often had components of social darwinism and scientific racism.

RELIGION AND SCIENCE

There are two major opinions regarding the relatioship between science and religion. Religion and science are mutually conflicting and Religion and science are not mutually opposing-

The View that Religion and Science are Mutually Conflicting

Religion is based on faith and rituals whereas science depends on observations experiments, verifications, proofs and facts. Ritualism, religious fundamentalism and fanaticism rooted in religion are very much opposed to science. According to Kingsley Davis there are two important causes for the conflict between religion and science. Science deals with the known or the empirical world. Religion is concerned with the unknown or supernatural world.

Science could not give an account of the origin of man earlier so religion filled in the gap by giving its own account of that. Later with its progress science too could give a satisfactory explanation of that. Here a conflict rose between the two as the scientist could not accept the religious account as true even though he lived among the people who believed in religious explanation. This situation created tension between him and the ordinary people or the religious leader. The second cause of conflict is that science believes in empirical truth whereas religion pursues the nonempirical truth: Davis writes the scientific pursuit of empirical truth as the highest goal is exactly the opposite of religious pursuit of nonempirical truth. Thus the scientist develops his scepticism about religious beliefs and explanations concerning creation of heaven and hell, life after death, miracles etc.

The View that Religion and Science are not Mutually Opposing

Viewed analytically science and religion need not be at conflict. Science deals with what is known. It is potential knowledge based on sensory evidences. Religious beliefs refer to the world beyond the senses. If they cannot be proved by the methods of science they cannot be disproved also. It is wrong to say that religion is based on emotion and science on thought. Infact both are based on thought though this is applied to different types of reality.

According to K. Davis it is possible for a scientist to have belief in God and still work as a good biologist or a physicist. His and his behaviour in church appropriate to religious situation with no feeling of incongruity. Even the attitude of scientist towards religion has not been that of a hostile one. Scientific truth is that which is known by the evidence of the senses. Religious truth is that which is known by revelations, by faith. An attempt to reconcile the two can promote mutual respect across the barrier. Any reconciliation which attempts to combine them can only undermine both. Religion is a social reality.

The persistence of religion throughout the ages proofs its survival value. It is rendering services to the humanity. Scientific investigators agree that religion like other institutions has its roots in certain human needs. Hence it was felt to be a necessity and continues to be a necessary thing.

Magic

The phenomenon of magic is closely associated with religion. Magic is often regarded as a form of religion. However they are different. They represent two aspects of the same –empirical power. Max Weber used the term magic to refer to religious action believed to be automatically effective, whether the goal is empirical or non-empirical. Malinowski defines magic as the use of supernatural means to try to obtain empirical ends. He however distinguished magic and religion.

British anthropologist James Frazer in his Golden Bough has spoken of two aspects of magic: Magic by imitation and Magic by contagion. In magic by imitation an individual imitates what he wants or expects to happen. If an individual wants rainfall to take place he may fill his mouth with water and squirt it around in different directions. Magic by contagion is based on the belief that whatever would come into contact with the supernatural power will be swayed by it. Thus the forehead of a person may be rubbed off with some ashes so that he may be free from headaches.

Magic and Science

Magic is often called a type of primitive science. This view is based on some analogies. Magic like science pursues practical ends, conceives that certain effects follow certain causes takes an impersonal attitude towards causation and has little to do with morality. Inspite of this magic is in many ways opposite of science. Magic relies on supernatural causation. It unscientifically believes that some effect is produced because of the mystical power associated with the spell, rite or object.

In magic the facts are not used to test the theory as in science. On the other hand the theory that is the magical procedure is always assumed to be right. Here the elements of faith and wishful thinking enter. A failure in magical performances is therefore attributed to a failure to carry out the procedures correctly and not to the procedure itself. The function of magic is to give confidence and a sense of security. For this reason the individual must have a non-rational faith in its adequacy.

Hence it can exist side by side with perfectly good scientific and technological practices. Magic deals in absolutes whereas science deals in probabilities. Science is tentative and K. Davis says magic may become less important but it is not going to disappear as technology and science advance.

WEBER'S: SOCIOLOGY OF RELIGION

Weber's work in the field of sociology of religion started with the essay *The Protestant Ethic and the Spirit of Capitalism*, which grew out of heavy "field work" among Protestant sects in America, and continued with the analysis of *The Religion of China: Confucianism and Taoism*, *The Religion of India: The Sociology of Hinduism and Buddhism*, and *Ancient Judaism*. His work on other religions was interrupted by his sudden death in 1920, which prevented him from following *Ancient Judaism* with studies of Psalms, Book of Jacob, Talmudic Jewry, early Christianity and Islam. His three main themes were the effect of religious ideas on economic activities, the relation between social stratification and religious ideas, and the distinguishable characteristics of Western civilization.

His goal was to find reasons for the different development paths of the cultures of the Occident and the Orient, although without judging or valuing them, like some of the contemporary thinkers who followed the social Darwinist paradigm; Weber wanted primarily to explain the distinctive elements of the Western civilization. In the analysis of his findings, Weber maintained that Calvinist (and more widely, Protestant) religious ideas had a major impact on the social innovation and development of the economic system of Europe and the United States, but noted that they were not the only factors in this development. Other notable factors mentioned by Weber included the rationalism of scientific pursuit, merging observation with mathematics, science of scholarship and jurisprudence, rational systematization of government administration, and economic enterprise. In the end, the study of the sociology of religion, according to Weber, focused on one distinguishing part of the Western culture, the decline of beliefs in magic, or what he referred to as "disenchantment of the world".

The Protestant Ethic and the Spirit of Capitalism

Weber's essay *The Protestant Ethic and the Spirit of*

Capitalism (*Die protestantische Ethik und der Geist des Kapitalismus*) is his most famous work. It is argued that this work should not be viewed as a detailed study of Protestantism, but rather as an introduction into Weber's later works, especially his studies of interaction between various religious ideas and economic behaviour. In *The Protestant Ethic and the Spirit of Capitalism*, Weber put forward the thesis that Calvinist ethic and ideas influenced the development of capitalism. He noted the shift of Europe's economic centre after the Reformation away from Catholic countries such as France, Spain and Italy, and toward Protestant countries such as the Netherlands, England, Scotland and Germany. Weber also noted that societies having more Protestants were those that have a more developed capitalist economy. Christian religious devotion had historically been accompanied by rejection of mundane affairs, including economic pursuit. Weber showed that certain types of Protestantism – notably Calvinism – were supportive of rational pursuit of economic gain and worldly activities dedicated to it, seeing them as endowed with moral and spiritual significance. Weber argued that there were many reasons to look for the origins of modern capitalism in the religious ideas of the Reformation. This theory is often viewed as a reversal of Marx's thesis that the economic "base" of society determines all other aspects of it.

Weber abandoned research into Protestantism because his colleague Ernst Troeltsch, a professional theologian, had begun work on the book *The Social Teachings of the Christian Churches and Sects*. Another reason for Weber's decision was that Troeltsch's work already achieved what he desired in that area, which is laying groundwork for comparative analysis of religion and society. The phrase "work ethic" used in modern commentary is a derivative of the "Protestant ethic" discussed by Weber. It was adopted when the idea of the Protestant ethic was generalised to apply to the Japanese people, Jews and other non-Christians.

Confucianism and Taoism

The Religion of China: Confucianism and Taoism was Weber's second major work on the sociology of religion. Weber focused on those aspects of Chinese society that were different from those of Western Europe and especially contrasted with Puritanism, and posed a question why capitalism did not develop in China.

He focused on the issues of Chinese urban development, Chinese patrimonialism and officialdom, and Chinese religion, as the areas in which Chinese development differed most distinctively from the European route.

According to Weber, Confucianism and Puritanism are mutually exclusive types of rational thought, each attempting to prescribe a way of life based on religious dogma. Notably, they both valued self control and restraint, and did not oppose accumulation of wealth. However, to both those qualities where just means to the final goal, and here they were divided by a key difference.

The Confucianism goal was "a cultured status position", while Puritanism's goal was to create individuals who are "tools of God". The intensity of belief and enthusiasm for action were rare in Confucianism, but common in Protestantism. Therefore, Weber states that it was this difference in social attitudes and mentality, shaped by the respective, dominant religions, that contributed to the development of capitalism in the West and the absence of it in China.

The Sociology of Hinduism and Buddhism

The Religion of India: The Sociology of Hinduism and Buddhism was Weber's third major work on the sociology of religion. In this work he deals with the structure of Indian society, with the orthodox doctrines of Hinduism and the heterodox doctrines of Buddhism, with modifications brought by the influence of popular religiosity, and finally with the impact of religious beliefs on the secular ethic of Indian society.

Weber ended his research of society and religion in India by bringing in insights from his previous work on China to discuss similarities of the Asian belief systems. He notes that the beliefs saw the meaning of life as otherwoldy mystical experience. The social world is fundamentally divided between the educated elite, following the guidance of a prophet or wise man, and the uneducated masses whose believes are centred on magic. In Asia, there was no Messianic prophecy to *plan and meaning to the everyday life of educated and uneducated alike.* Weber juxtaposed such Messianic prophecies, notably from the Near East region to those found on the Asiatic mainland, focusing more on exemplary ways to live one's life. It was those differences that prevented the countries of the Occident from following the paths of the earlier Chinese and Indian civilizations. His next work, Ancient Judaism was an attempt to prove this theory.

Ancient Judaism

In *Ancient Judaism*, his fourth major work on the sociology of religion, Weber attempted to explain the factors which resulted in the early differences between Oriental and Occidental religiosity. It is especially visible when the innerworldly asceticism developed by Western Christianity is contrasted with mystical contemplation of the kind developed in India. Weber noted that some aspects of Christianity sought to conquer and change the world, rather than withdraw from its imperfections. This fundamental characteristic of Christianity (when compared to Far Eastern religions) stems originally from ancient Jewish prophecy.

Weber notes that Judaism not only fathered Christianity and Islam, but was crucial to the rise of modern Occident state, as its influence were as important to those of Hellenistic and Roman cultures.

Weber's premature death in 1920 prevented him from following Ancient Judaism with his planned analysis of Psalms, Book of Jacob, Talmudic Jewry, early Christianity and Islam.

6

The Neo-Marxist Synthesis of Marx and Weber on Class

STRUCTURE VERSUS ACTION

One of the most fundamental differences between classical Marxist and Weberian theory is the different importance they assign to human agency in the explanation of social phenomena. In the analysis of social class, as in other areas, Marxist theory places much greater causal weight on the functioning of objective structures that constrain human behaviour in predictable channels. Such structures are viewed as being imbued with a substantial capacity for self-reproduction, but also as giving rise to developmental tendencies that, in the long run, are contradictory.

The most important such structure is the "mode of production," which Marx conceives as a historically specific complex of social relations through which human societies collectively produce their material means of existence. Social classes are defined in relation to the mode of production as an objective structure of positions, related to one another in terms of the production and appropriation of a surplus product. Marxists often speak of class as a structure of "empty places," in the sense that class positions entail material interests, capacities, and constraints that exist objectively and independently of the particular persons who occupy those positions and that condition their behaviour. In this manner, Marxist class theory abstracts from the consciousness or motives of concrete human agents to the logic of the supraindividual structure.

By comparison, Weberian theory assigns a much greater causal importance to human agency. Supraindividual structures are either rejected as legitimate explanatory concepts on the basis of a commitment to methodological individualism, or treated as merely the provisional outcome of contingently reproduced patterns of social action. In Weberian theory, classes are not the effect of an objective structure, such as the mode of production, but an outcome of the motivated behaviour of knowledgeable human actors. More specifically, classes are identified with a particular form of social action—namely, action that, from the standpoint of its subjective meaning, seeks to restrict access to valued resources with an orientation to maximizing their return on the market. The nature and effects of social classes therefore cannot be deduced from the logic of the mode of production, but must be studied in terms of the meaning systems implicated in social action. At the risk of oversimplification, this difference between Marxist and Weberian theory can be viewed as a disagreement over the possible and appropriate forms of abstraction in social theory, with Marxists defending a higher level of abstraction (and a different form of causality) than Weberians are willing to accept. Marxists would not necessarily claim that there is nothing to be gained in studying social classes from the standpoint of social action, but would argue that restricting the analysis solely to this level precludes an understanding of the underlying causal forces, thereby producing an exaggerated impression of the indeterminacy of social phenomena. Weberians, on the other hand, believe that Marxist theory promises more than it can possibly deliver and thus that it will be forever caught up in a fruitless process of seeking to impose objective patterns on what are, in fact, only the diverse and contingent outcomes of human agency.

Weberian critiques of Marxism often take the structuralist aspect of Marxist theory as a reason for its rejection, arguing that Marxism gives insufficient attention to the role of conscious agency and volition in the shaping of social events. Indeed, two of the most influential recent Weberian critiques of Marxism—

Frank Parkin's *Marxism and Class Theory: A Bourgeois Critique* (1979) and Anthony Giddens' *A Contemporary Critique of Historical Materialism* (1981)—make this a central point in their indictment of Marxism. These authors make essentially two kinds of arguments. First, they maintain that the framing of Marxist explanations in terms of the logic of the mode of production constitutes a form of functionalism, which they reject on a variety of grounds: Functionalist explanations are teleological; they falsely impute "needs" to the social system; and so on. Second, they argue that Marxism reduces human actors to the passive "bearers" of social relations, lacking any knowledge or intentionality. This they claim is especially problematic for a theory, such as Marxism, that also purports to be a guide to political action.

Several things can be said about these criticisms. First, they ignore the extensive debate within Marxism during the last decade over the legitimacy of functionalist explanations. Although functionalist arguments can indeed be found in Marxist writings (Giddens cites the example of Marxists "explaining" unemployment in terms of capitalism's "need" for a reserve army of labour), I think it is fair to say that most contemporary Marxists would themselves find such explanations if not illegitimate then certainly incomplete. Much of recent Marxist theory and research can be seen as an attempt to go beyond simple functionalist arguments about the place of particular institutions or practices within capitalism to more specific explanations of the *mechanisms* by which those institutions or practices are created and reproduced. In some cases the intentionality of human actors is invoked to account for the functionality of a given institution, as for example in "instrumentalist" explanations of why the state functions in the interests of the capitalist class. Here the effectivity of the social structure operates primarily by conditioning the interests and capacities for action of contending social classes. In other instances the functional correspondence between certain institutions and the logic of capitalism is explained by selection mechanisms and feedback processes in which intentionality plays a much more restricted role, as in explanations of capitalist behaviour in terms of a natural selection model of competition between firms or explanations of state policy in terms of the constraints of business confidence. Structural explanations of this kind may be correct or incorrect, but they cannot simply be dismissed on logical grounds.

Second, such critiques ignore the variation in the extent and manner in which human agency is incorporated in contemporary Marxist theory. Although extreme structuralist versions of Marxism can be found (Althusser is the favorite target of Weberian critics), most substantive Marxist investigations ascribe a significant role to human agency in their explanation of social events. This is particularly true in the area of class analysis. At the one extreme, Marxists such as Thompson analyze social classes almost exclusively in terms of human agency. Consider, for example, Thompson's definition of class in his *The Making of the English Working Class.*

By class I understand an historical phenomenon, unifying a number of disparate and seemingly unconnected events, both in the raw material of experience and in consciousness. I emphasize that it is an *historical* phenomenon. I do not see class as a "structure", nor even as a "category", but as something which in fact happens (and can be shown to have happened) in human relationships.... Class is defined by men as they live their own history, and, in the end, this is its only definition. One could not ask for a stronger statement of the primacy of agency over structure in the formation of social classes.

Other Marxists place a more equal emphasis on objective structures and human agency, viewing the two as reciprocally conditioned by one another. A good example is Przeworski, who analyzes classes as the effect of concrete historical struggles that are conditioned by objective structures but also react back upon and transform those structures. In Przeworski's words, Classes must thus be viewed as effects of struggles structured by objective conditions that are simultaneously economic, political, and ideological.... Precisely because class formation is an effect of struggles, outcomes of this process are at each moment of history to some extent indeterminate. Thompson and Przeworski are perhaps exceptional among Marxist theorists in the importance they attribute to human agency, but even when Marxists ascribe a degree of primacy to structural factors this seldom means that human agency is omitted from their analysis. A survey of recent Marxist writings on class reveals a variety of ways in which human agency is incorporated within a broader structural framework. In the first, important aspects of class relations are seen as structurally *underdetermined* in the sense that objective structures merely impose a general directionality upon social development and/or constrain social patterns within certain limits, whereas the pace and concrete form of that development and/or the selection among possible outcomes is determined (through struggle) by human agency. A good example would be my own study of the variation in the size and composition of intermediate classes among advanced capitalist societies (Burris, 1980). There I analyze the structural basis of developmental trends that are common to all advanced capitalist societies (e.g., the growth of the new middle class), but I also emphasize the manner in which those trends vary among societies as a result of distinctive national patterns of class struggle.

A second approach treats certain aspects of class relations as structurally *overdetermined*—that is, as subject to multiple and contradictory determinations and therefore, to some extent, indeterminate. A good example is Wright's (1978a) conception of intermediate class positions as "contradictory class locations." In Wright's view, such positions as managers and professionals are "objectively torn between class locations" in the sense that they occupy contradictory positions on different dimensions of capitalist class relations. For this reason, Wright argues, their place in the class struggle is objectively indeterminate and therefore especially susceptible to political and ideological forces. According to a third view, the structural determination of class is *mediated* by human agency in ways that are more than epiphenomenal. A good example is the Ehrenreich's analysis of the formation of what they call the "PMC" or "professional-managerial class." The Ehrenreichs identify a number of structural tendencies that condition the formation of this class—notably, the growth and concentration of a social surplus in forms that allow it to be strategically used for the reproduction of capitalist class relations—but go on to argue that the institutional changes associated with the emergence of the PMC "do not simply 'develop,' they require the effort of more or less conscious agents". Like other Marxist instrumentalists, the Ehrenreichs view structural factors as important only insofar as they shape the interests and political resources of contending classes. Whether or how those resources are actually mobilized in the service of class interests can only be understood from the standpoint of an analysis of human agency. The focus of their research is therefore upon the historical process by which specific actors (mainly far-sighted capitalists and middle-class reformers) consciously engineered a transformation of the class structure.

Finally, even when it figures nowhere else in the analysis, human agency almost always assumes an important role in contemporary Marxist accounts of the process by which structurally defined classes are formed (or fail to be formed) into organized collectivities. Whereas classical Marxism treated this transition as relatively unproblematic, even inevitable, contemporary Marxists have tended to view it as much more indeterminate. Typical in this regard is Wright's statement of the relationship between class structure and what he calls "class formation" —that is, historically specific forms of class organization. The class structure itself does not generate a unique pattern of class formation; rather, it determines the underlying probabilities of different types of class formations. Which of these alternatives actually occurs will depend upon a range of factors that are structurally contingent to the class structure itself. Class structure thus remains the structural foundation for class formations, but it is only through the specific historical analysis of given societies that it is possible to explain what kind of actual formation is built upon that foundation.

Overall, it would appear that contemporary Marxists are by no means reluctant to incorporate human agency into their analysis of class, the exact mix between structure and agency to be decided by the nature of the topic under investigation. Their work may be criticized on many grounds. The precise relationship they envision between structure and agency is sometimes poorly or incompletely theorized. But, whatever their shortcomings, they cannot be accused of ignoring the role of human agency in social life.

By contrast, among the Weberian critics of Marxism one often encounters an a priori refusal to entertain any form of structural explanation. Whereas Weberian arguments for the importance of human agency served as a useful corrective to the more one-sided structuralist versions of Marxism, in relation to the greater part of contemporary Marxist theory it is the Weberian critics who appear onesided. This is particularly true of Parkin, who rejects any structural basis to class (such as property relations, bureaucratic authority, or the division of labour) and seeks to ground classes purely in the exclusionary endeavours of human actors. This leads to an entirely circular form of argument in which class relations are seen as providing the bases of power that are mobilized in exclusionary actions, which in turn produce social classes. Compared with Parkin, Giddens' theory of "structuration"—seeking as it does to combine both structure and agency within a single theoretical framework—is more consistent with the spirit of contemporary Marxism, even though, as critics have noted, his rather frail conception of social structure tends to collapse into his more robust conception of social action.

UNIDIMENSIONAL VERSUS MULTIDIMENSIONAL VIEWS

A second difference between the classical Marxist and Weberian theories of class concerns the relative importance of class as compared with other forms of oppression or other bases of association and struggle. For Marx class is the single most important division around which social groups organize and contend for political power. Class struggle is therefore the primary vehicle of epochal social change. For Weber, the importance of class divisions is historically variable and contingent. Class relations coexist with other forms of oppression and other bases of association that are independent of class and potentially no less important for the organization of particular societies or the transition between types of society.

Contemporary Weberian critics of Marxism have made the primacy of class one of the main targets of their critique.

Parkin, for example, begins his assault on Marxism with the assertion that "now that racial, ethnic, and religious conflicts have moved toward the centre of the political stage in many industrial societies, any general model of class or stratification that does not fully incorporate this fact must forfeit all credibility" (Parkin, 1979, p. 9). Giddens is more sympathetic to the Marxist view that class relations have a "centrality in the dynamics of power" within capitalist society, but denies that this was true of precapitalist society. He also criticizes Marxism for what he claims is its inability to accommodate nonclass forms of domination (e.g., national, ethnic, and sexual oppression) in anything other than a "class reductionist" way.

Although the primacy or otherwise of class remains a major point of disagreement between contemporary Marxists and Weberians, the distance between them on this issue is no longer as great as the above critiques imply. Most Marxists would continue to defend some notion of the primacy of class relations; nevertheless, the thrust of contemporary Marxism has been decidedly in the direction of a more multidimensional viewpoint. A brief survey of recent Marxist writings on race and gender will illustrate this point. In both instances contemporary Marxists have accorded a considerable degree of autonomy to nonclass forms of oppression. Disagreements remain as to the most appropriate way of conceptualizing these forms of oppression, their degree of autonomy, and the precise manner in which they are articulated with capitalist class relations, but few Marxists today would argue that such forms of oppression can be treated as a mere reflex of class relations. Among Marxist feminists there is by now a well-established tradition of analysing women's position as an interaction between two distinct but interconnected structures: capitalist class relations and patriarchal gender relations. Mitchell (1974) was among the first to elabourate such an analysis. In her view the distinctiveness of women's oppression is located in the formation of sexual identities that, following Althusser, she conceptualizes as an ideological process that is "relatively autonomous" of the production relations that define social classes. A more systematic presentation of this view is found in McDonough and Harrison's (1978) essay "Patriarchy and

Relations of Production." They argue that "women are placed simultaneously in two separate but linked structures, those of class and patriarchy." The former they conceptualize as a structure of exploitation based in the appropriation of surplus labour through the social relations of production; the latter is conceptualized as a separate structure based in the control of female sexuality and fertility through the "social relations of reproduction." The form of each of these structures varies historically, they argue, within the limits set by the influence of the other structure. This perspective is developed further by Barrett (1980), who makes the additional point that the articulation of patriarchal relations within the capitalist mode of production must be conceptualized as the outcome of structurally conditioned but historically contingent patterns of struggle that can never be reduced to a simple functional logic.

A similar trend toward a more multi-dimensional view can be found in recent Marxist writings on race and ethnicity. Indeed, many Marxists make a direct analogy between racial divisions and sexual divisions, arguing, as does Edwards (1979), that both of these divisions reflect historical processes that are distinct from those of capitalism as a mode of production. The histories of racism and sexism, intimately linked though they are to that of capitalism, are not subsets of the latter. Accordingly, the dynamics of racial and sexual divisions require separate analyses.

The same point is underlined by Wright in his discussion of the relation between race and class in the determination of income inequality. The underlying premise of a Marxist class analysis is that, while the diverse dimensions of social inequality cannot be reduced to class inequality, class relations nevertheless play a decisive role in shaping other forms of inequality.... The empirical and theoretical problem is to sort out the complex interplay of racism and class relations, not to absorb the former into the latter.

Where Marxist analyses differ from Weberian analyses is not over the question of whether racial divisions are in some measure autonomous of class divisions, but over how the distinctiveness of racial divisions is to be conceptualized.

Weberian theorists typically subsume racial divisions under the general category of *status* group formation, whereas Marxists tend to conceptualize racial oppression as a variant of *national* or colonial oppression.

Just as Marxists hold different conceptions of patriarchy as the distinct basis of women's oppression, they also disagree over the nature and implications of national oppression in specific historical contexts. For example, at an earlier point in American history Marxist analyses of the oppression of Blacks tended to build upon the concept of a "Black Nation" as a distinct territorial entity, whereas more recent Marxist analyses have tended to favour some conception of "internal colonialism." Despite these differences, there is at least one common thread running through most contemporary Marxist analyses of race and ethnicity. This is the notion that the situation of racial minorities must be treated as an *interaction* between class and national oppression, neither of which can be subsumed under the other. This viewpoint is perhaps best summarized by Geschwender in his book *Racial Stratification in America*:

> There are valuable features incorporated in both the internal colonial (or submerged nation) model and the capitalist exploitation (or class) model. Each describes a portion of reality and provides valuable insights regarding the American system of racial stratification. Neither is sufficiently general to subsume the other. Therefore it is necessary to select elements from each of these two models to develop a comprehensive model with utility for the analysis of racial stratification in America.

Similar statements can be found in Baron (1975), Reich (1981) and other recent Marxist writings on racial inequality. If there is a weak point in these analyses, it is not the one alleged by Giddens: that Marxists are incapable of addressing nonclass forms of oppression in anything but a class reductionist manner. It is rather that, having abandoned class reductionism, contemporary Marxists are hard pressed to explain why class should be accorded *any* degree of primacy over other bases of political struggle. One can indeed point to a growing number of "post-Marxist" theorists for whom the rejection of class reductionism served as merely a stepping stone to the abandonment of the class primacy thesis altogether. Among contemporary Marxists, one encounters a number of nonreductionist arguments for the primacy of class, none of which is without problems. First, there is the simple empirical claim that Marxist class categories can be shown to have stronger effects on life chances, cultural patterns, or political consciousness than alternative bases of stratification. Much of the recent effort in Marxist class analysis has been devoted to demonstrating this fact, and the results are generally impressive, but this is ultimately a weak defense of the class primacy thesis. Many Weberians (Giddens, for example) would not dispute the centrality of class in contemporary capitalist society, but would argue that this is a wholly contingent state of affairs and indicates nothing about the general primacy of class.

Second, there is the evolutionary claim that only class relations have an internal logic that generates systematic tendencies toward cumulative and progressive social change. This is a much stronger argument for the class primacy thesis and is defended by such Marxists as G. A. Cohen and Erik Olin Wright. The problem with this defense is that it typically requires placing the development of the productive forces at the center of the historical process—a thesis that most contemporary Marxists are reluctant to advocate because of its association with "technological determinism" and its vulgarization in official Soviet Marxism.

Third, there is the straightforward materialist argument that, however autonomous and consequential various nonclass forms of domination may be, control over the material means of production remains the basic source of power in society. Whatever their motives or origins, effective political struggles must therefore assume a class form in the sense that they must ultimately draw upon and seek to restructure access to these material resources. My impression is that this is the version of the class primacy thesis that most contemporary Marxists would adhere to, at least implicitly. The problem with this defense is that it presumes precisely what is most contested by Weberian theory: that material resources are necessarily more important bases of power than political or ideological resources. As we shall see in the next section, this claim is often compromised by Marxist themselves by the importance they assign to political and ideological relations in the definition of social class.

EXPLOITATION VERSUS DOMINATION

A third difference between classical Marxist and Weberian theory concerns the relationship between exploitation and domination, or more generally between economic relations and political/ideological relations. By "exploitation" I refer here to the capacity of an individual or class to appropriate the labour of another, whereas "domination" refers to the ability to command the obedience of another. For Marx, class relations, conceived as relations of economic exploitation, are clearly paramount. Relations of political and ideological domination are secondary in the sense that they arise either as a means of securing the conditions for exploitation (as in the laws that guarantee the rights of private property), as a means of realizing or intensifying the degree of exploitation (as in the various forms of capitalist domination over workers at the point of production), or as a means of stabilizing and reproducing the relations of exploitation (as in the powers that capitalists exercise through the state, the media, etc.).

For Weber, relations of domination are in no sense subordinate to the goal of exploitation. Individuals sometimes seek dominance over others as a way of exploiting their labour, but they also pursue it for the social prestige it entails, and sometimes they pursue it purely for its own sake. If anything, domination is the more fundamental concept in Weberian theory. In Weber's writings the meaning systems that underpin different forms of authority (traditional, charismatic, rationallegal) are more important in defining the nature of societies than any typology based on forms of exploitation. Economic conflicts between classes are seen by Weber as merely one instance of the more general phenomenon of political struggles between dominant (privileged) and subordinate (disprivileged) collectivities. Following in this tradition, modern Weberians such as Parkin (1979, p. 46) and Giddens (1981, p. 60) treat exploitation as but a subspecies of the more general phenomenon of domination. Although classical Marxist and Weberian theory present a clear choice between an exploitation-based and a domination-based theory of society, recent developments in Marxist theory have tended to blur this distinction.

This is especially true in the area of class analysis and, more specifically, in the analysis of what is commonly referred to as the "new middle class." One of the main concerns of recent Marxist theory has been to clarify the class position of such groups as salaried managers and professionals. The classical Marxist definition of "ownership versus non-ownership of the means of production," understood as the foundation of capitalist relations of exploitation, offers little help here, since by this criterion all wage and salary earners would be classified as working class. Yet, common sense suggests that this is too heterogeneous a concept of the working class to be of any use in predicting the actual or potential organization, consciousness, and political behaviour of social groups in capitalist society. Most contemporary Marxists have responded to this problem by proposing more elabourate criteria of class position by which certain groups of wage and salary earners could be distinguished from the working class. The various efforts in this direction differ considerably in the precise criteria they propose and thus in the boundary that they identify between working-class and non-working-class positions. Yet, virtually all of them share one thing in common: In each instance the operative criterion is defined more in terms of domination than in terms of exploitation, a fact that has not gone unnoticed by recent Weberian commentators.

The class theories of Guglielmo Carchedi, Nicos Poulantzas, and Erik Olin Wright all illustrate this point. For Carchedi (1977), the criterion that divides wage and salary earners into working-class and newmiddle-class components is the distinction between what he calls the "function of the collective worker" and the "global function of capital." The former is defined by Carchedi as "the production of use-values within a complex and differentiated labour process"; the latter is defined as "the control and surveillance of the labour process"—a form of control that Carchedi interprets as essential to the expropriation of surplus value and not merely a technical condition of production. Workers and the new middle class are alike in that both are separated from ownership of the means of production; however, the latter are distinguished from the working class by their participation (in varying degrees) in the global function of capital—that is, by their exercise of supervisory authority. In Poulantzas' (1975) theory the working class is distinguished from the new middle class (or what he calls the "new petty bourgeoisie") by three criteria. In addition to the basic economic criterion of class position (which he defines as the distinction between productive and unproductive labour), Poulantzas maintains that political and ideological relations also enter into the structural determination of class. By political and ideological relations he means those relations which secure the reproduction of the dominant mode of exploitation. At the political level this is accomplished through the relations of supervision and authority within the capitalist enterprise, which Poulantzas, like Carchedi, interprets as involving not just the technical coordination of labour but also the enforcement of capitalist domination over workers. This places managers and supervisors in an antagonistic relation to the working class. At the ideological level Poulantzas identifies the basic class relation as the division between mental and manual labour, which he claims reinforces the subordination of workers to capital by excluding them from the "secret knowledge" of production. As the bearers of this relation of ideological domination, professionals, technicians, and other mental workers are classified as part of the new petty bourgeoisie along with managers and supervisors.

In Wright's (1978a) original theory of contradictory class locations, class positions are defined by a combination of three criteria: control over investment capital, control over the physical means of production, and control over labour. Among wage and salary earners, this yields three types of class locations. The working class is defined as that group which occupies a subordinate position (no control) on all three of these dimensions. Managers and supervisors occupy a contradictory class location in that, like workers, they are excluded from control over investments, but unlike workers they exercise a degree of control over the physical means of production and over the labour of others. "Semiautonomous workers" (essentially non-supervisory professionals and technicians) occupy a distinct contradictory class location. Like workers they are excluded from control over both investment capital and the labour of others, but unlike workers, they retain a degree of control over their immediate physical means of production and over their own direct activity within the labour process.

What characterizes all of these theories is the tendency for relations of exploitation to be displaced by relations of domination and subordination, at least insofar as the definition of the new middle class is concerned. Weberians such as Parkin (1979) have interpreted this as a tacit admission by contemporary Marxists of the superiority of Weberian theory. Whether or not this conclusion follows, it is certainly true that the increased importance these theorists attach to authority relations does not square easily with some of the traditional arguments for the superiority of Marxist class analysis. For instance, Marxists often criticize Weberian and other non-Marxist conceptions of class for their *gradational* nature. This, they argue, generates an indeterminate plurality of positions with no meaningful boundaries between classes as discrete social groups. Yet criteria such as the exercise of supervisory authority, control over the physical means of production, or autonomy in the labour process are also matters of degree. Virtually all workers retain some minimal control over their own labour or their immediate instruments of production. At what point then does the level of control become sufficient to exclude them from the working class? Second, Marxists often claim as a virtue of their theory that it yields an unambiguous asymmetry of material interests from which one can deduce probable patterns of political opposition. This is arguably true for the concept of exploitation, but it is less clear that relations of domination and subordination entail any necessary asymmetry of interests. A plausible case can perhaps be made that the domination of managers over workers is asymmetrical in this sense. Whether the "semi-autonomy" or "secret knowledge" of non-supervisory professionals means that their interests are inherently opposed to those of workers lacking such authority is much more questionable.

Finally, there is the problem to which I alluded in the previous section. To the extent that Marxists integrate relations of domination into their definition of class, it becomes increasingly difficult to defend either the general primacy of economic relations over political and ideological relations or the more specific claim of the primacy of class over nonclass forms of domination. This is especially true when, as is the case in all three theories examined above, differences in authority take precedence over similarities of economic characteristics in defining the boundaries between classes. It should be noted that one of the three theorists examined above has concluded that the problems associated with incorporating domination into the Marxist conception of class are so great that such efforts should be abandoned. In his latest writings, Wright (1985) has rejected his earlier theory of contradictory class locations and proposed an alternative way of conceptualizing the class position of salaried managers and professionals. As we shall see in the next section, however, this has resulted merely in the substitution of one form of convergence with Weberian theory for another.

PRODUCTION VERSUS MARKET RELATIONS

A final distinction between classical Marxist and Weberian theory concerns the relative importance of production versus market relations in the definition of class. Whereas Marx locates the basic class division in the relations of production, Weber defines classes in terms of the differential access to market rewards. In a sense, this difference condenses within itself each of the three previously discussed distinctions. Marx conceptualizes production as an objective structure of relations between classes, whereas Weber analyzes market relations from the standpoint of the motives and strategies of human agents as they struggle to increase their share of societal rewards. Marx's concern with exploitation also leads him to focus on production, since he views market transactions as relations of free and equal exchange and argues that it is only in the process of production that the appropriation of surplus labour takes place. Finally, production relations are conceived by Marx as polarized along a single dimension between exploiters and exploited, whereas Weber sees a multiplicity of bases around which groups organize in their struggle to gain privileged access to the market. In this instance, it has been primarily Weberians who have been criticized by Marxists for the deficiencies of their conception of class. By focusing on the myriad strategies by which groups compete for market rewards, Marxists argue, Weberians fail to appreciate the even more fundamental conflicts that characterize the relations of production. A representative statement of this critique is presented by Crompton and Gubbay in their book, *Economy and Class Structure.*

> Our major criticism of the Weberian approach to social class centres on the starting-point of his theoretical analysis of the class structure of capitalist societies—the market.... Property relations logically precede market relationships, and therefore in order to understand the nature of class structures we must direct our attention in the first place to this underlying structure—the capitalist mode of production, and its associated relations of production. Putting the same thing in a slightly different and simpler way, we feel that to study the market without also taking into account the relations of production which underlie the market gives at best an incomplete, and at worst a misleading, account of the class structure.

Most contemporary Marxists would defend some notion of the primacy of production relations over market relations. Once again, however, recent developments in Marxist theory have tended to undermine the distinctiveness of the Marxist perspective in the direction of a greater openness to Weberian viewpoints. Among Marxist political economists, for example, there is a growing school of "Sraffian" theorists who argue that capital accumulation is better analysed from the standpoint of market phenomena (wages, prices, etc.) than in terms of production values as defined by the labour theory of value (Steedman, 1977). In one of the more provocative works of recent Marxist theory, John Roemer (1982) extends this perspective to the analysis of class and exploitation. Through a detailed analysis of the flows of surplus labour from one category of actors to another in the course of various exchange relations, Roemer shows that, given an unequal distribution of property rights in the means of production, market exchange results in an exploitative transfer of labour from the property-poor to the property-rich, regardless of the nature of the relations of production. From this he concludes that the institution of wage labour and the domination of capitalists over workers at the point of production are incidental to the functioning of exploitation and the definition of classes in capitalist society. What matters is the institution of market exchange and the unequal distribution of different forms of property.

It is on the basis of Roemer's work that Erik Olin Wright has sought to reconceptualize the class position of salaried managers and professionals. Wright (1985) now argues that class is exclusively a relationship of exploitation, rather than a complex unity of exploitation and domination relations. The dominant form of exploitation in capitalist society is that based on the private ownership of the means of production, but there are also subsidiary forms of exploitation that derive from the unequal distribution of other productive assets. One such asset is skills—especially those whose supply is artificially restricted through credentialist mechanisms. A second is what Wright calls "organization assets," by which he means control over the conditions for the coordination of labour. Within this framework, salaried managers and professionals are distinguished from the working class by their disproportionate share of one or the other (or both) of these subsidiary assets. Such differentials in skill and organization assets, Wright argues, enable them (via the mechanism of market exchange) to exploit the labour of other workers, even as they themselves are exploitated by capitalists.

Whether this reconceptualization successfully exorcizes the concept of domination from the Marxist definition of class is an open question, given that by Wright's own admission the "ownership" of "organization assets" is rather difficult to distinguish from the exercise of hierarchical authority. But even accepting this distinction, it is clear that Wright has closed one door to Weberianism only by opening another: He has eliminated domination from the definition of class only by elevating the importance of market relations. Wright (1985, p. 107-108) defends the Marxist pedigree of his new theory by arguing that Weberians treat market relations from a culturalist standpoint (i.e., in terms of the meaning systems that shape social action), whereas he conceptualizes market relations from a materialist standpoint (i.e., in terms of objective patterns of exploitation that exist independently of the subjective states of actors). Yet the very introduction of such concepts as "skills" and "credentials" into the definition of class produces an inevitable slide toward a culturalist form of analysis. As both Marxists and Weberians have argued, what passes for "skill" in a given society or what is certified by credentials is very much a social construction and therefore dependent upon the subjective states of actors.

At the present time, few Marxists would be willing to follow Roemer and Wright in redefining class divisions from the standpoint of market exchange; however, there is another way in which market relations have assumed a more widespread importance in Marxist class analysis. This is in the analysis of fractional divisions *within* classes, and especially within the working class. During the past decade Marxist theorists have elabourated the concept of "labour market segmentation" in an effort to account for persistent divisions within the working class. According to this perspective, the failure of workers to unite as a class reflects more than just cultural divisions or false consciousness; it is rooted in objective differences in the conditions under which various fractions of workers sell their labour and corresponding differences in the nature of the jobs they come to occupy. Different variants of this theory propose different explanations for the existence of segmented labour markets. Some theorists follow the traditional Weberian perspective in attributing split labour markets to the exclusionary efforts of more privileged workers (Bonacich, 1976). Others attribute labour market segmentation to the divide-and-rule strategies of capitalists or to preexisting differences in the structure of jobs (Edwards, 1975; 1979). But regardless of whether labour market segmentation is viewed exclusively as a product of market competition or as a derivative of the underlying structure of production, market relations per se occupy an important place in the analysis, as only through the segmentation of labour markets are differences in the nature of jobs are translated into divisions between concrete fractions of workers.

Contemporary Marxists have thus broadened the focus of their analysis from the traditional Marxist concern with production relations to give greater attention to the social relations of the marketplace. To understand the reasons for this shift one need only look at the substantive issues that have preoccupied Marxist class analysis in recent years. First is the question of the class position of salaried managers and professionals. However one locates these groups within the social relations of production, it is clear that market phenomena, such as the closure of mobility opportunities through credentialism, play an important role in the recruitment, legitimation, and reproduction of these class positions. Second is the problem of the political disunity of the working class, which, as we have seen, has been addressed through the concept of labour market segmentation. Third, is the related issue of the gender and racial divisions and their articulation with capitalist class relations. Here too the closure of market opportunities has been seen as a crucial link between nonclass forms of inequality and the structure of class positions. One occasionally hears solemn pronouncements from certain Marxist quarters to the effect that market relations belong to the realm of "mere appearances," whereas only production relations reveal the "inner essense" of capitalist society. If this is true, however, then Marxism itself has become increasingly entangled in the web of "mere appearances."

7

The Protestant Ethic and the Spirit of Capitalism

The Protestant Ethic and the Spirit of Capitalism is a book written by Max Weber, a German sociologist, economist, and politician, in 1904 and 1905 that began as a series of essays. The original edition was in German. Considered a founding text in economic sociology and sociology in general, the book was translated into English for the first time by Talcott Parsons and appeared in 1930. In the book, Weber wrote that capitalism in northern Europe evolved when the Protestant (particularly Calvinist) ethic influenced large numbers of people to engage in work in the secular world, developing their own enterprises and engaging in trade and the accumulation of wealth for investment. In other words, the Protestant work ethic was a force behind an unplanned and uncoordinated mass action that influenced the development of capitalism. This idea is also known as "the Weber thesis". Weber, however, rejected deterministic approaches, and presented the Protestant Ethic as merely one in a number of 'elective affinities' leading toward capitalist modernity. Weber's term Protestant work ethic has become very widely known. The work relates significantly to the cultural "rationalization" and so-called "disenchantment" which Weber associated with the modern West.

Book Contents

The book is not a detailed study of Protestantism but rather an introduction into Weber's later studies of interaction between various religious ideas and economics. In the book, Weber argues that Puritan ethics and ideas influenced the development of capitalism. Religious devotion, however, is usually accompanied by a rejection of worldly affairs, including the pursuit of wealth and possessions.

To illustrate and provide an example, Weber quotes the ethical writings of Benjamin Franklin: "Remember, that *time is money*. He that can earn ten shillings a day by his labour, and goes abroad, or sits idle, one half of that day, though he spends but sixpence during his diversion or idleness, ought not to reckon *that* the only expense; he has really spent, or rather thrown away, five shillings besides.[...]Remember, that money is the *prolific, generating nature*. Money can beget money, and its offspring can beget more, and so on. Five shillings turned is six, turned again is seven and threepence, and so on, till it becomes a hundred pounds. The more there is of it, the more it produces every turning, so that the profits rise quicker and quicker. He that kills a breeding sow, destroys all her offspring to the thousandth generation. He that murders a crown, destroys all that it might have produced, even scores of pounds. (Italics in the original)"

Weber notes that this is not a philosophy of mere greed, but a statement laden with moral language. Indeed, Franklin claims that God revealed to him the usefulness of virtue. The Reformation profoundly affected the view of work, dignifying even the most mundane professions as adding to the common good and thus blessed by God, as much as any "sacred" calling. A common illustration is that of a cobbler, hunched over his work, who devotes his entire effort to the praise of God.

To emphasize the work ethic in Protestantism relative to Catholics, he notes a common problem that industrialists face when employing precapitalist labourers: Agricultural entrepreneurs will try to encourage time spent harvesting by offering a higher wage, with the expectation that labourers will see time spent working as more valuable and so engage it longer. However, in precapitalist societies this often results in labourers spending *less* time harvesting. Laborers judge that they can earn the same, while spending less time working and having more leisure. He also notes that societies having more Protestants are those that have a more developed capitalist economy. It is particularly advantageous in technical occupations for workers to be extremely devoted to their craft. To view the craft as an end in itself, or as a "calling" would serve this need well. This attitude is well-noted in certain classes which have endured religious education, especially of a Pietist background.

He defines spirit of capitalism as the ideas and *esprit* that favour the rational pursuit of economic gain: "We shall nevertheless provisionally use the expression 'spirit of capitalism' for that attitude which, *in the pursuit of a calling [berufsmaßig]*, strives systematically for profit for its own sake in the manner exemplified by Benjamin Franklin." The rationalization is partially a product of the fact that Luther and his religious descendants read the Old Testament and New with equal weight, and so is due to greater influence of Jewish thought.

Weber points out that such a spirit is not limited to Western culture if one considers it as the attitude of individuals, but that such individuals — heroic entrepreneurs, as he calls them — could not by themselves establish a new economic order (capitalism). He further noted that the spirit of capitalism could be divorced from religion, and that those passionate capitalists of his era were either passionate against the Church or at least indifferent to it. Desire for profit with minimum effort and seeing work as a burden to be avoided, and doing no more than what was enough for modest life, were common attitudes. As he wrote in his essays: "In order that a manner of life well adapted to the peculiarities of the capitalism... could come to dominate others, it had to originate somewhere, and not in isolated individuals alone, but as a way of life common to the whole groups of man."

After defining the "spirit of capitalism," Weber argues that there are many reasons to find its origins in the religious ideas of the Reformation. Many others like William Petty, Montesquieu, Henry Thomas Buckle, John Keats have noted the affinity between Protestantism and the development of commercialism. Weber shows that certain branches of

Protestantism had supported worldly activities dedicated to economic gain, seeing them as endowed with moral and spiritual significance. This recognition was not a goal in itself; rather they were a byproduct of other doctrines of faith that encouraged planning, hard work and self-denial in the pursuit of worldly riches.

Weber traced the origins of the Protestant ethic to the Reformation, though he acknowledged some respect for secular everyday labour as early as the Middle Ages. The Roman Catholic Church assured salvation to individuals who accepted the church's sacraments and submitted to the clerical authority. However, the Reformation had effectively removed such assurances. From a psychological viewpoint, the average person had difficulty adjusting to this new worldview, and only the most devout believers or "religious geniuses" within Protestantism, such as Martin Luther, were able to make this adjustment, according to Weber.

In the absence of such assurances from religious authority, Weber argued that Protestants began to look for other "signs" that they were saved. Calvin and his followers taught a doctrine of double predestination, in which from the beginning God chose some people for salvation and others for damnation. The inability to influence one's own salvation presented a very difficult problem for Calvin's followers. It became an absolute duty to believe that one was chosen for salvation, and to dispel any doubt about that: lack of self-confidence was evidence of insufficient faith and a sign of damnation. So, self-confidence took the place of priestly assurance of God's grace.

Worldly success became one measure of that self-confidence. Luther made an early endorsement of Europe's emerging labour divisions. Weber identifies the applicability of Luther's conclusions, noting that a "vocation" from God was no longer limited to the clergy or church, but applied to any occupation or trade.

However, Weber saw the fulfilment of the Protestant ethic not in Lutheranism, which was too concerned with the reception of divine spirit in the soul, but in Calvinistic forms of Christianity. The trend was carried further still in Pietism.

The Baptists diluted the concept of the calling relative to Calvinists, but other aspects made its congregants fertile soil for the development of capitalism—namely, a lack of paralyzing ascetism, the refusal to accept state office and thereby develop *un*politically, and the doctrine of control by conscience which caused rigorous honesty.

What Weber found, in simple terms:

- According to the new Protestant religions, an individual was religiously compelled to follow a secular vocation with as much zeal as possible. A person living according to this world view was more likely to accumulate money.
- The new religions (in particular, Calvinism and other more austere Protestant sects) effectively forbade wastefully *using* hard earned money and identified the purchase of luxuries as a sin. Donations to an individual's church or congregation was limited due to the rejection by certain Protestant sects of icons. Finally, donation of money to the poor or to charity was generally frowned on as it was seen as furthering beggary. This social condition was perceived as laziness, burdening their fellow man, and an affront to God; by not working, one failed to glorify God.

The manner in which this paradox was resolved, Weber argued, was the investment of this money, which gave an extreme boost to nascent capitalism. By the time Weber wrote his essay, he believed that the religious underpinnings of the Protestant ethic had largely gone from society. He cited the writings of Benjamin Franklin, which emphasized frugality, hard work and thrift, but were mostly free of spiritual content. Weber also attributed the success of mass production partly to the Protestant ethic. Only after expensive luxuries were disdained, could individuals accept the uniform products, such as clothes and furniture, that industrialization offered.

In his remarkably prescient conclusion to the book, Weber lamented that the loss of religious underpinning to capitalism's spirit has led to a kind of involuntary servitude to mechanized industry. "The Puritan wanted to work in calling; we are forced to do so. For when asceticism was carried out of monastic cells into everyday life, and began to dominate worldly morality, it did its part in building the tremendous cosmos of the modern economic order. This order is now bound to the technical and economic conditions of machine production which today determine the lives of all the individuals who are born into this mechanism, not only those directly concerned with economic acquisition, with irresistible force. Perhaps it will so determine them until the last ton of fossilized coal is burnt. In Baxter's view the care for external goods should only lie on the shoulders of the 'saint like a light cloak, which can be thrown aside at any moment.' But fate decreed that the cloak should become an iron cage.

Weber maintained that while Puritan religious ideas had significantly impacted the development of economic system in Europe and United States, there were other factors in play, as well. They included the rationalism in scientific pursuit, growing connections between observation and mathematics, development of scholarship and jurisprudence, rational systematisation of government administration (development of bureaucracy) and advances in entrepreneurship. In the end, the study of Protestant ethic, according to Weber, investigated a part of the detachment from magic, that *disenchantment of the world* that could be seen as a unique characteristic of Western culture.

In the final endnotes Weber states that he abandoned research into Protestantism because his colleague Ernst Troeltsch, a professional theologian, had begun work on *The Social Teachings of the Christian Churches and Sects*. Another reason for Weber's decision was that Troeltsch's work already achieved what he desired in that area, which is laying groundwork for comparative analysis of religion and society. Weber moved beyond Protestantism with his research but would continue research into sociology of religion with in his later works (the study of Judaism and the religions of China and India).

This book is also Weber's first brush with the concept of rationalization. His idea of modern capitalism as growing out of the religious pursuit of wealth meant a change to a rational means of existence, wealth. That is to say, at some point the

Calvinist rationale informing the "spirit" of capitalism became unreliant on the underlying religious movement behind it, leaving only rational capitalism. In essence then, Weber's "Spirit of Capitalism" is effectively and more broadly a Spirit of Rationalization. The essay can also be interpreted as one of Weber's criticisms of Karl Marx and his theories. While Marx's historical materialism held that all human institutions-including religion-were based on economic foundations, *The Protestant Ethic* turns this theory on its head by implying that a religious movement fostered capitalism, not the other way around.

Other scholars have taken a more nuanced view of Weber's argument. Weber states in the closing of this essay, "it is, of course, not my aim to substitute for a one-sided materialistic an equally one-sided spiritualistic causal interpretation of culture and history. Each is equally possible, but each if it does not serve as the preparation, but as the conclusion of an investigation, accomplishes equally little in the interest of historical truth." Weber's argument can be understood as an attempt to deepen the understanding of the cultural origins of capitalism, which does not exclude the historical materialist origins described by Marx.

ASCETICISM AND THE SPIRIT OF CAPITALISM

Richard Baxter; Meaning of Work; Justification of Profit; Jewish vs. Puritan Capitalism; Puritanism and Culture; Saving and Capital; Paradox of Asceticism and Rich; Serving Both Worlds; Citizenry Capitalistic Ethic; Iron Cage of Capitalism.

Spirit of Capitalism

The first, and probably most vital, feature of the spirit of capitalism was that it invested "economizing" with high moral significance. The individual engages in capitalistic economizing not only for the expediency of making a living, but in the expectation that such activity would test his inner resources and thus affirm his moral worth. In this regard, the American novelist Walker Percy observed, "As long as I am getting rich, I feel well. It is my Presbyterian blood."

A major effect of this spirit, as Durkheim noted, is that the entrepreneur performs his tasks with an earnestness of purpose that places them at the center of his life, and endows them with intrinsic dignity. There is nothing degrading about them. Such an approach to monetary gain is markedly different from the sordid passion of greed, for monetary gain was not to be used for luxury or self-indulgent bodily comfort, but rather was to be saved, and accumulated. Neither could the resulting frugality be mistaken for miserliness, as the accumulated resources were to be reinvested in worthy enterprises. The spirit of capitalism constituted a sort of moral "habitus" which burdened the possessor of money with a steward's obligation toward his own possessions.

Likewise, the individual entrepreneur isn't allowed to become overly absorbed into or preoccupied with himself. His existence revolves around an objective concern outside himself, which unceasingly demands his devotion and thus, becomes a test of his self-worth. By its very nature, these economic practices require reference to a goal; however, increase in capital becomes the ultimate point of reference.

Ultimately, the point of the spirit of capitalism is to attribute moral significance to entrepreneurial activity and lend meaning to the existence of those committed to it.

Criticisms

The economist and historian Henryk Grossman criticises Weber's analysis on two fronts. Firstly with reference to Marx's extensive work showing the stringent legal measures taken against poverty and vagabondage that was a reaction to the massive enclosure of the commons in England. And, secondly, in Grossman's own work showing how this "bloody legislation" against those that had been put off their land was effected across Europe and especially in France. For Grossman this legislation, the outlawing of idleness and the poorhouses they instituted physically forced people from serfdom into wage-labour. For him, this general fact was not related to protestantism and so capitalism came largely by force and not by any vocational training regarding an inner-worldliness of protestanism. Thus Grossman solves the central crux of Weber's analysis: his puzzlement over how enough people were recruited into early capitalist manufacturing. Grossman shows how people were in fact forced to obey capitalist principles not on any religious grounds but rather from legalistic grounds of force made by those who held power and wanted more production for their own benefit but also, often in their own view, for their nation's benefit. However, it is possible that the Protestant "work ethic" reinforced or legitimized these legal measures within a larger cultural context.

In a paper published on November 10, 2009, Harvard economist David Cantoni tested Weber's Protestant hypothesis using population and economic growth in second-millennium Germany as the data set, with negative results. Cantoni writes:

"Using population figures in a dataset comprising 276 cities in the years 1300-1900, I find no effects of Protestantism on economic growth. The finding is robust to the inclusion of a variety of controls, and does not appear to depend on data selection or small sample size. In addition, Protestantism has no effect when interacted with other likely determinants of economic development. I also analyze the endogeneity of religious choice; instrumental variables estimates of the effects of Protestantism are similar to the OLS results. "

Literacy and the Spirit of Capitalism

It has recently been suggested that Protestantism has indeed influenced positively the capitalist development of respective social systems not so much through the "Protestant ethics" but rather through the promotion of literacy.

Indeed, the ability to read was essential for Protestants (unlike Catholics) to perform their religious duty " to read the Bible. The reading of Holy Scripture was not just unnecessary for Catholic laymen, for a long time it was even prohibited for them. The edict of the Toulouse Synod (1229) prohibited the Catholic laymen from possessing copies of the Bible. Soon after that, a decision by the Tarragon Synod spread this prohibition to ecclesiastic people as well. In 1408, the Oxford Synod absolutely prohibited translations of the Holy Scripture. From the very beginning, Protestant groups did not accept this prohibition. Thus, Luther translated in 1522–1534 first the New Testament, and then the Old Testament, into German, so that any German-speaking person could read the Holy Scripture in his or her native language. Moreover, the Protestants viewed reading the Holy Scripture as a religious duty of any Christian. As a result, the level of literacy and education was, in general, higher for Protestants than it was for Catholics and for followers of other confessions that did not provide religious stimuli for learning literacy. It has been shown that literate populations have many more opportunities to obtain and utilize the achievements of modernization than illiterate ones. On the other hand, literate people could be characterized by a greater innovative-activity level, which provides opportunities for modernization, development, and economic growth. Empirical tests have confirmed the presence of a rather strong and highly significant correlation between the early introduction of mass literacy and subsequent high rates of capitalist economic development.

Becker and Wossmann at the University of Munich showed that literacy levels differing in religious areas can sufficiently explain the economic gaps cited by Weber. The results were supported even under a concentric diffusion model of Protestantism using distance from Wittenberg as a model.

THE SPIRIT OF CAPITALISM

In the title of this study is used the somewhat pretentious phrase, the *spirit* of capitalism. What is to be understood by it? The attempt to give anything like a definition of it brings out certain difficulties which are in the very nature of this type of investigation. If any object can be found to which this term can be applied with any understandable meaning, it can only be an historical individual, i.e. a complex of elements associated in historical reality which we unite into a conceptual whole from the standpoint of their cultural significance.

Such an historical concept, however, since it refers in its content to a phenomenon significant for its unique individuality, cannot be defined according to the formula *genetic proximity, differential specification,* but it must be gradually put together out of the individual parts which are taken from historical reality to make it up. Thus the final and definitive concept cannot stand at the beginning of the investigation, but must come at the end. We must, in other words, work out in the course of the discussion, as its most important result, the best conceptual formulation of what we here understand by the spirit of capitalism, that is the best from the point of view which interests us here. This point of view (the one of which we shall speak later) is, further, by no means the only possible one from which the historical phenomena we are investigating can be analysed. Other standpoints would, for this as for every historical phenomenon, yield other characteristics as the essential ones. The result is that it is by no means necessary to understand by the spirit of capitalism only what it will come to mean to us for the purposes of our analysis. This is a necessary result of the nature of historical concepts which attempt for their methodological purposes not to grasp historical reality in abstract general formula, but in concrete genetic sets of relations which are inevitably of a specifically unique and individual character.

Thus, if we try to determine the object, the analysis and historical explanation of which we are attempting, it cannot be in the form of a conceptual definition, but at least in the beginning only a provisional description of what is here meant by the spirit of capitalism. Such a description is, however, indispensable in order clearly to understand the object of the investigation. For this purpose we turn to a document of that spirit which contains what we are looking for in almost classical purity, and at the same time has the advantage of being free from all direct relationship to religion, being thus, for our purposes, free of preconceptions.

Time is money. He that can earn ten shillings a day by his labour, and goes abroad, or sits idle, one half of that day, though he spends but sixpence during his diversion or idleness, ought not to reckon *that* the only expense; he has really spent, or rather thrown away, five shillings besides. "Remember, that *credit is* money. If a man lets his money lie in my hands after it is due, he gives me the interest, or so much as I can make of it during that time. This amounts to a considerable sum where a man has good and large credit, and makes good use of it. "Remember, that money is of the prolific, generating nature. Money can beget money, and its offspring can beget more, and so on. Five shillings turned is six, turned again it is seven and threepence, and so on, till it becomes a hundred pounds. The more there is of it, the more it produces every turning, so that the profits rise quicker and quicker. He that kills a breeding-sow, destroys all her offspring to the thousandth generation. He that murders a crown, destroys all that it might have produced, even scores of pounds."

"Remember this saying, *The good paymaster is lord of another man's purse.* He that is known to pay punctually and exactly to the time he promises, may at any time, and on any occasion, raise all the money his friends can spare. This is sometimes of great use. After industry and frugality, nothing contributes more to the raising of a young man in the world than punctuality and justice in all his dealings; therefore never keep borrowed money an hour beyond the time you promised, lest a disappointment shut up your friend's purse for ever.

"The most trifling actions that affect a man's credit are to be regarded. The sound of your hammer at five in the morning, or eight at night, heard by a creditor, makes him easy six months longer; but if he sees you at a billiard-table, or hears your voice at a tavern, when you should be at work, he sends for his money the next day; demands it, before he can receive it, in a lump. "It shows, besides, that you are mindful of what you owe; it makes you appear a careful as well as an honest man, and that still increases your credit.

"Beware of thinking all your own that you possess, and of living accordingly. It is a mistake that many people who have credit fall into. To prevent this, keep an exact account for some time both of your expenses and your income. If you take the pains at first to mention particulars, it will have this good effect: you will discover how wonderfully small, trifling expenses mount up to large sums, and will discern what might have been, and may for the future be saved, without occasioning any great inconvenience."

"For six pounds a year you may have the use of one hundred pounds, provided you are a man of known prudence and honesty.

"He that spends a groat a day idly, spends idly above six pounds a year, which is the price for the use of one hundred pounds.

"He that wastes idly a groat's worth of his time per day, one day with another, wastes the privilege of using one hundred pounds each day.

"He that idly loses five shillings' worth of time loses five shillings, and might as prudently throw five shillings into the sea.

"He that loses five shillings, not only loses that sum, but all the advantage that might be made by turning it in dealing, which by the time that a young man becomes old, will amount to a considerable sum of money."

It is Benjamin Franklin who preaches to us in these sentences, the same which Ferdinand Kürnberger satirizes in his clever and malicious *Picture of American Culture* as the supposed confession of faith of the Yankee. That it is the spirit of capitalism which here speaks in characteristic fashion, no one will doubt, however little we may wish to claim that everything which could be understood as pertaining to that spirit is contained in it. Let us pause a moment to consider this passage, thc philosophy of which Kürnberger sums up in the words, "They make tallow out of cattle and money out of men". The peculiarity of this philosophy of avarice appears to be the ideal of the honest man of recognized credit, and above all the idea of a duty of the individual toward the increase of his capital, which is assumed as an end in itself. Truly what is here preached is not simply a means of making one's way in the world, but a peculiar ethic. The infraction of its rules is treated not as foolishness but as forgetfulness of duty. That is the essence of the matter. It is not mere business astuteness, that sort of thing is common enough, it is an ethos. *This is* the quality which interests us.

When Jacob Fugger, in speaking to a business associate who had retired and who wanted to persuade him to do the same, since he had made enough money and should let others have a chance, rejected that as pusillanimity and answered that "he (Fugger) thought otherwise, he wanted to make money as long as he could", the spirit of his statement is evidently quite different from that of Franklin. What in the former case was an expression of commercial daring and a personal inclination morally neutral, in the latter takes on the character of an ethically coloured maxim for the conduct of life. The concept spirit of capitalism is here used in this specific sense, it is the spirit of modern capitalism. For that we are here dealing only with Western European and American capitalism is obvious from the way in which the problem was stated. Capitalism existed in China, India, Babylon, in the classic world, and in the Middle Ages. But in all these cases, as we shall see, this particular ethos was lacking.

Now, all Franklin's moral attitudes are coloured with utilitarianism. Honesty is useful, because it assures credit; so are punctuality, industry, frugality, and that is the reason they are virtues. A logical deduction from this would be that where, for instance, the appearance of honesty serves the same purpose, that would suffice, and an unnecessary surplus of this virtue would evidently appear to Franklin's eyes as unproductive waste. And as a matter of fact, the story in his autobiography of his conversion to those virtues, or the discussion of the value of a strict maintenance of the appearance of modesty, the assiduous belittlement of one's own deserts in order to gain general recognition later, confirms this impression. According to Franklin, those virtues, like all others, are only in so far virtues as they are actually useful to the individual, and the surrogate of mere appearance is always sufficient when it accomplishes the end in view. It is a conclusion which is inevitable for strict utilitarianism. The impression of many Germans that the virtues professed by Americanism are pure hypocrisy seems to have been confirmed by this striking case. But in fact the matter is not by any means so simple. Benjamin Franklin's own character, as it appears in the really unusual candidness of his autobiography, belies that suspicion. The circumstance that he ascribes his recognition of the utility of virtue to a divine revelation which was intended to lead him in the path of righteousness, shows that something more than mere garnishing for purely egocentric motives is involved.

In fact, the *superior good* of this ethic, the earning of more and more money, combined with the strict avoidance of all spontaneous enjoyment of life, is above all completely devoid of any eudaemonistic, not to say hedonistic, admixture. It is thought of so purely as an end in itself, that from the point of view of the happiness of, or utility to, the single individual, it appears entirely transcendental and absolutely irrational. Man is dominated by the making of money, by acquisition as the ultimate purpose of his life. Economic acquisition is no longer subordinated to man as the means for the satisfaction of his material needs. This reversal of what we should call the natural relationship, so irrational from a naive point of view, is evidently as definitely a leading principle of capitalism as it is foreign to all peoples not under capitalistic influence. At the same time it expresses a type of feeling which is closely connected with certain religious ideas. If we thus ask, why should "money be made out of men", Benjamin Franklin himself, although he was a colourless deist, answers in his autobiography with a quotation from the Bible, which his strict Calvinistic father drummed into him again and again in his youth: "Seest thou a man diligent in his business? He shall stand before kings" (Proverbs 22:29). The earning of money within the modern economic order is, so long as it is done legally, the result and the expression of virtuc and proficiency in a calling; and this virtue and proficiency are, as it is now not difficult to see, the real Alpha and Omega of Franklin's ethic, as expressed in the passages we have quoted, as well as in all his works without exception.

And in truth this peculiar idea, so familiar to us today, but in reality so little a matter of course, of one's duty in a calling, is what is most characteristic of the social ethic of capitalistic culture, and is in a sense the fundamental basis of it. It is an obligation which the individual is supposed to feel and does feel towards the content of his professional activity, no matter in what it consists, in particular no matter whether it appears on the surface as a utilization of his personal powers, or only of his material possessions (as capital).

Of course, this conception has not appeared only under capitalistic conditions. On the contrary, we shall later trace its origins back to a time previous to the advent of capitalism. Still less, naturally, do we maintain that a conscious acceptance of these ethical maxims on the part of the individuals, entrepreneurs or labourers, in modern capitalistic enterprises, is a condition of the further existence of present-day capitalism.

The capitalistic economy of the present day is an immense cosmos into which the individual is born, and which presents itself to him, at least as an individual, as an unalterable order of things in which he must live. It forces the individual, in so far as he is involved in the system of market relationships, to conform to capitalistic rules of action. The manufacturer who in the long run acts counter to these norms, will just as inevitably be eliminated from the economic scene as the worker who cannot or will not adapt himself to them will be thrown into the streets without a job.

Thus the capitalism of today, which has come to dominate economic life, educates and selects the economic subjects which it needs through a process of economic survival of the fittest. But here one can easily see the limits of the concept of selection as a means of historical explanation. In order that a manner of life so well adapted to the peculiarities of capitalism could be selected at all, i.e. should come to dominate others, it had to originate somewhere, and not in isolated individuals alone, but as a way of life common to whole groups of men. This origin is what really needs explanation. Concerning the doctrine of the more naive historical materialism, that such ideas originate as a reflection or superstructure of economic situations, we shall speak more in detail below.

At this point it will suffice for our purpose to call attention to the fact that without doubt, in the country of Benjamin Franklin's birth (Massachusetts), the spirit of capitalism (in the sense we have attached to it) was present before the capitalistic order. There were complaints of a peculiarly calculating sort of profit-seeking in New England, as distinguished from other parts of America, as early as 1632. It is further undoubted that capitalism remained far less developed in some of the neighbouring colonies, the later Southern States of the United States of America, in spite of the fact that these latter were founded by large capitalists for business motives, while the New England colonies were founded by preachers and seminary graduates with the help of small citizen, craftsmen and yeomen, for religious reasons. In this case the causal relation is certainly the reverse of that suggested by the materialistic standpoint.

But the origin and history of such ideas is much more complex than the theorists of the superstructure suppose. The spirit of capitalism, in the sense in which we are using the term, had to fight its way to supremacy against a whole world of hostile forces. A state of mind such as that expressed in the passages we have quoted from Franklin, and which called forth the applause of a whole people, would both in ancient times and in the Middle Ages have been proscribed as the lowest sort of avarice and as an attitude entirely lacking in self-respect. It is, in fact, still regularly thus looked upon by all those social groups which are least involved in or adapted to modem capitalistic conditions. This is not wholly because the instinct of acquisition was in those times unknown or undeveloped, as has often been said. Nor because the greed for gold, was then, or now, less powerful outside of citizen capitalism than within its peculiar sphere, as the illusions of modem romanticists are wont to believe. The difference between the capitalistic and pre-capitalistic spirits is not to be found at this point. The greed of the Chinese Mandarin, the old Roman aristocrat, or the modern peasant, can stand up to any comparison. And the *greed for gold* of a Neapolitan cab-driver or *barcaiuolo,* and certainly of Asiatic representatives of similar trades, as well as of the craftsmen of southern European or Asiatic countries, is, as anyone can find out for himself, very much more intense, and especially more unscrupulous than that of, say, an Englishman in similar circumstances.

The universal reign of absolute unscrupulousness in the pursuit of selfish interests by the making of money has been a specific characteristic of precisely those countries whose citizen-capitalistic development, measured according to Occidental standards, has remained backward. As every employer knows, the lack *of conscience* of the labourers of such countries, for instance Italy as compared with Germany, has been, and to a certain extent still is, one of the principal obstacles to their capitalistic development. Capitalism cannot make use of the labour of those who practise the doctrine of undisciplined *liberal arbitration,* any more than it can make use of the business man who seems absolutely unscrupulous in his dealings with others, as we can learn from Franklin.

Hence the difference does not lie in the degree of development of any impulse to make money. The *greed for gold is* as old as the history of man. But we shall see that those who submitted to it without reserve as an uncontrolled impulse, such as the Dutch sea-captain who "would go through hell for gain, even though he scorched his sails", were by no means the representatives of that attitude of mind from which the specifically modem capitalistic spirit as a mass phenomenon is derived, and that is what matters. At all periods of history, wherever it was possible, there has been ruthless acquisition, bound to no ethical norms whatever. Like war and piracy, trade has often been unrestrained in its relations with foreigners and those outside the group. The double ethic has permitted here what was forbidden in dealings among brothers.

Capitalistic acquisition as an adventure has been at home in all types of economic society which have known trade with the use of money and which have offered it opportunities, through *commenda,* farming of taxes, State loans, financing of wars, ducal courts and officeholders. Likewise the inner attitude of the adventurer, which laughs at all ethical limitations, has been universal. Absolute and conscious ruthlessness in acquisition has often stood in the closest connection with the strictest conformity to tradition. Moreover, with the breakdown of tradition and the more or less complete extension of free economic enterprise, even to within the social group, the new thing has not generally been ethically justified and encouraged, but only tolerated as a fact. And this fact has been treated either as ethically indifferent or as reprehensible, but unfortunately unavoidable. This has not only been the normal attitude of all ethical teachings, but, what is more important, also that expressed in the practical action of the average man of pre-capitalistic times, pre-capitalistic in the sense that the rational utilization of capital in a permanent enterprise and the rational capitalistic organization of labour had not yet become dominant forces in the determination of economic activity. Now just this attitude was one of the strongest inner obstacles which the adaptation of men to the conditions of an ordered citizen-capitalistic economy has encountered everywhere.

The most important opponent with which the spirit of capitalism, in the sense of a definite standard of life claiming ethical sanction, has had to struggle, was that type of attitude and reaction to new situations which we may designate as traditionalism. In this case also every attempt at a final definition must be held in abeyance. On the other hand, we must try to make the provisional meaning clear by citing a few cases. We will begin from below, with the labourers. One of the technical means which the modem employer uses in order to secure the greatest possible amount of work from his men is the device of piece-rates. In agriculture, for instance, the gathering of the harvest is a case where the greatest possible intensity of labour is called for, since, the weather being uncertain, the difference between high profit and heavy loss may depend on the speed with which the harvesting can be done.

Hence a system of piece-rates is almost universal in this case. And since the interest of the employer in a speeding up of harvesting increases with the increase of the results and the intensity of the work, the attempt has again and again been made, by increasing the piecerates of the workmen, thereby giving them an opportunity to earn what is for them a very high wage, to interest them in increasing their own efficiency. But a peculiar difficulty has been met with surprising frequency: raising the piece-rates has often had the result that not more but less has been accomplished in the same time, because the worker reacted to the increase not by increasing but by decreasing the amount of his work. A man, for instance, who at the rate of 1 mark per acre mowed 2 1/2 acres per day and earned 2 1/2 marks, when the rate was raised to 1.25 marks per acre mowed, not 3 acres, as he might easily have done, thus earning 3.75 marks, but only 2 acres, so that he could still earn the 2 1/2 marks to which he was accustomed. The opportunity of earning more was less attractive than that of working less. He did not ask: how much can I earn in a day if I do as much work as possible? But: how much must I work in order to earn the wage, 2 1/2 marks, which I earned before and which takes care of my traditional needs? This is an example of what is here meant by traditionalism. A man does not "by nature" wish to earn more and more money, but simply to live as he is accustomed to live and to earn as much as is necessary for that purpose. Wherever modem capitalism has begun its work of increasing the productivity of human labour by increasing its intensity, it has encountered the immensely stubborn resistance of this leading trait of pre-capitalistic labour. And today it encounters it the more, the more backward (from a capitalistic point of view) the labouring forces are with which it has to deal.

Another obvious possibility, to return to our example, since the appeal to the acquisitive instinct through higher wage-rates failed, would have been to try the opposite policy, to force the worker by reduction of his wage-rates to work harder to earn the same amount than he did before. Low wages and high profits seem even today to a superficial observer to stand in correlation; everything which is paid out in wages seems to involve a corresponding reduction of profits. That road capitalism has taken again and again since its beginning. For centuries it was an article of faith, that low wages were productive, i.e. that they increased the material results of labour so that, as Pieter de la Cour, on this point, as we shall see, quite in the spirit of the old Calvinism, said long ago, the people only work because and so long as they are poor.

But the effectiveness of this apparently so efficient method has its limits. Of course the presence of a surplus population which it can hire cheaply in the labour market is a necessity for the development of capitalism. But though too large a reserve army may in certain cases favour its quantitative expansion, it checks its qualitative development, especially the transition to types of enterprise which make more intensive use of labour. Low wages are by no means identical with cheap labour. From a purely quantitative point of view the efficiency of labour decreases with a wage which is physiologically insufficient, which may in the long run even mean a survival of the unfit. The present-day average Silesian mows, when he exerts himself to the full, little more than two-thirds as much land as the better paid and nourished Pomeranian or Mecklenburger, and the Pole, the further East he comes from, accomplishes progressively less than the German. Low wages fail even from a purely business point of view wherever it is a question of producing goods which require any sort of skilled labour, or the use of expensive machinery which is easily damaged, or in general wherever any great amount of sharp attention or of initiative is required. Here low wages do not pay, and their effect is the opposite of what was intended. For not only is a developed sense of responsibility absolutely indispensable, but in general also an attitude which, at least during working hours, is freed from continual calculations of how the customary wage may be earned with a maximum of comfort and a minimum of exertion. Labour must, on the contrary, be performed as if it were an absolute end in itself, a calling. But such an attitude is by no means a product of nature. It cannot be evoked by low wages or high ones alone, but can only be the product of a long and arduous process of education. Today, capitalism, once in the saddle, can recruit its labouring force in all industrial countries with comparative ease. In the past this was in every case an extremely difficult problem. And even today it could probably not get along without the support of a powerful ally along the way, which, as we shall see below, was at hand at the time of its development.

What is meant can again best be explained by means of an example. The type of backward traditional form of labour is today very often exemplified by women workers, especially unmarried ones. An almost universal complaint of employers of girls, for instance German girls, is that they are almost entirely unable and unwilling to give up methods of work inherited or once learned in favour of more efficient ones, to adapt themselves to new methods, to learn and to concentrate their intelligence, or even to use it at all. Explanations of the possibility of making work easier, above all more profitable to themselves, generally encounter a complete lack of understanding. Increases of piece-rates are without avail against the stone wall of habit. In general it is otherwise, and that is a point of no little importance from our view-point, only with girls having a specifically religious, especially a Pietistic, background. One often hears, and statistical investigation confirms it, that by far the best chances of economic education are found among this group. The ability of mental concentration, as well as the absolutely essential feeling of obligation to one's job, are here most often combined with a strict economy which calculates the possibility of high earning, and a cool self-control and frugality which enormously increase performance. This provides the most favourable foundation for the conception of labour as an end in itself, as a calling which is necessary to capitalism: the chances of overcoming traditionalism are greatest on account of the religious upbringing. This observation of present-day capitalism in itself suggests that it is worth while to ask how this connection of adaptability to capitalism with religious factors may have come about in the days of the early development of capitalism. For that they were even then present in much the same form can be inferred from numerous facts. For instance, the dislike and the persecution which Methodist workmen in the eighteenth century met at the hands of their comrades were not solely nor even principally the result of their religious eccentricities, England had seen many of those and more striking ones. It rested rather, as the destruction of their tools, repeatedly mentioned in the reports, suggests, upon their specific willingness to work as we should say today.

However, let us again return to the present, and this time to the entrepreneur, in order to clarify the meaning of traditionalism in his case.

Sombart, in his discussions of the genesis of capitalism has distinguished between the satisfaction of needs and acquisition as the two great leading principles in economic history. In the former case the attainment of the goods necessary to meet personal needs, in the latter a struggle for profit free from the limits set by needs, have been the ends controlling the form and direction of economic activity. What he calls the economy of needs seems at first glance to be identical with what is here described as economic traditionalism. That may be the case if the concept of needs is limited to traditional needs. But if that is not done, a number of economic types which must be considered capitalistic according to the definition of capital which Sombart gives in another part of his work, would be excluded from the category of acquisitive economy and put into that of needs economy. Enterprises, namely, which are carried on by private entrepreneurs by utilizing capital (money or goods with a money value) to make a profit, purchasing the means of production and selling the product, i.e. undoubted capitalistic enterprises, may at the same time have a traditionalistic character. This has, in the course even of modem economic history, not been merely an occasional case, but rather the rule, with continual interruptions from repeated and increasingly powerful conquests of the capitalistic spirit. To be sure the capitalistic form of an enterprise and the spirit in which it is run generally stand in some sort of adequate relationship to each other, but not in one of necessary interdependence. Nevertheless, we provisionally use the expression spirit of (modern) capitalism to describe that attitude which seeks profit rationally and systematically in the manner which we have illustrated by the example of Benjamin Franklin. This, however, is justified by the historical fact that attitude of mind has on the one hand found its most suitable expression in capitalistic enterprise, while on the other the enterprise has derived its most suitable motive force from the spirit of capitalism.

But the two may very well occur separately. Benjamin Franklin was filled with the spirit of capitalism at a time when his printing business did not differ in form from any handicraft enterprise. And we shall see that at the beginning of modem times it was by no means the capitalistic entrepreneurs of the commercial aristocracy, who were either the sole or the predominant bearers of the attitude we have here called the spirit of capitalism. It was much more the rising strata of the lower industrial middle classes. Even in the nineteenth century its classical representatives were not the elegant gentlemen of Liverpool and Hamburg, with their commercial fortunes handed down for generations, but the self-made parvenus of Manchester and Westphalia, who often rose from very modest circumstances. As early as the sixteenth century the situation was similar; the industries which arose at that time were mostly created by parvenus.

The management, for instance, of a bank, a wholesale export business, a large retail establishment, or of a large putting-out enterprise dealing with goods produced in homes, is certainly only possible in the form of a capitalistic enterprise.

Nevertheless, they may all be carried on in a traditionalistic spirit. In fact, the business of a large bank of issue cannot be carried on in any other way. The foreign trade of whole epochs has rested on the basis of monopolies and legal privileges of strictly traditional character.

In retail trade—and we are not here talking of the small men without capital who are continually crying out for Government aid—the revolution which is making an end of the old traditionalism is still in full swing. It is the same development which broke up the old puttingout system, to which modern domestic labour is related only in form. How this revolution takes place and what is its significance may, in spite of the fact these things are so familiar, be again brought out by a concrete example.

Until about the middle of the past century the life of a putter-out was, at least in many of the branches of the Continental textile industry, what we should today consider very comfortable. We may imagine its routine somewhat as follows: The peasants came with their cloth, often (in the case of linen) principally or entirely made from raw material which the peasant himself had produced, to the town in which the putterout lived, and after a careful, often official, appraisal of the quality, received the customary price for it. The putter-out's customers, for markets any appreciable distance away, were middlemen, who also came to him, generally not yet following samples, but seeking traditional qualities, and bought from his warehouse, or, long before delivery, placed orders which were probably in turn passed on to the peasants. Personal canvassing of customers took place, if at all, only at long intervals. Otherwise correspondence sufficed, though the sending of samples slowly gained ground. The number of business hours was very moderate, perhaps five to six a day, sometimes considerably less; in the rush season, where there was one, more. Earnings were moderate; enough to lead a respectable life and in good times to put away a little. On the whole, relations among competitors were relatively good, with a large degree of agreement on the fundamentals of business. A long daily visit to the tavern, with often plenty to drink, and a congenial circle of friends, made life comfortable and leisurely.

The form of organization was in every respect capitalistic; the entrepreneur's activity was of a purely business character; the use of capital, turned over in the business, was indispensable; and finally, the objective aspect of the economic process, the book-keeping, was rational. But it was traditionalistic business, if one considers the spirit which animated the entrepreneur: the traditional manner of life, the traditional rate of profit, the traditional amount of work, the traditional manner of regulating the relationships with labour, and the essentially traditional circle of customers and the manner of attracting new ones. All these dominated the conduct of the business, were at the basis, one may say, of the *ethos* of this group of business men.

Now at some time this leisureliness was suddenly destroyed, and often entirely without any essential change in the form of organization, such as the transition to a unified factory, to mechanical weaving, etc. What happened was, on the contrary, often no more than this: some young man from one of the putting-out families went out into the country, carefully chose weavers for his employ, greatly increased the rigour of his supervision of their work, and thus turned them from peasants into labourers. On the other hand, he would begin to change his marketing methods by so far as possible going directly to the final consumer, would take the details into his own hands, would personally solicit customers, visiting them every year, and above all would adapt the quality of the product directly to their needs and wishes. At the same time he began to introduce the principle of low prices and large turnover. There was repeated what everywhere and always is the result of such a process of rationalization: those who would not follow suit had to go out of business. The idyllic state collapsed under the pressure of a bitter competitive struggle, respectable fortunes were made, and not lent out at interest, but always reinvested in the business. The old leisurely and comfortable attitude toward life gave way to a hard frugality in which some participated and came to the top, because they did not wish to consume but to earn, while others who wished to keep on with the old ways were forced to curtail their consumption.

And, what is most important in this connection, it was not generally in such cases a stream of new money invested in the industry which brought about this revolution—in several cases known to me the whole revolutionary process was set in motion with a few thousands of capital borrowed from relations—but the new spirit, the spirit of modem capitalism, had set to work. The question of the motive forces in the expansion of modem capitalism is not in the first instance a question of the origin of the capital sums which were available for capitalistic uses, but, above all, of the development of the spirit of capitalism. Where it appears and is able to work itself out, it produces its own capital and monetary supplies as the means to its ends, but the reverse is not true. Its entry on the scene was not generally peaceful. A flood of mistrust, sometimes of hatred, above all of moral indignation, regularly opposed itself to the first innovator. Often—I know of several cases of the sort—regular legends of mysterious shady spots in his previous life have been produced. It is very easy not to recognize that only an unusually strong character could save an entrepreneur of this new type from the loss of his temperate self-control and from both moral and economic shipwreck. Furthermore, along with clarity of vision and ability to act, it is only by virtue of very definite and highly developed ethical qualities that it has been possible for him to command the absolutely indispensable confidence of his customers and workmen. Nothing else could have given him the strength to overcome the innumerable obstacles, above all the infinitely more intensive work which is demanded of the modem entrepreneur. But these are ethical qualities of quite a different sort from those adapted to the traditionalism of the past.

And, as a rule, it has been neither daredevil and unscrupulous speculators, economic adventurers such as we meet at all periods of economic history, nor simply great financiers who have carried through this change, outwardly so inconspicuous, but nevertheless so decisive for the penetration of economic life with the new spirit. On the contrary, they were men who had grown up in the hard school of life, calculating and daring at the same time, above all temperate and reliable, shrewd and completely devoted to their business, with strictly citizen opinions and principles. One is tempted to think that these personal moral qualities have not the slightest relation to any ethical maxims, to say nothing of religious ideas, but that the essential relation between them is negative. The ability to free oneself from the common tradition, a sort of liberal enlightenment, seems likely to be the most suitable basis for such a business man's success. And today that is generally precisely the case. Any relationship between religious beliefs and conduct is generally absent, and where any exists, at least in Germany, it tends to be of the negative sort. The people filled with the spirit of capitalism today tend to be indifferent, if not hostile, to the Church. The thought of the pious boredom of paradise has little attraction for their active natures; religion appears to them as a means of drawing people away from labour in this world. If you ask them what is the meaning of their restless activity, why they are never satisfied with what they have, thus appearing so senseless to any purely worldly view of life, they would perhaps give the answer, if they know any at all: "to provide for my children and grandchildren". But more often and, since that motive is not peculiar to them, but was just as effective for the traditionalist, more correctly, simply: that business with its continuous work has become a necessary part of their lives. That is in fact the only possible motivation, but it at the same time expresses what is, seen from the viewpoint of personal happiness, so irrational about this sort of life, where a man exists for the sake of his business, instead of the reverse.

Of course, the desire for the power and recognition which the mere fact of wealth brings plays its part. When the imagination of a whole people has once been turned toward purely quantitative bigness, as in the United States, this romanticism of numbers exercises an irresistible appeal to the poets among business men. Otherwise it is in general not the real leaders, and especially not the permanently successful entrepreneurs, who are taken in by it. In particular, the resort to entailed estates and the nobility, with sons whose conduct at the university and in the officers' corps tries to cover up their social origin, as has been the typical history of German capitalistic parvenu families, is a product of later decadence. The ideal type of the capitalistic entrepreneur, as it has been represented even in Germany by occasional outstanding examples, has no relation to such more or less refined climbers.

He avoids ostentation and unnecessary expenditure, as well as conscious enjoyment of his power, and is embarrassed by the outward signs of the social recognition which he receives. His manner of life is, in other words, often, and we shall have to investigate the historical significance of just this important fact, distinguished by a certain ascetic tendency, as appears clearly enough in the sermon of Franklin which we have quoted. It is, namely, by no means exceptional, but rather the rule, for him to have a sort of modesty which is essentially more honest than the reserve which Franklin so shrewdly recommends. He gets nothing out of his wealth for himself, except the irrational sense of having done his job well.

But it is just that which seems to the pre-capitalistic man so incomprehensible and mysterious, so unworthy and contemptible. That anyone should be able to make it the sole purpose of his life-work, to sink into the grave weighed down with a great material load of money and goods, seems to him explicable only as the product of a perverse instinct, the *greed for gold.*

At present under our individualistic political, legal, and economic institutions, with the forms of organization and general structure which are peculiar to our economic order, this spirit of capitalism might be understandable, as has been said, purely as a result of adaptation. The capitalistic system so needs this devotion to the calling of making money, it is an attitude toward material goods which is so well suited to that system, so intimately bound up with the conditions of survival in the economic struggle for existence, that there can today no longer be any question of a necessary connection of that acquisitive manner of life with any single *worldview.* In fact, it no longer needs the support of any religious forces, and feels the attempts of religion to influence economic life, in so far as they can still be felt at all, to be as much an unjustified interference as its regulation by the State. In such circumstances men's commercial and social interests do tend to determine their opinions and attitudes. Whoever does not adapt his manner of life to the conditions of capitalistic success must go under, or at least cannot rise. But these are phenomena of a time in which modern capitalism has become dominant and has become emancipated from its old supports. But as it could at one time destroy the old forms of medieval regulation of economic life only in alliance with the growing power of the modern State, the same, we may say provisionally, may have been the case in its relations with religious forces. Whether and in what sense that was the case, it is our task to investigate. For that the conception of moneymaking as an end in itself to which people were bound, as a calling, was contrary to the ethical feelings of whole epochs, it is hardly necessary to prove. The dogma "*You cannot serve God and mammon*" (Matthew 6:24) which was incorporated into the canon law and applied to the activities of the merchant, and which at that time (like the passage in the gospel about interest) was considered genuine, as well as St. Thomas's characterization of the desire for gain as *turpitudo* (which term even included unavoidable and hence ethically justified profit-making), already contained a high degree of concession on the part of the Catholic doctrine to the financial powers with which the Church had such intimate political relations in the Italian cities, as compared with the much more radically anti-chrematistic views of comparatively wide circles. But even where the doctrine was still better accommodated to the facts, as for instance with Anthony of Florence, the feeling was never quite overcome, that activity directed to acquisition for its own sake was at bottom a *pudendum* which was to be tolerated only because of the unalterable necessities of life in this world.

Some moralists of that time, especially of the nominalistic school, accepted developed capitalistic business forms as inevitable, and attempted to justify them, especially commerce, as necessary. The *industry* developed in it they were able to regard, though not without contradictions, as a legitimate source of profit, and hence ethically unobjectionable. But the dominant doctrine rejected the spirit of capitalistic acquisition as *turpitudo*, or at least could not give it a positive ethical sanction. An ethical attitude like that of Benjamin Franklin would have been simply unthinkable. This was, above all, the attitude of capitalistic circles themselves. Their life-work was, so long as they clung to the tradition of the Church, at best something morally indifferent. It was tolerated, but was still, even if only on account of the continual danger of collision with the Church's doctrine on usury, somewhat dangerous to salvation. Quite considerable sums, as the sources show, went at the death of rich people to religious institutions as conscience money, at times even back to former debtors as *usury* which had been unjustly taken from them. It was otherwise, along with heretical and other tendencies looked upon with disapproval, only in those parts of the commercial aristocracy which were already emancipated from the tradition. But even sceptics and people indifferent to the Church often reconciled themselves with it by gifts, because it was a sort of insurance against the uncertainties of what might come after death, or because (at least according to the very widely held latter view) an external obedience to the commands of the Church was sufficient to insure salvation. Here the either non-moral or immoral character of their action in the opinion of the participants themselves comes clearly to light.

Now, how could activity, which was at best ethically tolerated, turn into a calling in the sense of Benjamin Franklin? The fact to be explained historically is that in the most highly capitalistic centre of that time, in Florence of the fourteenth and fifteenth centuries, the money and capital market of all the great political Powers, this attitude was considered ethically unjustifiable, or at best to be tolerated. But in the backwoods small citizen circumstances of Pennsylvania in the eighteenth century, where business threatened for simple lack of money to fall back into barter, where there was hardly a sign of large enterprise, where only the earliest beginnings of banking were to be found, the same thing was considered the essence of moral conduct, even commanded in the name of duty.

To speak here of a reflection of material conditions in the ideal superstructure would be patent nonsense. What was the background of ideas which could account for the sort of activity apparently directed toward profit alone as a calling toward which the individual feels himself to have an ethical obligation? For it was this idea which gave the way of life of the new entrepreneur its ethical foundation and justification. The attempt has been made, particularly by Sombart, in what are often judicious and effective observations, to depict economic rationalism as the salient feature of modern economic life as a whole. Undoubtedly with justification, if by that is meant the extension of the productivity of labour which has, through the subordination of the process of production to scientific points of view, relieved it from its dependence upon the natural organic limitations of the human individual.

Now this process of rationalization in the field of technique and economic organization undoubtedly determines an important part of the ideals of life of modern citizen society. Labour in the service of a rational organization for the provision of humanity with material goods has without doubt always appeared to representatives of the capitalistic spirit as one of the most important purposes of their life-work. It is only necessary, for instance, to read Franklin's account of his efforts in the service of civic improvements in Philadelphia clearly to apprehend this obvious truth. And the joy and pride of having given employment to numerous people, of having had a part in the economic progress of his home town in the sense referring to figures of population and volume of trade which capitalism associated with the word, all these things obviously are part of the specific and undoubtedly idealistic satisfactions in life to modern men of business. Similarly it is one of the fundamental characteristics of an individualistic capitalistic economy that it is rationalized on the basis of rigorous calculation, directed with foresight and caution toward the economic success which is sought in sharp contrast to the hand-to-mouth existence of the peasant, and to the privileged traditionalism of the guild craftsman and of the adventurers' capitalism, oriented to the exploitation of political opportunities and irrational speculation.

It might thus seem that the development of the spirit of capitalism is best understood as part of the development of rationalism as a whole, and could be deduced from the fundamental position of rationalism on the basic problems of life. In the process Protestantism would only have to be considered in so far as it had formed a stage prior to the development of a purely rationalistic philosophy. But any serious attempt to carry this thesis through makes it evident that such a simple way of putting the question will not work, simply because of the fact that the history of rationalism shows a development which by no means follows parallel lines in the various departments of life. The rationalization of private law, for instance, if it is thought of as a logical simplification and rearrangement of the content of the law, was achieved in the highest hitherto known degree in the Roman law of late antiquity.

But it remained most backward in some of the countries with the highest degree of economic rationalization, notably in England, where the Renaissance of Roman Law was overcome by the power of the great legal corporations, while it has always retained its supremacy in the Catholic countries of Southern Europe. The worldly rational philosophy of the eighteenth century did not find favour alone or even principally in the countries of highest capitalistic development.

The doctrines of Voltaire are even today the common property of broad upper, and what is practically more important, middle-class groups in the Romance Catholic countries. Finally, if under practical rationalism is understood the type of attitude which sees and judges the world consciously in terms of the worldly interests of the individual ego, then this view of life was and is the special peculiarity of the peoples of the *liberal arbitration,* such as the Italians and the French are in very flesh and blood. But we have already convinced ourselves that this is by no means the soil in which that relationship of a man to his calling as a task, which is necessary to capitalism, has preeminently grown. In fact, one may—this simple proposition, which is often forgotten, should be placed at the beginning of every study which essays to deal with rationalism—rationalize life from fundamentally different basic points of view and in very different directions. Rationalism is an historical concept which covers a whole world of different things. It will be our task to find out whose intellectual child the particular concrete form of rational thought was, from which the idea of a calling and the devotion to labour in the calling has grown, which is, as we have seen, so irrational from the standpoint of purely eudamonistic self-interest, but which has been and still is one of the most characteristic elements of our capitalistic culture. We are here particularly interested in the origin of precisely the irrational element which lies in this, as in every conception of a calling.

8

Max Weber: Methodology of the Social Sciences

OBJECTIVITY IN SOCIAL SCIENCE AND SOCIAL POLICY

The purpose of this new journal (where this essay appeared) is "the education of judgement about practical social problems" and "the criticism of practical social policy."

Questions to be addressed: What is the validity of the value-judgements which are uttered by the critic? In what sense, if the criterion of scientific knowledge is to be found in the 'objective' validity of its results, has he (the critic) remained within the sphere of scientific discussion? In what sense are there in general 'objectively valid truths' in those disciplines concerned with social and cultural phenomena?

The science of social institutions and culture arose for practical considerations, with the purpose of producing value-judgement as measures of state policy. Knowledge of what "is" was conflated with knowledge of what "should be"; this was because natural laws and evolutionary principles dominated the field. This journal will try to reject this conflation, since "it can never be the task of an empirical science to provide binding norms and ideals from which the directives for immediate personal activity can be derived." Value-judgements should not be eliminated, but subjected to scientific criticism. Science can help an actor choose between alternative ends by analysing the appropriateness of a means for an end, and by providing information on what a desired end will cost in terms of the loss of other values. The acting person can then choose from among the values involved according to his own conscience or personal view. Science can show him that all choosing involves the espousal of certain values.

Every science of cultural life must arrive at a rational understanding of the ideas which underlie every concrete end. Science can judge these ideas and ends ONLY according to a logical and historically defined standard of value which can be elevated to a certain "level of explicitness" beyond individual sentiment. Science can tell a person what s/he can do, not what s/he should do. Put another way, treating the ideas as a coherent system of thought, science can point out to an actor what is possible within his or her value system, and what would be contradictory to that value system.

Problems of social policy are not based on purely technical considerations of specific ends, but involve disputes about the normative standards of value which lie in the domain of general cultural values. This conflict over general cultural values does not occur solely between 'class interests' but between general views on life and the universe as well (take that, Karl).

It is *not possible* to establish and to demonstrate as scientifically valid 'a principle' for practical social science from which the norms for the solution of practical problems can be unambiguously derived. While social science needs the discussion of practical problems in terms of fundamental principles, that is, the reduction of unreflective value-judgements to the premises from which they are logically derived, the search for a "lowest common denominator" of in the form of generally valid value judgements is not empirical, impractical and entirely meaningless. We cannot establish on the basis of ethical imperatives or norms for concretely condition individual conduct, normatively desirable cultural values.

Objective science must distinguish between value judgements and empirical knowledge, and try to see factual truths. However, value-judgements of the practical interest of the scientist will always be significant in determining the focus of attention of analytical activity (my values direct me in what

I think are interesting or important questions or matters to investigate — this gets called, value-relevance elsewhere: there is no harm, according to Max, in allowing your values, personal interests or social commitments to guide you in the selection of research topics; however, once you start researching, you need value-neutrality).

This journal will pursue logical analysis of the content of ideals, while not ignoring how ideals motivate value-judgements. It will present social policy, i.e., the statement of ideals, in addition to social science, i.e., the analysis of facts. In non-scientific discussions of policy, it must be made clear where the investigator stops analysing and where the evaluating and acting person begins to present his sentiments (make value judgements). Again, individual sentiments don't have to be eliminated, nor can they be, but they should be kept strictly separate from scientific analysis. "An attitude of moral indifference has not connection with scientific 'objectivity'."

As said before, every recognition of a scientific problem reflects specific motives and values on the part of the investigator. This journal, a good journal, will try to avoid developing on a character on the basis of the values of its common contributors.

A social science problem is one which throws light on the "the fundamental socio-economic problem: the scarcity of means" For us, phenomena have the following cultural significance (since we are interested in socio-economic data), "economic," "economically-relevant," "economically-conditioned." This journal (thus, by extension, our buddy Max), considers all of these as important since material interests influence all aspects of culture w/o exception. Our science, the science of economic cultural phenomena seeks particular causes for these phenomena, so it is also interested in historical knowledge. We want to investigate the general cultural significance of the socio-economic structure of the human community and its historical forms of organization. Treatment of these social problems will (hopefully) result in solutions for social policy.

This limited scope (focus on the socio-economic aspect of cultural life) is deliberately one-sided, because general social science is ambiguous without some specification of the way in which this social is to be investigated. This journal is interested, however, in the economic interp of history, not the materialist conception of history as a causal formula (take that, Karl). Karl's materialist conception is popular among laymen and dilettantes (not to mention, so I hear, hat-wearing, feminist vegetarians) who are not satisfied until they find economic causes for every freakin' thing under the sun.

The explanation of everything by economic causes alone is never exhaustive in any sense whatsoever in any sphere of cultural phenomena, not even in the economic sphere itself. We choose this one-sided approach, however, as a way to investigate cultural reality by specific technical means and using qualitatively similar categories (remember, though, material interests are found in every aspect of culture). There is no absolutely objective scientific analysis of culture independent of special and one-sided viewpoints according to which social phenomena are selected, analysed, and organized for expository purposes. These view points are necessary in order to engage in an empirical science of concrete reality which seeks to understand the cultural significance of individual events in their contemporary manifestations and the causes of their being historical so and not otherwise. The infinite multiplicity of life means that we can select only a segment of it for scientific investigation.

Ideal Type: Formulated by exaggerating one side of reality, or selecting multiple aspects of reality and synthesizing them into a unified analytical construct. The analysis of reality is concerned, for Max, "with the configuration into which (hypothetical!) 'factors' are arranged to form a cultural phenomena which is historically significant to us" (75). The ideal type is derived inductively from the real world. You compare the type with empirical reality to see how it differs. Then, you look for the causes of the deviations.

MAX WEBER: METHODOLOGY OF THE SOCIAL SCIENCES

Value-judgements are practical evaluations of the unsatisfactory or satisfactory character of phenomena subject to our influence. In teaching, a lecture should be different from a speech, and teachers should not impose their ideas on their students simply because students are prevented from leaving and from protesting. There is no specialized qualification for personal prophesy, and for that reason it is not entitled to freedom from external control. Students should gain from teachers today: 1) the ability to fulfil a given task in a workmanlike fashion; 2) the ability to recognize facts, even those which may be personally uncomfortable, and to distinguish them from his/her own evaluations; 3) learn to subordinate himself to his task and repress the impulse to exhibit his personal tastes or other sentiments unnecessarily.

The unresolvable question—unresolvable because it is ultimately a question of evaluation—as to whether one may, must, or should champion certain practical values in teaching, should not be confused with the purely logical discussion of the relationship of value-judgements to empirical disciplines such as sociology.

The distinction between empirical statements of fact and value-judgments is difficult. However, all recognizable value judgements should be made rigorously explicit to both the researcher him/herself and his/her audience.

Weber does not believe in value free sociology, he believes in striving for value-neutral sociology.

The specific function of science is to ask questions about the things which convention makes self-evident.

"Understanding" explanations do justice to a person who really or evidently thinks differently. They are scientifically valuable 1) for the purposes of a causal analysis which seeks to establish the motives of human actions and 2) for the communication of really divergent evaluations when one is in discussion with a person who really or apparently has different evaluations from one's self.

The shallowness of our routinized daily existence in the most significant sense of the word consist in the fact that the persons who are caught up in it do not become aware, and above all do not wish to become aware, of the motley of irreconcilably antagonistic values that they hold... value-spheres cross and interpenetrate.

The discussion of value-judgements can have only the following functions:

1) the elabouration and explication of ultimate, internally consistent value-axioms, from which the divergent attitudes are derived. People are often in error, not only about their opponents' evaluations, but also their own. The procedure for this analysis begins with concrete particular evaluations and analyses their meanings and then moves to the more general level of irreducible evaluations. It is not empirical and it produces no new knowledge of facts. It's validity flows from its logic.

2) deduction of implications for those accepting certain value-judgements which follow from certain irreducible value axioms when these axioms alone are used to evaluate certain situations of fact. This deduction depends partly on logic, and partly on empirical observation for the most complete casuistic analyses of all such empirical situations subject to practical evaluation.

3) determination of the factual consequences which the realization of a given practical evaluation must have: 1) in the event of being bound to certain indispensable means, 2) in the event of the inevitability of certain, not directly desired repercussions (these empirical observations may lead us to determine the end cannot be achieved, or that in its achievement there may be other, undesired consequences which make our end too dangerous to pursue. We may be made to reconsider our ends, means and repercussions, so that they become a new problem for us, or we may discover new axioms which we had not previously taken into consideration).

Problems in social science are selected by value-relevance — relevance for values of the researcher/problem-selector. The task of a value-neutral science, once the problem of interest is chosen, is the reduction of, say, a communist standpoint to its most rational and internally consistent form, and the empirical investigation the pre-conditions for its existence and its practical consequences. This analyses, though, can never tell us whether or not we should be communists; no science can. Strictly empirical analysis can provide a solution to a problem only where it is a question of a means adequate to the realization of an absolutely unambiguous end. When the normatively valid is the object of empirical investigation, its normative validity is disregarded. Its existence and not its validity is what concerns the investigator.

An example of what NOT to do: Because the state is tremendously important and has a great deal of power in modern life, people conclude that it represents the ultimate value and that all social actions should be evaluated in terms of their relations to its interests. This is an inadmissible deduction of a value-judgement from a statement of fact. Bad, bad, bad.

SOCIAL PSYCHOLOGY OF THE WORLD RELIGIONS

The world religions, to Max, are Confucianism, Hinduism, Buddhism, Christianity and Islam, and they are chosen because they have a large number of followers, and for no other reason. He will also consider Judaism, since it is an important precursor to Christianity and Islam and because of its significance for the development of the economic ethic of the West.

The term 'economic ethic' points to the practical impulses for action which are founded in the psychological and pragmatic contexts of religion. The religious determination of life conduct is only one of the determinants of the economic ethic. The religiously determined way of life is itself profoundly influenced by economic and political factors.

Those strata which are decisive in stamping the characteristic features of an economic ethic may change in the course of history; nevertheless, as a rule one may determine the strata whose styles of life have been at least predominately decisive for certain religions. For example, Confucianism was the status ethic of prebendaries, men with literary educations who were characterized by a secular rationalism. Christianity began its course as a doctrine of itinerant artisan journeymen.

It is not the case for Weber that "the ruling ideas of any epoch are the ideas of the ruling classes," however. And, however incisive the social influences, economically and politically determined, may have been upon a religious ethic in a particular case, it receives its stamp primarily from religious sources, and most predominantly from the content of its annunciation and promise.

One of the foci of religious ethics has been the evaluation of suffering. By treating suffering as a symptom of secret guilt and of a crime in the sight of G/god/s, religion has psychologically met a very important need. The fortunate is seldom satisfied with the fact of being fortunate. Beyond this, he needs to know that he has a right to his good fortune. Good fortune wants to be legitimate fortune. Religion provides the theodicy of good fortune for those who are fortunate.

Salvation religions are religions of suffering. Under the pressure of typical and ever-recurrent distress, the religiosity of a 'redeemer' evolved. This religiosity presupposed the myth of a saviour, hence (at least relatively) a rational view of the world. In Judaism, the term messiah was originally attached to the saviours from political distress, as transmitted by the hero sagas. In Judaism, and in this clear-cut fashion only in it and under very particular other conditions, the suffering of a people's community, rather than the suffering of an individual, became the object of hope for religious salvation. The usual rule was that the saviour bore an individual and universal character at the same time that he was ready to guarantee salvation to the individual and to any individual who would turn to him.

The tribal and local gods, gods of the city and the empire, have taken care only of the interests that concern the collectivity as a whole. In the community cult, the community as such turned to its god. The individual, however, turned to the sorcerer and magician for help with his personal evils. Hereditary dynasties of mystagogues or trained personnel under a head determined in accordance with certain rules developed. Collective religious arrangements for individual suffering per se, and for salvation from it, originated in this fashion. The typical service of magicians and priests becomes the determination of the factors to be blamed for suffering; that is, the confession of sins. Where religious development was decisively influenced by prophecy, sin was no longer merely a magical offence: it was a sign of disbelief in the prophet and his commandments.

While prophets have not generally been descendants of depressed classes, it has generally been the depressed classes who need a redeemer. Thus, most prophetically announced religious of redemption have been located in the less-favoured social strata. For these, such religiosity has been either a substitute for, or a rational supplement to, magic.

The need for an ethical interpretation of suffering and of the meaning of the distribution of fortunes among men increased with the growing rationality of conceptions of the world. There have been three rationally satisfactory answers to questions about the basis of the incongruity between destiny and merit: Karma, dualism (from Zoroastrianism) and the predestination decree of the deus abscondidus (the absconded god; kind of a cool phrase). These solutions are rationally closed, and are found in pure form only as exceptions.

Ecstatic states (orgies, quietistic edification, contemplative mortification, etc.) have been sought first of all, for the sake of the emotional value they offered the devout. Rationalized religions have sublimated the orgy into the sacrament. Every hierocratic and official authority of a church fights against virtuoso religion and its autonomous development. The church is the holder of institutionalized grace, and seeks to organize the religiosity of the masses.

The kind of empirical state of bliss or experience of rebirth that is sought after as the supreme value by a religion has varied according to the character of the stratum that was foremost in adopting it. The conception of the idea of redemption is very old, if one understands by it a liberation from sickness, hunger, etc., ultimately from suffering and death. However, redemption attained a specific significance only where it expressed a systematic and rationalized image of the world and represented a stand in the face of the world. Not ideas, but material and ideal interests, directly govern men's conduct. Yet very frequently the world images that have been created by ideas have, like switchmen, determined the tracks along which action has been pushed by the dynamic of interest. From what and for what one wished to be redeemed, and let us not forget, could be redeemed, depended upon one's image of the world.

Behind every religion lies a stand toward something in the actual world which is experienced as specifically senseless. Thus, the demand has been implied: the world order, in its totality, could, and should somehow be a meaningful cosmos. The various great ways of leading a rational and methodical life have been characterized by irrational presuppositions, which have been accepted simply as given and incorporated into life. What these presuppositions have been is historically and socially determined, to a very large extent, through the peculiarity of those strata that have been the carriers of the ways of life during its formative and decisive period. The interest situation of these strata, as determined socially and psychologically, has made for their peculiarity.

Where prophecy has provided a religious basis, this basis could be one of two fundamental types of prophesy: exemplary and emissary. Exemplary prophesy points the way to salvation by exemplary living (usually contemplative and apathetic-ecstatic ways of life). Emissary prophesy addresses its demands to the world in the name of a god. These demands are ethical, and often of an active acetic character.

The civic strata, conditioned by the nature of their life, which is greatly detached from economic bonds to nature, tend toward a practical rationalism in conduct. Their whole existence has been based on technological or economic calculations and upon the mastery of nature and man. These strata tend toward religions of active asceticism. Wherever the direction of the whole way of life has been methodically rationalized, it has been profoundly determined by the ultimate values toward which this rationalism has been directed.

All kinds of practical ethics that are systematically and unambiguously oriented toward fixed goals of salvation are rational, partly in the same sense as formal method is rational, and partly in the sense that they distinguish between valid norms and what is empirically given. All ruling powers need legitimacy, which comes in three kinds... In the main, it has been the work of jurists to give birth to modern Western states, as well as modern Western churches. Jurists work in the realm of formal rationalization, they follow procedures, etc. With the triumph of formalistic (rather than substantive) juristic rationalism, the legal type of domination appeared in the West.

NATURAL SCIENCE, SOCIAL SCIENCE, AND VALUE RELEVANCE

Weber rejected both the positivist contention that the cognitive aims of the natural and the social sciences were basically the same and the opposing German historicist doctrine that in the realm of Kultur and Geist (that is, in the domain of history) it is impossible to make legitimate generalizations because human actions are not subject to the regularities that govern the world of nature. Against the historicists Weber argued that the method of science, whether its subject matter be things or men, always proceeds by abstraction and generalization. Against the positivists, he took the stand that man, in contrast to things, could be understood not only in external manifestations, that is, in behavior, but also in the underlying motivations. And against both these approaches Weber emphasized the value-bound problem choices of the investigator and the value-neutral methods of social research.

According to Weber, differences between the natural sciences and the social sciences arise from differences in the cognitive intentions of the investigator, not from the alleged inapplicability of scientific and generalizing methods to the subject matter of human action. What distinguishes the natural and social sciences is not an inherent difference in methods of investigation, but rather the differing interests and aims of the scientist. Both types of science involve abstraction. The richness of the world of facts, both in nature and in history, is such that a total explanation in either realm is doomed to fail. Even in physics it is impossible to predict future events in all their concrete detail. No one, for example, can calculate in advance the dispersion of the fragments of an exploding shell. Prediction becomes possible only within a system of conceptualizations that excludes concern for those concrete facts not caught in the net of abstractions. Both the natural and the social sciences must abstract from the manifold aspects of reality; they always involve selection.

The natural scientist is primarily interested in those aspects of natural events that can be formulated in terms of abstract laws. While the social scientist may wish to search for such lawful abstract generalizations in human behavior, he is also interested in particular qualities of human actors and in the meaning they ascribe to their actions. Any scientific method must make a selection from the infinite variety of empirical reality. When the social scientist adopts a generalizing method, he abstracts from random unique aspects of the reality he considers; concrete individual actions are conceived as "cases" or "instances," which are subsumed under theoretical generalizations. The individualizing approach, in contrast, neglects generic elements and concentrates attention on particular features of phenomena or concrete historical actors. Both methods are defensible, provided neither is alleged to encompass phenomena in their totality. Neither method is privileged or inherently superior to the other.

What particular problem attracts a scholar, and what level of explanation is sought, depends, Weber argues, on the values and interests of the investigator. The choice of problems is always "value relevant." "There is no absolutely 'objective' scientific analysis of culture or... of 'social phenomena' independent of special and 'one-sided' viewpoints according to which— expressly or tacitly, consciously or unconsciously— they are selected, analysed and organized for expository purposes." What is considered "worthy to be known" depends upon the perspective of the inquiring scholar. Hence there is no insurmountable chasm between the procedures of the natural and the social scientist, but they differ in their cognitive intentions and explanatory projects.

When the objection is raised that rational knowledge of causal sequences may be attained in the world of nature, but that the human world in not susceptible to rational explanation because of its unpredictability and irrationality, Weber counters by turning the tables. Our knowledge of nature must always be, as it were, from the outside. We can only observe external courses of events and record their uniformities. But in regard to human action, we can do more than write protocols of recurrent sequences of events; we can attempt to impute motives by interpreting men's actions and words. With this method, he of course opposes the positivists as well. "Social facts are in the last resort *intelligible* facts." We can understand (*verstehen*) human action by penetrating to the subjective meanings that actors attach to their own behavior and to the behavior of others. A sociology of the chicken yard can only account for regularities of behavior—in other words, for a pecking order. A sociology of human groups has the inestimable advantage of access to the subjective aspects of action, to the realm of meaning and motivation. Hence Weber's definition of sociology as "that science which aims at the *interpretative understanding (Verstehen)* of social behavior in order to gain an explanation of its causes, its course, and it effects."

The notion of interpretative understanding did not originate with Weber. It was first advanced by the historian Droysen and was used extensively by such scholars as Dilthey. But for them the method was meant to extol intuition over rational-causal explanation. Weber, in contrast, saw in it only a preliminary step in the establishment of causal relationships. The grasping of subjective meaning of an activity, Weber argued, is facilitated through empathy *(Einfuehlung)* and a reliving *(Nacherbleben)* of the experience to be analysed. But any interpretative explanation *(verstehende Erklaerung)* must become a causal explanation if it is to reach the dignity of a scientific proposition. *Verstehen* and causal explanation are correlative rather than opposed principles of method in the social sciences. Immediate intuitions of meaning can be transformed into valid knowledge only if they can be incorporated into theoretical structures that aim at causal explanation.

Against the objection that this manner of interpretation is subject to the danger of contamination from the values held by the scientific investigator, Weber countered that interpretations can be submitted to the test of evidence. This, he argued, is to be distinguished from the fact that the choice of subject matter—as distinct from the choice of interpretation—stems from the investigator's value orientation, which may be the case with the natural scientist as well.

Weber insisted that a value element inevitable entered into the selection of the problem an investigator chooses to attack. There are no intrinsically scientific criteria for the selection of topics; here every man must follow his own demon, his own moral stance, but this in no way invalidates the objectivity of the social sciences. The question of whether a statement is true of false is logically distinct from that of its relevance to values. *Wertbeziehung* (value relevance) touches upon the selection of the problem, not upon thc interpretation of phenomena. As Parsons put it, "Once a phenomenon is descriptively given, the establishment of causal relations between it and either its antecedents or its consequences is possible only through the application, explicitly or implicitly, of a formal schema of proof that is independent of any value system, except the value of scientific proof." Hence, the relativity of value orientations leading to different cognitive choices has nothing to do with questions of scientific validity. What are relativized in this view are not the findings but the problems. Value relevance must be distinguished from value-neutrality, since they refer to two different orders of ideas. In the first place, ethical neutrality implies that once the social scientist had chosen his problem in terms of its relevance to his values, he must hold values—his own or those of others—in abeyance while he follows the guidelines his data reveal. He cannot impose his values on the data and he is compelled to pursue his line of inquiry whether or not the results turn out to be inimical to what he holds dear. A geneticist of liberal persuasion, for example, should not abandon his line of inquiry if his findings suggest that differences in intelligence are associated with biological traits. Value neutrality, in this first meaning of the term, refers to the normative injunction that men of science should be governed by the ethos of science in their role as scientists, but emphatically not in their role as citizens.

In addition, value neutrality refers no less importantly to another order of considerations; the disjunction between the world of facts and the world of values, the impossibility of deriving "ought statements" from "is statements." An empirical science, Weber contended, can never advise anyone what he *should* do, though it may help him to clarify for himself what he can or wants to do.

The scientific treatment of value judgments may not only understand and empatically analyze the desired ends and the ideals which underline them; it can also "judge" them critically. This criticism can... be no more than a formal logical judgment of historically given value judgments and ideas, a testing of the ideals according to the postulate of the internal *consistency* of the desired end.... It can assist [the acting person] in becoming aware of the ultimate standards of value which he does not make explicit to himself, or which he must presuppose in order to be logical.... As to whether the person expressing these value judgments *should* adhere to these ultimate standards is his personal affair; it involves will and conscience, not empirical knowledge.

Weber was fundamentally at odds with those who argued for a morality based on science. In this respect he was as opposed to Durkheim as he would be to those psychoanalysts today who claim they have a scientific warranty to counsel "adjustment" or "self-actualization," as the case may be, to their patients.

Bibliography

Adams, Bert N. and R. A. Sydie: *Sociological Theory*, Thousand Oaks, Pine Forge, 2001

Brubaker, Rogers: *The Limits of Rationality*. London: Routledge, 1992.

Bruun, Hans Henrik: *Science, Values and Politics in Max Weber's Methodology*. Copenhagen: Munksgaard, 1972.

Burkey, Richard M.: *Ethnic and Racial Groups: the Dynamics of Dominance*, Menlo Park, Cummings, 1978.

Gellner, Ernest: *Legitimation of Belief*. Cambridge: Cambridge University Press, 1974.

Gerth, Hans and C. Wright Mills: *From Max Weber: Essays in Sociology*, New York, Oxford University Press, 1958.

Giddens, Anthony and David Held: *Classes, Power, and Conflict: Classical and Contemporary Debates*, Berkeley, University of California Press, 1982.

Goldman, Harvey: *Politics, Death, and the Devil: Self and Power in Max Weber and Thomas Mann*. Berkeley: University of California Press, 1992.

Hadden, Richard W.: *Sociological Theory: An Introduction to the Classical Tradition*, Peterborough, Broadview Press, 1997.

Hennis, Wilhelm: *Max Weber: Essays in Reconstruction*. London: Allen & Unwin, 1988.

Henrich, Dieter: *Die Einheit der Wissenschaftslehre Max Webers*. Tübingen: J. C. B. Mohr/Paul Siebeck, 1952.

Honigsheim, Paul: *The Unknown Max Weber*. New Brunswick, NJ: Transaction Publisher, 2003.

Hughes, H. S.: *Consciousness and Society: Reorientation of European Social Thought*. New York: Vintage Books, 1977.

Käsler, Dirk: *Max Weber: An Introduction to his Life and Work*. trans. P. Hurd. Chicago: University of Chicago Press, 1988.

Kim, Sung Ho.: *Max Weber's Politics of Civil Society*. Cambridge: Cambridge University Press, 2004.

Löwith, Karl: *Max Weber and Karl Marx*, London: Allen & Unwin, 1982.

Mommsen, Wolfgang: *Max Weber and German Politics, 1980-1920*, Chicago: University of Chicago Press, 1984.

Oakes, G. : *Roscher and Knies: The Logical Problems of Historical Economics*, New York: Free Press, 1903.

Roth, Guenther: *Max Webers deutschen-englische Familiengeschichte 1800-1950*. Tübingen: J. C. B. Mohr/ Paul Siebeck, 2001.

Stammer. Otto: *Max Weber and Sociology Today*. New York: Harper, 1971.

Strauss, Leo: *Natural Right and History*. Chicago: University of Chicago Press, 1950.

Swedberg, Richard: *The Max Weber Dictionary*. Stanford: Stanford University Press, 2005.

Taylor, Charles: *Sources of the Self: The Making of the Modern Identity*. Cambridge, MA: Harvard University Press, 1989.

Vattimo, Giani: *The End of Modernity: Nihilism and Hermeneutics inPostmodern Culture*, Baltimore: Johns Hopkins University Press, 1988.

Index

I

J

K

L

M

N

O

P

R

S

T

W

❑❑❑